2963311

B/SM1

RUSSELL 7/12
Knight of the Sword

KNIGHT OF THE SWORD

Sir Sidney Smith at the Breach of Acre, 9th May, 1799 (*from 'The Life and Correspondence of Admiral Sir William Sidney Smith' by John Barrow; London, Richard Bentley, 1848*).

KNIGHT OF THE SWORD

The Life and Letters of

ADMIRAL
SIR WILLIAM SIDNEY SMITH
G.C.B.

by

LORD RUSSELL OF LIVERPOOL

LONDON
VICTOR GOLLANCZ LTD
1964

Printed in Great Britain
by Ebenezer Baylis & Son Limited
The Trinity Press, Worcester, and London

ACKNOWLEDGEMENTS

I am most grateful to Her Majesty the Queen for graciously giving me permission to make use of material from the Royal Archives.

I also wish to express my thanks to Mr S. S. Wilson, C.B.E., Keeper of Public Records; Mr P. K. Kemp, Head of the Historical Section, Admiralty; Mr B. Cheeseman, Librarian, Colonial Office; Mr Godfrey Thompson, City Librarian, Leeds; The Earl of Harewood; Mr E. J. Davis, County Archivist, Buckinghamshire; The Director of the Swedish State Archives, and Capitaine de Vaisseau de Brossard, Chef du Service Historique, Ministère des Armées (Marine), Paris; for giving me access to documents relating to Admiral Sir Sidney Smith and other useful information;

To Lord Bruce for giving me access to certain correspondence between the 7th Earl of Elgin and Admiral Sir Sidney Smith;

To Mr E. T. Brown, Sir Tresham Lever, Bt., The Hon. Mrs F. W. Cunnack, Lieutenant-Colonel L. Ford, Brigadier E. Mockler-Ferryman, C.B., and Mr A. C. Pallot for placing certain notes, engravings and other information at my disposal;

To my wife for translating several documents from the original French, and to Miss M. W. Thurston for helping me with the research.

CONTENTS

I

EARLY DAYS

For William Sidney Smith, Knight Grand Cross of the Swedish Order of the Sword and Admiral in the Royal Navy, all the world was, undoubtedly, a stage on which, in a varied and exciting life, he played many parts.

Before he was thirteen years old he had seen active service in America and at Cape St Vincent. His greatest claim to fame was his defence of Acre, after which Napoleon said of him, "that man made me miss my destiny".

He fought with the Swedish Navy against the Russians in the gulf of Finland and, later, spent two years as a prisoner of war in the Abbaye and Temple prisons in Paris.

He also served for a short time with the Turkish navy, destroyed the French ships left behind in Toulon harbour when Lord Hood decided to evacuate it, and carried out a series of commando raids along the coast of Calabria.

Smith never stopped talking about his exploits and never minimised his talents. He was frequently referred to rather contemptuously by senior officers in his own service, many of whom both disliked and envied him, as the Knight of the Sword: hence the title of this book.

The defence of Acre left him, as Sir John Moore's Chief-of-Staff once said, "with a strong taste for inshore operations and an unbridled thirst for glory".

The practice of reporting annually on officers of the Royal Navy was not then in existence, but if it had been Sidney Smith's reports would have made interesting reading.

Little is known of his family and, although their surnames were the same, Lord Strangford, whose cousin Sidney Smith once claimed to be, was, in fact, no relation. Nevertheless he was the fourth generation to hold a commission in one of the services.

His father had been a captain in the Guards but resigned his commission, after the Battle of Minden, in disgust at the treatment of Lord George Germain for merely carrying out the orders of Ferdinand, Prince of Brunswick who was in command of the allied army. This Captain Smith had three sons, and Sidney was the second of them. The youngest, John Spencer, after serving a few years as an officer of the Guards, entered the Diplomatic Service and was chargé d'affaires in Constantinople during the time his brother Sidney was campaigning in Egypt and the Levant.

Even as a small boy Sidney Smith was quite a character. He had a complete contempt for danger, possessed a marked aptitude for inventiveness, a love of adventure and a dislike of subservience, all of which he retained throughout his service in the Royal Navy.

There is a story told about him at the age of eleven which shows that he already possessed two characteristics which were displayed on many occasions during his eventful life, a recklessness in running into danger and great resourcefulness in getting out of it with credit.

It was the custom, at his father's estate at Midgham in Berkshire, to hold family prayers every evening, and the signal that they were about to be said was given by a number of blasts on a horn. One evening young Sidney did not appear, not because he had failed to hear the summons but for the simple reason that he was not in a position to obey it. It was the first time Sidney had been absent and his father was, not unnaturally, somewhat alarmed and feared that the boy might have met with an accident.

A search was made through the grounds and he was eventually found, with a girl of his own age to whom he had lately been paying some attention, in a large wash-tub becalmed in the centre of a deep pond.

When the voyage began Sidney had been armed with a long pole which he used to navigate the tub like a punt, but, while he was temporarily distracted by his lady friend, the pole had gone overboard, leaving them without any means of navigation.

When the search party first caught sight of the future hero of many fights there he was, standing up in the rudderless craft calmly surveying the situation, his arms folded, looking not unlike the famous print of Napoleon on the island of St Helena.

The search party, which included Sidney's father, were not so happy about the situation. None of them could swim, it was getting dark and the girl was obviously getting panicky. Young Sidney, who was in no hurry and rather enjoyed, as he always did in later life, playing the leading role, eventually hailed the party on shore and told them to fasten the string of his kite on to the collar of his favourite dog which then swam out to him. The tow-line was then taken on board and Sidney's 'ship' quickly towed to safety.

By this time the girl was in hysterics but Sidney stepped ashore calm and unmoved. "Now, father," he said, "we had better go to prayers."

A few years' schooling were to follow at Tonbridge and Bath but neither school can have contributed much to his career, for shortly before his twelfth birthday he was appointed to H.M.S. *Tortoise* as a midshipman under Viscount Howe. This appointment he probably owed to his father, a gentleman usher to Queen Charlotte, and the Duke of Clarence, who was later to be his King and with whom he always remained on quite intimate terms; he served in the same fleet with him, though on a different ship, and a little more than five years later both fought their first action against the French fleet off the Chesapeake.

The method of entry for officers into the Navy during the eighteenth century was largely by 'interest'. It was possible for a father, provided he knew a member of the Board of Admiralty, or a serving admiral, to obtain a King's letter and armed with this the boy was appointed as a captain's servant in a sea-going ship.

The number of so-called 'servants' which a captain was allowed varied according to the size of the ship, and in a first-rate ship was twenty-four. They were not really servants but young boys who wished to make the sea their career. After about two years' service they were rated as able seamen, and later midshipmen, but in reality they were midshipmen all the time and messed in the gunroom. As a King's letter-boy or captain's servant they received no pay and were only put on the pay-roll when rated able seaman or midshipman.

The regulations provided that after six years at sea they could be examined in seamanship for the rank of lieutenant; so, in order to gain time, boys whose fathers had sufficient influence were frequently entered in ships at an absurdly early age, sometimes when only nine years old. The official minimum age for promotion to lieutenant was twenty, but this was often so difficult to prove that many obtained promotion while still much younger.

After attaining the rank of lieutenant future promotion depended partly on merit and partly on interest. An admiral was often prepared to accelerate the promotion of lieutenants who had good family connections and he would do the same if they were of outstanding merit.

There was never any purchase of commissions as in the Army and wealth had no part in promotion. Interest was probably the quickest way up the ladder although Nelson is an example of promotion through outstanding merit.

Sidney Smith did not have long to wait for his first promotion, for in September 1780 he was appointed to H.M.S. *Alcide* as lieutenant although his commission was not gazetted by the Admiralty until three years later, doubtless because of the regulation then in force that no officer could be so promoted until he had reached the age of nineteen. Even before this confirmation of his lieutenantcy, however, he was again promoted to the rank of commander on H.M. Sloop *Fury* and, in October 1782, only five years after he first joined the navy, he became Captain of H.M.S. *Alcmene*.

During these first few years of his service he kept up a continuous correspondence with his father and his letters disclose a command of the English language which must have been rare for one of his age.

In a letter from H.M.S. *Alcide* in November 1780 he wrote, "I wish everybody that calls Sir George Rodney's temper and judgment in question had been in the fleet those thirteen days, to windward of Martinique, in chase of the enemy's superior fleet. . . . Sir George only wanted reminding that there was such a person as me, for he no sooner was told I was arrived in the Greyhound than he packed me off on board the *Alcide* going out on a profitable cruise; as for his giving me a command, I am too young; besides he has more upon his list than he is likely to provide for in that way; perhaps he may recollect, in answer to my being too young, when he thinks of it, that I am as old as, and have been to sea much longer than his son who is a post-captain. He is very whimsical, and such a whim may take him, if he was reminded by somebody else besides me."

Smith remained in command of H.M.S. *Alcmene* until February 1784, by which time peace had been concluded, and on arrival at Spithead paid off the ship.

The Navy in peacetime he found too dull for his adventurous nature and decided to travel abroad for the purpose, as he himself wrote, "of further qualifying myself for my country's service".

His first port of call was Normandy, where he lived in Caen for nearly two years, and where he picked up a fluent knowledge of French which he spoke like a native. He also became very friendly with the d'Harcourt family and it was after his first visit to their château at Harcourt that he wrote the following letter to his eldest brother.

While enjoying the new found delights of life in France he kept his sailor's weather eye open wherever he went and made a reconnaissance of the new naval harbour which was then under construction at Cherbourg.

Caen, June 1785.

Dear Charles,

I sent off a letter today, 25th, and, according to promise, I now go on with what I had not room to say there. In the first place, you are not to suppose I had forgotten you during my absence from Caen. The truth is, I began two different letters, but being uncomfortable at an inn, tired, and neither pen nor paper fit to give vent to my ideas as fast as they came, I made such a chaos, that they would have been unintelligible to you, as they were even to me.

Now to begin, as far back as before my late journey. I have already described my pension (boarding-house), I visited all the people in the town, as is the custom for a stranger to do; and they went not an inch further than the custom, for having returned my visit, I heard no more of them; so I remained totally without evening society, except my land-lady's circle which, not being quite comme il faut, I generally preferred my books. At last the Duc d'Harcourt arrived. I delivered my letter at his crowded levee, and received an invitation to visit him at Harcourt, where he should have it more in his power to shew me civility. This reception was everything I could wish, in the eyes of beholders; and he repeated his invitation by two messages, one by his head-servant, the other by a gentleman. The next day he reviewed the regiment, and, in passing the line, stopped some minutes to speak to Captain Dalrymple and me, who were standing in front of the centre,—a mark of distinction he bestowed upon nobody else. He afterwards took us to the spot where he intended to stand, when the regiment marched by him, which second instance, you see, proved his attention to be more than mere form.

I visited him at his château (Harcourt), five leagues from hence, and then got better acquainted with him, and found his heart as good as his behaviour was affable. It was written in every peasant's countenance, how pleased they were to see him returned among them; and the hat was pulled off in a manner which indicated something more than mere respect.

The duke has broken through the French regular rules of gardening, in parterres and terraces, for the English way, following nature, and destroying a straight line with as much abhorrence as Queen Mary did a Protestant; giving as a reason, that if every one follows the *nature* of his ground, every man has an original. Madame la duchesse was there; she receives *les dames* from all the country round, and for as long as they choose; so there is always *beaucoup de monde* there; and I got so well acquainted with the Caen party, as to be invited since to their supper parties, so that I have lately been so much under obligation to speak French, that I am no longer distressed to express myself on any subject; and they are polite and charitable enough to listen with attention without laughing at my Anglicisms. My pronunciation is allowed to be perfect, for which I always thank my mother; and I understand whatever is said to me. This progress, you may suppose, begins to make my hours of relaxation more pleasant.

The duke commanded at Havre de Grace, when we were cruizing off with Commodore Johnston, so we of course talked over our different hopes and fears on that occasion, which is a pleasure worth all pain, and which I have experienced very often lately, as you will see when I come to my *tour*; scarce a day passing but I dined in company with some officer against whom I have been engaged more than once; one of them the son of Mons. de Guichen, who was in his ship, when engaged with the Sandwich on the 17th of April; he is still a garde de marine, or midshipman, though older than I am; so they suppose I must be a bishop of marines, or at least related to one, to be so far advanced so young.

But to finish with the château d'Harcourt; it is rather more modern than the time when every baron defended himself; and though that state of things terminated with them long before it did with us, that which succeeded seems still to exist, and I could easily fancy myself two hundred years back while I was there.

The great hall, in which we dined, is surrounded with family pictures larger than life, of knights in armour on horseback;—*les vassaux*, as they call the peasants, attending with complaints, to be decided by *le seigneur*; and many other circumstances, so like what has existed, but has ceased to exist with us. I don't know what progress the arts may have made at Paris, but in Normandy, every piece of household furniture is a most mis-shapen old-fashioned thing. The work of the ladies is still the making of a chair-seat with worsted, on a piece of coarse thin canvas, which when finished, looks something worse than a piece of Wilton carpet. *Apropos* to carpet, there is not such a thing in France. The bed-chambers are all paved, except a suite of rooms (whose only use seems to be to walk through) which are boarded with oak in squares, neatly enough, and dry rubbed; so that previous to a dance I was at lately, they were obliged to wet the floor with a mop (I beg pardon, there is not such a thing in France), a hair-broom. This same dance occurred upon a fête given to the colonel of the regiment, and as the Duc d'Harcourt spoke to him particularly about me, desiring him to introduce me, he was very anxious and punctual in his visits and messages, as I found on my return, which was but just in time. There I fell in love with a *démoiselle*, whose name I do not know. I was told it was *Tourville*, a grand-daughter of the admiral's, which would have been curious enough; but I have since seen Mademoiselle Tourville, and it was not her. You see I let the heart go as it will—as to the judgment, Englishmen are famous here, to a proverb, for its government of their actions, (so said the lady to Sterne, at Calais,) and it will never let me *marry* a Frenchman, as her connections and *acres* are con-comitants, neither of which a *capitaine de vaisseau Anglais* ought to have any business with. I shall probably see my mistress tonight where I sup, in consequence of an invitation, produced by le Duc d'Harcourt's desire, *au colonel du regiment*.

And now for more advantages which I have received from the *honnêteté de monseigneur*. All the world here talk of the great works going on at Cherbourg, which are nothing less than building a breakwater two miles and a half from the shore. His most Christian majesty having found the want of a port

in the channel, in the late war, fit for the reception of large
ships, is determined to make one at any expense, and it will
cost immensely; and if I have any judgment as to the force
of water, perhaps fail after all. The Duc d'Harcourt being
there, and having expressed himself that he had no objection
to us English seeing it—I went thither, and the day after,
two more English captains of men-of-war arrived from Caen
on the same errand; as, on the 7th of the month, one of the
wooden frames called cones, (from their form) was to be
sunk. Monsieur le duc received us most politely, desired us
to consider ourselves engaged to him while we stayed, and
conducted us to the place where these frames are constructed,
about half-tide mark on the beach. They are circular, 150
feet diameter at bottom, 60 feet high, and diminishing from
their conical form to 60 feet diameter at the top; built as
strong as a ship, except that worse wood is considered to
answer the purpose. The next morning at eight o'clock, it
was high water, spring-tide, when one of these cones was
floated by means of empty casks, which had been lashed
round its base at low water. We embarked with monsieur le
duc, and attended it as it was conducted (I am sorry to add,
in a very seaman-like manner,) to the place where it was to
be sunk in a line with the two already placed. In comparison
with the vessels which surrounded it, (one of which was
Wells's Raven,) it looked like a floating island. We mounted
one of the other cones, and had a fine view of its *enfoncement*,
which was performed by their cutting the casks away, two
or four at a time, on opposite sides, by means of a chopper
suspended over the lashings like a pile driver, wind and
weather being favourable. The whole of this operation
succeeded to admiration, and it now remains to be filled
with stones, as the one was on which we stood. The small
vessels threw in their first cargoes immediately, which, as its
contents are 50,000 tons, had not more effect than a handful
in a bushel. It will take about five weeks to fill it, and you
may easily conceive, that if a gale of wind should come on
before it is full, the wood-work above the stones will have no
more chance to stand against the violence of the waves, than
the wreck of a ship does: one *has* been half destroyed in this
manner, so will others probably, considering the difficulties
and immensity of the work, which is nothing less than moving
a mountain piece-meal, and carrying it a league into the

sea. 'Tis a most tremendous undertaking, and, without a compliment to my friends the French, a work *digne des Romains*. I am extremely glad I have seen it, as you may suppose, and particularly with the advantage of the protection of the governor of Normandie, and commander-in-chief *pour sa majesté*, which I find I have omitted to tell you the Duc d'Harcourt is.

I did not stay to see the launching of a second; not to tire monsieur le duc, who, I fear, put himself out of his way in some things by his attention to us. I stayed, however, one day longer than my brother officers, perhaps to evince my independence of them. This I passed very pleasantly with the French naval officers established at the port, *contre qui j'ai combattu, et avec qui j'ai fait connaissance*. The commandant also was very civil, and we compared notes on a certain afternoon in which he amused himself with firing on the Unicorn and Quebec. That cruize I formed the resolution, if ever I had the opportunity, to visit those parts of this coast made remarkable to us by any such event, and that opportunity being now come, I would not let it slip. Besides, Wraxall's Tour had raised a curiosity to see Mont St Michel. Though you may have read it, I desire you will send to Barratt's directly, and read all the first pages. You will find there my history, for I did everything he did, in better language than I could write it. I shall proceed therefore to the anecdotes which make the difference, and to do it more completely, I will begin my journey from Caen, which will be unintelligible to you, unless Barratt can furnish you with a *carte du pays*, or a sight of one.

You know I have a thing called a cabriolet, which I believe I have already described as extremely like that in which Gil Blas and Scipio, or Dr Sangrado (I forget which) performed a journey. In *this*, however, I did *not* go, but sacrificed the ease of that conveyance to my pocket. I must have had three horses to drag myself and servant, so I took two to ride. I was sheathed with Mr Brown's leather; and so far from repenting my scheme, found it much more pleasant, as I was at liberty to go out of the common road, to look at an old tower, or any thing remarkable. The horses went under the appellation of *chevaux quittés*, because you go without a conductor, and leave them where you take the others. I was told I should find them extremely hard, and so I should if I had not

learned to ride in England, and thereby practise what
nobody here has the least idea of, that is, rising in the stirrups,
for they bump it along like so many old women going to
market.

The first town I passed through was Bayeux, famous only
for its cathedral, it being the see and residence of the bishop
of this diocese, which includes Caen, where he has a palace,
but never resides,—luckily for us, as we have the use of his
garden, into which my windows look. I slept at Bayeux, and
set off at four o'clock the next morning. Having the whole
day before me, I could not resist the temptation a fine day
offered to visit my element, the sea, which was but two
leagues to the right. I rode along the edge of the cliffs to the
westward, which though not so high as Albion's, gave a
noble view as far as La Hogue on one side, and very near to
Havre de Grace on the other. I joined the great road again
before I reached Isigny, crossed the Petit Vey, and dined at
Carantan, after a wetting and a ride of eleven leagues.
Notwithstanding the rain, I walked to the church to pay my
respects to Wraxall's St Cecilia. I found nothing of the
enthusiastic in her air, it was more coquettish, and I grudged
the walk exceedingly, which Mr Wraxall's descriptive powers
had cost me. I went on to Valognes in the afternoon, seven
leagues further. The first part of the road was extremely like
the Bath road through Berkshire, lowland to the left,
terminating in a high ridge. Valognes has nothing remarkable; it once occupied more ground than at present, having
been a flourishing Roman colony, as is proved by the
amphitheatre, which has lately been found in digging. Next
morning I arrived at Cherbourg in very good time. You
know my history there.

The Duc d'Harcourt, understanding my intention to
return *en cercle par Mont St Michel*, recommended me to go
on as far as St Malo, and gave me a letter to the commandant.
I left Cherbourg in the afternoon, slept at Valognes, and
appropriated the next day to what you would not have
forgiven me, if I had not done, being in the neighbourhood.
I went to La Hogue,* there to read Admiral Russell's letter,
which I brought with me in a volume of Campbell's

* On the 17th of May, 1692, Admiral Russell discovered the French fleet, under
Count Tourville, off Cape La Hogue, and immediately engaged them; but so
thick a fog came on, that, for two or three days, nothing effectual could be done.
On clearing upon the twenty-second, the French were seen moving off: Russell

Admirals, from Caen, in the hopes of being able to do this very thing. I found nobody alive who remembered anything about *le brûlement*, as they called it, though I was told of one old woman who was old enough to have been alive then. Everybody's father was there, and served in such a battery, but I could get no certain account from them where King James was encamped, and Campbell does not lead to that at all. They pointed out where the wrecks are still visible at very low spring tides, and the fishing for iron is even now a profitable employment; they are between the island of Tatihou and La Hogue Point, before the village of St Vaas. I had read somewhere that the place from whence King James beheld the action was a kind of natural amphitheatre formed by the hills. I found a spot which answered this description, and flatter myself it was the very place; it is out of gunshot to the southward of the wrecks, but commands a fine view of all that could have passed. I could easily fill up the picture with the lively objects of ships on fire and explosions, as I am pretty well acquainted with their appearance; and, as Wraxall says, "felt that pleasure, which is natural to a thinking mind, at being on a spot famous for any historical event," mixed, however, with a painful sensation at the idea of what King James must have felt on seeing all his hopes vanish in thick clouds of smoke. I returned to Valognes that night, and arrived at Coutances early the next evening, and had the same view from the tower, at the setting of the sun, that Wraxall mentions. Next day dined at Granville; and knowing the geography of the country, instead of going round eighteen leagues by land, I took a passage by water, in a fishing boat, of five leagues to Cancale. The master was at Cancale, at our *brûlement*, with Sir James Wallace, and I had two fellow passengers, seamen, who had been in the action of the 12th of April. You may suppose I

---

pursued Tourville. Tourville ran ashore and cut away his masts, and two others followed him. The body of the fleet in the evening stood into La Hogue: the admiral ordered Sir George Rooke to follow with fire-ships, and all the boats well manned to destroy them; but they had got so far up the bay that none but small frigates and boats could advance near enough. Sir George ordered every boat to be manned and to board the enemy; and so terrified were the French, that, as our brave fellows entered on one side, the French crowded out on the other. The result was that, with the ships destroyed in the bay, and half a dozen of which Russell gave an account outside, the loss of the enemy was two ships of 104 guns and fourteen others of the line from 90 to 60 guns.

set them a going, and was highly entertained and amused
with their different accounts. As it was late before the tide
would let us leave Granville, it was near ten o'clock at night
before we arrived, fine smooth water, and moonlight. My
new friends piloted me to the *auberge*, stormed the people up,
got some fire in a *sabot*, and I insisted that we should all sit
down together to eat broiled mackerel, the only thing the
house produced. They seemed mightily pleased, and were
very anxious to know who I was, which was the only thing in
which I did not choose to satisfy them. English, and a seaman,
was all they could make out. I paid the reckoning, and had a
very good night's rest in a good bed, which the meanest house
in France always has, with linen bleached very white. The
next morning before I set off for St Malo I took a walk, with
my fisherman as a conductor, to see the marks of our bullets
in the rocks and houses. We talked over the whole business
very good-humouredly, and he told me he sold forty of our
shot for twelve sous a-piece, an illustration of the proverb,
" 'Tis an ill wind that blows nobody any good". I will give
you the rest of my history in another letter. This has im-
perceptibly spun to such a length, that the post hour is come
without my having written to my mother; therefore I beg
you to read this to her. Adieu.

Affectionately yours,
W. Sidney Smith

From France he went to Gibraltar and from there to
Morocco to 'spy out the land', and on the completion of this
visit he sent the following report, in the form of a letter, to the
Secretary of the Admiralty, and at the same time volunteered
his services in what he considered the probable event of his
country going to war with the Emperor of Morocco.

Tuy, in Gallicia, April 30th 1788.

Sir,
    I beg you will lay before my lords commissioners of the
admiralty, that in the month of May last, being at Gibraltar,
and a witness to the Emperor of Morocco's unreasonable
demands and imperious language, I judged a war with him
to be not far distant, and therefore undertook a journey
through his dominions, in order to acquire a knowledge of
his coasts, harbours, and force, so as to be of use in case of
such an event taking place; this knowledge so acquired seems

now to be called for by the Emperor of Morocco's having ordered his cruizers to be in readiness, if not actually to capture British vessels. I am, therefore, on my return to England in the earnest hope that their lordships will enable me to employ it to advantage in the protection of our trade, by giving me the command of a force adequate to the destruction of his inconsiderable naval force, even in his harbours. It consists of only seven frigates and three row galleys, independent of what adventurers may have joined him from the other Barbary states, and what prizes he may have taken and armed. I conceive the trade within the Straits of Gibraltar to be sufficiently protected by the squadron already in the Mediterranean; the chief danger lies from the ports of Laraiche, Salee, Mogadore, and Santa Cruz, *towards the Atlantic*, and a single squadron cannot perform both services of guarding *within* and *without* the Straits, because of the uncertainty and frequent impossibility of passing the gut when bound outwards.

A second separate squadron, therefore, to rendezvous and refit in Lagos Bay, appears necessary, which in my opinion need not consist of more than a fifty-gun ship, six frigates and sloops, and some small vessels; these latter should be of a similar construction to the emperor's galleys, as they will otherwise be likely to annoy our trade with impunity, from the difficulty of getting at them in calm seas and shoal harbours, which the frigates cannot approach, such as Arzilla, Mahmora, Enfifac and Azamore; besides these Laraiche, Salee, and Mogadore are the ports where his greatest force commonly assembles; the two former being bar-harbours are very difficult of access to an enemy, as well on account of the shoals as the good disposition of their batteries, which the French in their late expedition experienced to their cost; the latter (Mogadore) not being a bar-harbour is more easy of access, and, though fortified by a wall and protected by a greater *number* of guns, their injudicious position and distribution render it by no means impregnable to such a force as I have named above, if in such a position as I should hope to be able to place it, and aided by the disembarkation of such a detachment of troops as Gibraltar could easily furnish.

The forty-four gun ships, lately fitted as transports, appear to me a proper sort of ship for this service, from their weight of metal, their room, and their draught of water not being greater than the depth in those situations, which I sounded when there, and which then appeared the most favourable for such a design; besides this, their establishment, being that of a sloop, obviates the difficulty there might otherwise be of finding officers young enough to serve under the command of so young a one as I am; I hope their lordships will not consider this my inferiority of rank as an obstacle to grant me the honour I request, but rather trust that what I want, in professional experience and ability, will be made up by *local* knowledge and zeal for the public service; at the same time that they will pardon me, if that zeal carries me too far in thus making the proposition and offer of myself.

I have the honour to be

Yours most obedient humble servant,

W. Sidney Smith

Secretary of the Admiralty.

KNIGHT OF THE SWORD

When Sidney Smith returned from his Mediterranean trip in the autumn of 1788 England was still at peace, and he was no peacetime sailor. Bored stiff without the excitement for which his adventurous spirit always craved he spent twelve long tedious months waiting for trouble to break out somewhere. It was not long, however, before the prospect of another spell of active service opened up for him when war was declared in June 1788 between Russia and Sweden. In 1789, therefore, Smith applied for and was granted six months' leave of absence to visit Stockholm and St Petersburg, and at the same time gave an undertaking that it was not his intention to join the service of any foreign power.

After his arrival in Stockholm in November 1789 he lost little time in approaching Duke Karl of Sudermania at Karlskrone and asked whether he might be allowed to serve with the Swedish fleet. The Duke took an instant liking to this enthusiastic and persuasive young English naval officer and went with him to Stockholm where his request was handed to the King of Sweden.

Gustavus, the officers of whose navy had no experience of active service, welcomed the British captain's offer and wrote him the following letter:

Haga, January 17th 1790.

Colonel* Sidney Smith,

The great reputation you have acquired in serving your own country with equal success and valour, and the profound calm which England enjoys, not affording you any opportunity to display your talents at present, induce me to propose to you to enter into my service, during this war, and principally for the approaching campaign.

To offer you the same rank and appointments, which you enjoy in your own country, is only to offer you what you

* Colonel is the only term by which the rank of post-captain in the British navy can be compared with the similar rank in Sweden.

have a right to expect; but to offer you opportunities of distinguishing yourself anew, and of augmenting your reputation, by making yourself known in these northern seas as the *élève* of Rodney, Pigot, Howe, and Hood, is, I believe, to offer you a situation worthy of them and of yourself, which you will not resist, and the means of acquitting yourself towards your masters in the art of war, by extending their reputation, and the estimate they are already held in here.

I have destined a particular command for you, if you accept my offer, concerning which I will explain myself more in detail when I have your definitive answer.

I pray God to have you in his holy keeping.

Yours very affectionate,
Gustavus

This offer was almost too good to be true but he could not accept it without the Admiralty's permission, and how was this to be obtained? Fortunately for Smith he was able to persuade the British Minister in Stockholm to let him carry some important despatches to London where he would be able to request permission to accept King Gustavus' offer.

Meanwhile, the Duke of Sudermania, who was as anxious as his brother the King to acquire Smith's services, also wrote to him.

From His Royal Highness the Duke of Sudermania to Captain Sidney Smith

Stockholm, January 18th 1790.

My Dear Friend,

I have just learnt that the king has offered you the command of the light squadron. This news gives me the greatest pleasure, for two reasons; first, I am happy to have an able, skilful, and experienced man at the head of this department, uniting those qualities with the desire to do good, without attending to those interested individuals who ever annex their own private interests to military affairs, which is altogether to be found in you. And the second cause of my satisfaction is what regards me more particularly, for you know one would rather serve with a friend than an indifferent person; and, as the two fleets will ever be in situations mutually to require each other's assistance, it will be more agreeable to me to have to do with one, to whom I am particularly attached, than with one not so well known to me.

I am sorry, however, that this should occasion your precipitate departure. I offer up the most sincere prayers for your return, and that the king, your master, will please to give his consent to my desires.

As you have no carriage fit for your journey, I have given orders to my equerry to offer you a light and convenient one; see if it will suit you, or choose which you please among those I have. I write this without ceremony. Between friends one does not stand on such things.

Return as quick as you can, and bring some of your brave Englishmen with you, for we stand in need of officers. I shall offer up my prayers that your journey may be fortunate, and without accident, and I hope that that Being, who watched over you in your little boat, will do the same this time, and bring you in good health to the arms of your friends, among whom I beg you ever to reckon me.

I desire you will present my respects to the King, and my compliments to the Prince of Wales. From what you have told me of the Prince, I am desirous some day to make his acquaintance.

I need not give you new assurances of the interest I take in everything which concerns you. When I have once given my friendship, it is for life, and this sentiment will rest eternally in my heart, being yours for ever.

Charles,
Duke of Sudermania.

To Mr Sidney Smith, Colonel in the service
of His Majesty the King of England.

What happened on his arrival in London is told in Smith's own words:

With these grand objects in view, I left Stockholm, flattering myself, that as I was the bearer of the most authentic and recent intelligence from the north, so I should be an acceptable and welcome messenger. On my arrival, however, I found, by my reception, that I had been egregiously mistaken, since it was with difficulty that I obtained even the least degree of attention. This was, of course, a great disappointment to me, which I felt the more, considering the exertion and dispatch I had made on the journey from Stockholm, and the shock my health had suffered by travelling night and day in open carriages, in the worst season of the year.

At the end of six weeks, I ventured to represent by letter, with all respect, that the most unqualified negative could not be more unpalatable to the King of Sweden, or more prejudicial to his majesty's affairs, than this delay must be. To this, I received no answer whatever, and I had occasion to observe that this application I had made was considered as very unbecoming impatience in me.

Anxious still to ascertain whether I might not yet be the bearer of the joyful news, that assistance would be afforded from the allies, I waited till it was evident that there was no such intention; and as nothing was done till the spring advanced, I saw that if I did not set off forthwith, I should be too late for the opening of the campaign.

It was by now obvious that H.M. Government were not going to give Smith's request their official blessing and he had no alternative but to return on his own responsibility to Stockholm, and this he did. At that time his conduct was not an offence against English law for the Foreign Enlistment Act was not passed until 1870.* Nevertheless, it may seem surprising that the British naval authorities appear to have taken no disciplinary action against him, as it was, to say the least, unusual for a British officer to become a mercenary in the service of a foreign power engaged in a war in which his own country was not a belligerent.† Perhaps their lordships at the Admiralty preferred to have this stormy petrel usefully occupied far from home rather than have him making a nuisance of himself on their own doorstep.

So Sidney Smith set sail for the Baltic and, after a long and stormy passage, arrived at Karlocrona. He wrote to his friend the British Minister in Stockholm, Mr Liston, telling him why he had not put in at Stockholm.

"Having nothing to do at Stockholm," he wrote, "as I am

* Section 4 of this Act provides that any British subject who, without Her Majesty's licence and within or without Her Majesty's dominions, accepts, or agrees to accept a commission or engagement in the military or naval service of any foreign state at war with any foreign state at peace with Her Majesty shall be punishable by fine and/or imprisonment at the discretion of the court which convicts him.

† Although it was unusual there was, nevertheless, another officer of the Royal Navy serving on the other side, Captain Dennison, who was in command of the Russian frigate *Venus*, and who nearly succeeded in taking the King of Sweden prisoner off Cape Musalo.

not charged with any dispatch for you, I made no scruple of altering my destination and coming hither as the only chance I have of joining the duke (of Sudermania) before he meets the enemy, and also as the best mode of getting to Finland to make my report to the King and to say the little I am authorised to say as an acknowledgement of the message he sent by me".

This was, in fact, completely untrue as the British Secretary of State for Foreign Affairs had snubbed him and refused to regard him even as an unofficial envoy. Smith had not been authorised to give any message to the Swedish King.

He did not, however, allow the fact that he arrived too late to sail with the Duke's fleet to deter him. Under the false pretext of carrying important despatches to the King he managed to get permission to sail in the fast cutter *Dragon* to join the main fleet which he reached on 18th May near the mouth of the Gulf of Finland.

The Duke was delighted to see Smith as he was in need of cheerful company after the reverse which the Swedish fleet had suffered at Reval, losing two battleships.

Next day Smith sailed in the Duke's own yacht to Svenskund, which he reached on 21st May, and went on board the Royal Yacht from which he wrote the following letter to Liston.

*A bord de l'*Amphion, *le* 21 *Mai* 1790
Svenska Sund.

Dear Sir,

By the date of this you will observe that I am on board his majesty's yacht. I left His Royal Highness the Duke of Sudermania the day before yesterday, off Reval, in good health, though not in the best spirits, after the unfortunate attack on the enemy's fleet in the port.

I need not enter into the detail of that business, as you will probably have it at length in the gazettes—suffice it to say it was a most desperate undertaking, such as I should not have advised, or let pass, without a remonstrance, had I been with his royal highness; because, considering the position of the Russian fleet, and that they had full time to prepare themselves, it was next to impossible that it could be successful. Mons. De Grasse attempted the same thing against us at St Christopher's, with as little success, *we* having the same advantage as the Russians had, of a fixed position, while he had the disadvantage of being under way, and exposed to the whole fire of our line, drawn to a centre on each of his ships in succession. . . . His Majesty has placed me on board a little yacht which follows his galley, the *Seraphim*, on board of which he remains in action. I shall probably not be able to refrain from doing the same. I hope that will not be considered as serving. . . .

I remain,

Dear Sir, yours truly,

W. Sidney Smith

King Gustavus' naval staff, however, were not so pleased to have the cocky English captain with them. One of them, Captain Sillen, wrote in his diary, "We are most curious to know how the Englishman Smith is going to behave here. Some pretend to know for certain that he does not want to hold any post or position and that he will not even serve as a volunteer but merely intends to stay here for a while as a spectator after which he will return to the main fleet—this, it seems to me, would certainly be the wisest thing he could do."

That he would soon return to the main fleet was not a bad guess but Sillen could not have been further from the mark in thinking that Smith would be content to play the rôle of spectator. He did not know his Smith. This "adventurer", as another officer called him, "was given such wide powers to direct the fleet's movements that the flag captain became entirely dependent on him though he did everything he could to sabotage Smith's orders when he considered them unsuitable. On one occasion when this officer openly defied him Smith said, 'My dear Klint, you don't understand my position,' and there the matter rested."

But in the King's eyes and in his brother's Smith could do no wrong. "By the King and his staff he is regarded in an incomparable light," Sillen wrote, "and at table he is virtually the only subject of His Majesty's conversation. He retains all his English freedom of manner and says he is only here to satisfy his curiosity."

And so it remained until the end of the war when Sidney Smith returned to England where he was received in triumph and invested by King George III, at the request of the King of Sweden, with the Grand Cross of the Royal Swedish Order of the Sword as Knight Commander. All was forgiven and forgotten.

3

FIRESHIP CAPTAIN*

PEACE having now come to Sweden, and his own country not
being yet at war again, Sidney Smith had to look elsewhere for
adventure. Fortunately for him Lord Grenville, who was then
Secretary of State for Foreign Affairs, decided to send him to
Constantinople on a secret mission and gave him a sum of
£1,500 out of the Foreign Office Vote, for expenses.

This assignment could not have come at a more opportune
time for there were other reasons for Smith wanting to go to the
Dardanelles. The Russians and Turks were still fighting and he
thought that his having only recently fought in the Swedish
navy against the Russians might qualify him for a similar
appointment, as naval adviser to the Turks. Failing this, an
up-to-date and professional report on the naval and military
situation in that area might raise his stock a little at the
Admiralty where he was not, at the moment, exactly popular.

Furthermore, from a purely personal point of view, it would
be pleasant to see, once more, his old friend Liston, now Sir
Robert, and British Ambassador to the Porte, who was soon to
be relieved by Smith's own brother Spencer.

Practically nothing is known about his short stay in the Near
East except that there is a note amongst his papers to the effect
that his expenses amounted to considerably more than the sum
allotted to him by Lord Grenville:

1792. Expenses of a journey to Constantinople by land, and
residence there; examining the Black Sea, Sea of Marmora,
Dardanelles, Archipelago and Ionian Islands—beyond the
sum of fifteen hundred pounds furnished by the Foreign
Office for that purpose, but which was inadequate from the
unforeseen circumstance of war breaking out between Great
Britain and France.

There is, however, some evidence that he was serving in the

---

* After Sir Sidney's burning of the French fleet at Toulon Napoleon nicknamed
him 'Le Capitaine de Brûlot'.

Turkish Navy and stationed at Smyrna when he first heard the news that war had broken out between England and France. This was like the sound of a trumpet to the warhorse and he set about devising some way of joining the British forces with the least possible delay. He found that there were a number of British seamen stranded in Smyrna without employment and managed to buy a small vessel which he named the *Swallow Tender*, manned it with forty of these sailors, hoisted the English flag and sailed westward through the Mediterranean in search of the English fleet which he found at Toulon just before the evacuation of the port and the destruction of its magazines and arsenals.

In August 1793 a Royalist rising had broken out in Toulon, and its inhabitants, through Admiral Turgot who was in command of the French fleet there, approached Lord Hood, then Commander-in-Chief in the Mediterranean, and invited him to occupy the town and naval harbour in the name of Louis XVII.

The general committee of Toulon then made the following declaration:

It is the unanimous wish of the inhabitants of Toulon to reject a constitution which does not promote their happiness; to adopt a monarchic government, such as it was, by the constituent assembly of 1798; and, in consequence, they have proclaimed Louis XVII, the son of Louis XVI, King; and have sworn to acknowledge him, and no longer suffer the despotism of the tyrants who at this time govern France.

Lord Hood immediately issued this dramatic proclamation and then occupied the town and took over the harbour together with all its shipping which, he declared, he would hold in trust for Louis XVII until peace should be re-established in France.

PROCLAMATION

By the Right Honourable Samuel Lord Hood, Vice-Admiral of the Red, and Commander-in-chief of His Britannic Majesty's squadron in the Mediterranean, etc., to the Inhabitants of the Towns and Provinces in the South of France.

During four years you have been involved in a revolution which has plunged you in anarchy, and rendered you a prey to factious leaders. After having destroyed your government, trampled under foot the laws, assassinated the virtuous, and authorised the commission of crimes, they have endeavoured to propagate throughout Europe their destructive system of every social order. They have constantly held forth to you the idea of liberty, while they have been robbing you of it. Everywhere they have preached respect to persons and property, and everywhere in their name it has been violated. They have amused you with the sovereignty of the people, which they have constantly usurped. They have declaimed against the abuses of royalty in order to establish their tyranny upon the fragments of a throne still reeking with the blood of your legitimate sovereign. Frenchmen! you groan under the pressure of want and the privation of all specie; your commerce and your industry are annihilated, your agriculture is checked, and the want of provisions threatens you with a horrible famine. Behold, then, the faithful picture of your wretched condition. A situation so dreadful sensibly afflicts the coalesced Powers. They see no other remedy, but the re-establishment of the French monarchy. It is for this, and the acts of aggression committed by the executive power of France, that we have armed in conjunction with the other coalesced Powers. After mature reflection upon these leading objects, I come to offer you the force with which I am entrusted by my sovereign, in order to spare the further effusion of human blood, to crush with promptitude the factious, to re-establish a regular government in France, and thereby maintain peace and tranquillity in Europe. Decide, therefore, definitively, and with precision. Trust your hopes to the generosity of a *loyal* and *free* nation. In its name, I have just given an unequivocal testimony to the well-disposed inhabitants of Marseilles, by granting to the commissioners, sent on board the fleet under my command, a passport for procuring a quantity of grain, of which this great town now stands so much in need. Be explicit! and I fly to your succour, in order to break the chain which surrounds you, and to be the instrument of making many years of happiness succeed to four years of misery and anarchy, in which your deluded country has been involved.

Given on board his Britannic Majesty's ship *Victory*, off Toulon, this 23rd day of August, 1793.

Hood

The decision to occupy Toulon was a rash one, as the Navy on its own was not of sufficient strength to hold it without re-inforcements, and apparently no arrangements had been made in advance to supply any. The Spaniards had considerable forces in the vicinity but the Spanish Admiral, when requested by Lord Hood to assist, politely declined. Nor was this all. The French sailors, commanded by a Royalist admiral, were rapidly becoming mutinous; they got rid of their commander and appointed a revolutionary in his place.

By the middle of December it became fairly obvious that the Allies could not hold out any longer and at a Council of War presided over by Lord Hood it was decided that preparations would have to be made immediately for a possible withdrawal. This would mean abandoning the Royalists in Toulon to the wolves, but the council resolved to inform the inhabitants that if it were found necessary to retreat "the combined powers would use every possible means to carry off such of them as might wish to leave".

Meanwhile, although Smith had joined Hood's fleet, he was still on half-pay and had not been given any appointment. When it was finally decided to evacuate Toulon Smith volun-teered to burn the French ships which had to be left behind, a task that was carried out so badly that several which were reported as burnt and destroyed were identified in later years as still in active service. The blame for this, however, cannot be laid at his door. It was because our Spanish allies fled before they had completed their part of the operation. Napoleon himself, speaking of the burning of the ships said, "Sir Sidney Smith set them on fire and they would all have been burned if the Spaniards had behaved well."

The details of this operation were duly reported to Lord Hood.

Sir Sidney Smith to Lord Hood. Detailing the result of his operations, the work of the preceding night.

Agreeably to your lordship's orders I proceeded with the *Swallow Tender*, three English, and three Spanish gun-boats, to the arsenal, and immediately began making the necessary preparations for burning the French ships and stores therein; we found the dock-gates well secured by the judicious arrangements of the governor; and although the dock-yard people had already substituted the three-coloured cockade for the white one, I did not think it safe to attempt the securing any of them, considering the small force I had with me, and considering that a contest of any kind would occupy our whole attention and prevent us from accomplishing our preparations.

The galley-slaves, to the number of at least 600, shewed themselves jealous spectators of our operations,—their disposition to oppose us was evident, and being unchained (which was unusual) rendered it necessary to keep a watchful eye on them. I accordingly restrained them on board the galleys, by pointing the guns of the *Swallow Tender* and one of the gun-boats on them, in such a manner as to enfilade the quay on which they must land to come to us; assuring them at the same time that no harm should happen to them if they remained quiet. The enemy kept up a cross fire of shot and shells on the spot from Malbousquet and the neighbouring hills, which contributed to keep the galley-slaves in subjection, and operated in every respect favourably for us, by keeping the republican party in the town within their houses, while it occasioned little interruption to our work of preparing and placing combustible matter in the different storehouses and on board the ships such was the steadiness of the few brave seamen I had under my command. A great multitude of the enemy continued to draw down the hill towards the dock-yard wall, and, as the night closed in, they came near enough to pour in an irregular though quick fire on us from the *boulangerie*, and the heights which overlook it; we kept them at bay by discharges of grape-shot from time to time, which prevented their coming so near as to discover the insufficiency of our force to repel a closer attack. A gun-boat was stationed to flank the wall on the outside, and two field-pieces were placed within against the wicket, usually frequented by the workmen, of whom we were particularly apprehensive.

About eight o'clock, I had the satisfaction to see Lieutenant Gore towing in the *Vulcan* fireship. Captain Hare, her commander, placed her, agreeably to my directions, in a most masterly manner, across the tier of men of war; and the additional force of her guns and men diminished my apprehensions of the galley-slaves rising on us, as their murmurs and occasional tumultuous debates ceased entirely on her appearance; the only noise heard among them was the

2

hammer knocking off their fetters, which humanity forbade my opposing, as they might thereby be more at liberty to save themselves, on the conflagration taking place around them; in this situation we continued to wait most anxiously for the hour concerted with the governor for the inflammation of the trains; the moment the signal was made we had the satisfaction to see the flames rise in every quarter. Lieutenant Tupper was charged with the burning of the general magazine, the pitch, tar, tallow, and oil store-houses, and succeeded most perfectly, the hemp magazine was included in this blaze. The weather being nearly calm was unfavourable to the spreading of the flames, but 250 barrels of tar, divided among the deals and other timber, insured the rapid ignition of that whole quarter which Lieutenant Tupper had undertaken.

The mast-house was equally well set on fire by Lieutenant Middleton of the *Britannia*. Lieutenant Pater of the *Britannia* continued in a most daring manner to brave the flames, in order to complete the work where the fire seemed to have caught imperfectly; I was obliged to call him off, lest his retreat should become impracticable; his situation was the more perilous, as the enemy's fire redoubled as soon as the amazing blaze of light rendered us distinct objects for their aim.

Lieutenant Ironmonger, of the Royals, remained with the guard at the gate till the last, long after the Spanish guard was withdrawn, and was brought safely off by Captain Edge of the *Alert*, to whom I had confided the important service of closing our retreat, and bringing off our detached parties, which were saved to a man. I was sorry to find myself deprived of the further services of Captain Hare; he had performed that of placing his fire-ship to admiration, but was blown into the water, and much scorched by the explosion of her priming, when in the act of putting the match to it. Lieutenant Gore was also much burnt, and I was consequently deprived of him also, which I regretted the more, from the recollection of his bravery and activity in the warm service of Fort Mulgrave. Mr Eales, midshipman, who was also with him on this occasion, deserves every praise for his conduct throughout this service. The guns of the fire-ship going off on both sides, as they heated, in the direction that was given them, towards those quarters from whence we were most apprehensive of the enemy forcing their way in upon us, checked their career; their shouts and republican songs, which we could hear distinctly, continued till they, as well as ourselves, were in a manner thunderstruck by the explosion of some thousand barrels of powder on board the *Iris* frigate, lying in the inner road without us, and which had been injudiciously set on fire by the Spanish boats, in going off, instead of being sunk as ordered; the concussion of air, and the shower of falling timber ignited, were such as nearly to have destroyed the whole of us. Lieutenant Patey of the *Terrible*, with his whole boat's crew, nearly perished; the boat was blown to pieces, but the men were picked up alive. The *Union* gun-boat, which was nearest to the *Iris*, suffered considerably, Mr Young being killed, with three men, and the vessel shaken to pieces.

I had given it in charge to the Spanish officers, to fire the ships in the basin before the town, but they returned and reported that various obstacles had prevented their entering it; we attempted it together, as soon as we had completed the business in the arsenal, but were repulsed in our attempt to cut the boom, by repeated volleys of musketry from the flag-ship and the wall of the *Batterie Royale*. The cannon of this battery had been spiked by the judicious precautions taken by the governor, previous to the evacuation of the town. The rear of our column being by this time out of the eastern gate, the horrid cries of the poor inhabitants announced that the villainous part of the community had got the upper hand; boats, full of men, women and children, pushed from the shore, even without oars, claiming our protection from the knife of the assassin, by the most sacred of all ties,—professed friendship: we accordingly kept our station, for the purpose of affording them an asylum. Many straggling Neapolitan soldiers, whose undisciplined conduct had separated them from the main body, were among the number thus driven into the water. We received them as more particularly belonging to us, repulsing their pursuers by our fire; nor did we quit the shore till we had received all who were there to claim our assistance. The failure of our attempt on the ships in the basin before the town, owing to the insufficiency of our force, made me regret that the Spanish gun-boats had been withdrawn from me to perform the service. The Adjutant Don Pedro Cotiella, Don Francisco Riguelme, and Don Francisco Truxillo remained with me to the last; and I feel bound to bear testimony to the zeal and activity with which they performed the most essential services, during the whole of this business, as far as the insufficiency of their force allowed; it being reduced, by the retreat of the gun-boats, to a single felucca and a mortar-boat, which had expended its ammunition, but contained thirty men with cutlasses.

We now proceeded to burn the *Hero* and *Themistocles*, two seventy-four gun ships, lying in the Inner Road; our approach to them had hitherto been impracticable in boats, as the French prisoners, which had been left in the latter ship, were still in possession of her, and had shewn a determination to resist our attempt to come on board. The scene of conflagration around them, heightened by the late tremendous explosion, had, however, awakened their fears for their lives; thinking this to be the case, I addressed them, expressing my readiness to land them in a place of safety, if they would submit; and they most thankfully accepted the offer, shewing themselves to be completely intimidated, and very grateful for our humane intentions towards them, in not attempting to burn them with the ship; it was necessary to proceed with precaution as they were more numerous than ourselves. We at length completed their disembarkation, and then set her on fire; on this occasion I had nearly lost my valuable friend and assistant, Lieutenant Miller of the *Windsor Castle*, who had stayed so long on board to ensure the fire taking, that it gained on him suddenly; and it was not without being much scorched and the risk of being suffocated that we could approach the ship to take him in; the loss to the service would have been very great had we not succeeded in our endeavours to save him. Mr Knight, midshipman, of the *Windsor Castle*, who was in the boat with me, shewed much activity and address, on this occasion, as well as firmness throughout the day.

The explosion of a second powder vessel, equally unexpected, and with a shock even greater than the first, again put us in the most imminent danger of perishing; and, when it is considered that we were within the sphere of the falling timber, it is next to miraculous that no one piece of the many, which made the water foam round us, happened to touch either the *Swallow* or the three boats with me.

Having now set fire to everything within our reach,

exhausted our combustible preparations, and our strength, to such a degree, that the men absolutely dropped on the oars, we directed our course to join the fleet, running the gauntlet under a few ill directed shots from the forts of Balaqué and Aiguilette, now occupied by the enemy, but fortunately without loss of any kind, we proceeded to the place appointed for the embarkation of the troops, and took off as many as we could carry.

It would be injustice to those officers whom I have omitted to name, from their not having been so immediately under my eye, if I did not acknowledge myself indebted to them all for their extraordinary exertions in the execution of this great national object; the quickness with which the conflagration took effect, on my signal, its extent and duration, are the best evidences that every officer and man was ready at his post, and firm under most perilous circumstances. I, therefore, subjoin a list of the whole who were employed on this service.

We can ascertain that the fire extended to at least ten sail of the line, how much further we cannot say. The loss of the general magazine, and of the quantity of pitch, tar, rosin, hemp, timber, cordage, and gun-powder, must considerably impede the equipment of the few ships that remain. I am sorry to have been obliged to leave any, but I hope your lordship will be satisfied that we did as much as our circumscribed means enabled us to do in a limited time.

W. Sidney Smith

All things considered Sidney Smith had not done too badly. When he volunteered to undertake this dangerous and difficult operation he knew the hazards involved and there was literally no time in which to make adequate preparation.

Only a few hours before it was due to start Hood sent him two letters impressing its importance upon him. "You *must* burn every French ship you possibly can," the Admiral wrote, "consult the governor as to the proper hour of doing it, on account of the bringing off the troops."

On the morning of 15th January 1794 Smith arrived in London with a despatch from Lord Hood giving details of the evacuation.

Victory, Hierces Bay, Dec. 20 1793.

Sir,

It is my duty to acquaint you, that I have been obliged to

evacuate Toulon, and to retire from the harbour to this anchorage.

It became unavoidably necessary that the retreat should not be deferred beyond that night, as the enemy commanded the town and ships by their shot and shells; I therefore, agreeable to the governor's plan, directed the boats of the fleet to assemble by eleven o'clock near Fort La Malgue, and am happy to say the whole of the troops were brought off, to the number of near 8000, without the loss of a man; and, in the execution of this service I have infinite pleasure in acknowledging my very great obligations to Captain Elphinstone for his unremitting zeal and exertion, who saw the last man off, and it is a very comfortable satisfaction to me that several thousands of the meritorious inhabitants of Toulon were sheltered in his majesty's ships. . . . Circumstances which had taken place made the retreat absolutely necessary to be effected as soon as possible, and prevented the execution of a settled arrangement for destroying the French ships and arsenal. I ordered the *Vulcan* fire-ship to bed primed, and Sir Sidney Smith, who joined me from Smyrna about a fortnight ago, having offered his service to burn the ships, I put Captain Hare under his orders, with the Lieutenants Tupper and Gore of the *Victory*, Lieutenant Pater of the *Britannia*, and Lieutenant R. W. Miller of the *Windsor Castle*. Ten of the enemy's ships of the line in the arsenal, with the mast-house, great store-house, hemp-house, and other buildings, were totally destroyed. . . .

Don Langara* undertook to destroy the ships in the basin, but, I am informed, found it not practicable; and, as the Spanish troops had the guarding of the powder-vessels, which contained the powder of the ships I ordered into the basin and arsenal on my coming here, as well as that from the distant magazines within the enemy's reach, I requested the Spanish admiral would be pleased to give orders for their being scuttled and sunk; but instead of doing that, the officer to whom that duty was intrusted, blew them up, by which two fine gun-boats which I had ordered to attend Sir Sidney Smith were shook to pieces. The lieutenant commanding one of them was killed, and several seamen badly wounded. I am sorry to add, that Lieutenant Goddard, of the *Victory*, who commanded the seamen upon the heights of

* The Admiral in command of the Spanish fleet.

Grasse, was wounded, but I hope and trust not dangerously.

I beg to refer you for further particulars to General Dundas, respecting the evacuation of Toulon; and to Sir Sidney Smith as to the burning of the enemy's ships etc. on which service he very much distinguished himself, and he gives great praise to Captain Hare, of the fire-ships, as well as to all the lieutenants employed under him. . . .

I have the honour, etc.

Hood

Admiral Collingwood, however, was not at all pleased.

"Our miscarriage at Toulon is truly provoking," he wrote, "the more so as gross mismanagement alone could have prevented its being totally destroyed. Lord Hood was in good luck to get possession of it, but was not general enough to discover how critical his situation was there. No preparation was made for the destruction either of ships or arsenal; and at last perhaps it was put into as bad hands as could be found—Sir Sidney Smith, who arrived there a few days before and had no public situation either in the fleet or army, but was wandering to gratify his curiosity—you know how it was executed. The ships should have been prepared for sinking as soon as he got possession of them, loading them deep with ballast and stones, and making a porthole in them near the edge of the water; and then placing the ships in those parts of the harbour which would most effectually injure it. If the necessity for sinking the ships did not arise they would be uninjured; if it did they might have all been put under water in half an hour."

Collingwood's comments, however, are not surprising for Sir Sidney was to him like a red rag is to a bull.

The final scenes in Toulon had not been very creditable and Smith described them in a letter written to Sir William Hamilton in Naples before he left for London.

"The idea of *sauve qui peut*", he wrote, "seemed to possess everybody. The fleets of the different nations, alarmed at the idea of being burnt by red hot shot or shells from Fort Mulgrave (now in possession of the enemy) weighed anchor, and crowded out of the road in such haste, as to alarm the troops on shore, lest they should be left behind; indeed many of the Neapolitan and Spanish soldiers would have been so left, had not the English squadron stayed to receive them, after the ships of their own nations were gone. This I aver to be the fact, and

I wonder by what system of reasoning an admiral can consider himself responsible to his sovereign for the safety of *the fleet alone*, when the army is equally under his care; yet this was the language.

The little order that had been hitherto preserved on shore was destroyed by this precipitation, which gave the retreat every appearance of a most disgraceful flight. This disagreeable scene was heightened, and one's feelings tortured, by the lamentations of women and children, who, with their husbands or fathers, were obliged to leave their homes and their property, to save their lives, under the certainty of a public execution, if they escaped the massacre to be expected, on an enraged and merciless enemy entering the town. The impatience of officers and brutality of the soldiers, in claiming a preference at the place of embarkation, increased the confusion,—in short the whole of this horrid scene is not describable—a few muskets fired in the town, perhaps from the windows, by some mad-headed republican, raised a cry that their party had made a revolution in the town; the tumult and pressure, on this alarm, became such that many were forced into the water and drowned."

A terrible fate befell those Royalists who were unable to get away or who, for some reason, decided to remain behind, and Sidney Smith described one of the incidents that happened in these words:

"The royalists and the liberated convicts had been driven into the great square of Toulon, and were compressed together in one huge mass. Bonaparte, who then commanded the artillery, fired upon the people, and mowed them down like grass; those who had escaped his fire threw themselves upon the ground, hoping to avoid their threatened doom, when the future emperor of the French, taking advantage of the first moment of awful stillness which prevailed after the roaring of the cannon, exclaimed in a loud voice, 'The vengeance of the French republic is satisfied—rise and go to your homes', which summons the wretched people no sooner attempted to obey than a second murderous discharge of his artillery hurled them into eternity."

4

LION OF THE SEA

UPON his return to England Smith was well received in Government circles and highly commended by Lord Spencer for his destruction of an important section of the French fleet. He got little praise, however, from most of his seniors in the service who were jealous of him. Nelson was particularly sarcastic about the Toulon operation. "We have just got accounts that the French fleet is at sea," he wrote some twelve months afterwards, "twenty-two sail of the line. Sir Sidney Smith did not burn them all. Lord Hood mistook the man: there is an old song, 'Great talkers do the least we see'."

With the Admiralty, however, this last exploit had done Smith no harm and, only six months after his return, he was appointed to command the frigate *Diamond*, then stationed with the Channel fleet whose main duty was blockading the French Channel ports.

His first duty was to take Lord Spencer, who had just taken over the Admiralty, across the Channel to Flushing *en route* for Vienna and the First Lord appears to have spent most of the voyage listening to Sir Sidney's views on how the war at sea should be conducted. It must have been an intriguing experience, even though it doubtless tried the First Lord's patience to the utmost for Smith was never short of ideas nor was he ever hesitant in putting them forward.

About three weeks later Spencer wrote the following to William Windham, the Secretary of State for War:*

> I promised Sir Sidney Smith to write to you something about what he calls his ideas, but my own ideas have really been so turned and twisted and humbled about ever since, that I protest his have been pretty nearly shaken out of my head. In general, however, I remember he said a good deal about the French coasting ships which, by their being very flat bottomed, can run into shoal water where none of our

* The Windham Papers. Vol. I.

2*

Ships-of-War can follow them, and of course he is very desirous of having a fleet of flat-bottomed vessels at his command to go and break them all to pieces. He does not seem to think much of the scheme about Calais, but he has an idea that something might be done at Havre. He is certainly an odd eccentric man, but he is very clever, and has a great deal of contrivance about him, and if he could some-how be put into activity without giving offence to the more regular and orderly sort of Geniuses, who I believe all look upon him as a Fellow of the College of Physicians does upon a Quack doctor, he might be of great service.

A few days later Windham received the following letter from Sidney Smith:

Captain Sir W. Sidney Smith to William Windham
                    Diamond, at Plymouth, August 13, 1794.
PRIVATE

I agree entirely that the best way of acting against France, either in order to make a diversion to save Holland, to ward off a threatened attack on this country, or to make an impression on the centre of the enemy's country so as to effectuate the great object of the war, is by a *descent on their coasts*. The *point of attack* must depend on intelligence to be obtained, and the extent of the force that may be destined to carry the plan into effect. I am of opinion that the coast must be destitute of sufficient strength to defend it by the concentration of their forces in the formation of their great armies, but I am by no means of opinion that they are so liable to be surprised as the Duc de Levis seems to apprehend, for their intelligence is so good and their establishment of Coast signals is so perfectly well arranged and so well attended to that intelligence is quickly conveyed from one point to another. The *attempt* might be made to surprise, but it should be with such a force as would be equal to pro-ceeding by open assault when discovered, which is not impracticable on the very gates of a place inadequately garrisoned and irregularly fortified on one side.

A ruler laid on the map, from London to Paris shews the strait line of *shortest distance* to be by way of Dieppe or Havre and Rouen, and it is to be remembered that there is no chain of fortified places requiring regular sieges by that route.

Having received the latter part of my education at Caen in

Normandy, I have had opportunity of being acquainted with the Normans, and I am inclined to give credit to the Duc de Levis's assertion that Normandy and the Southern part of Picardy are disaffected to the convention, or at least to the Jacobin System; and consequently that they might be induced to shew themselves if a sufficient force was at hand, as a central point round which to rally; but my experience at Toulon has proved to me that this never can be expected if the *white flag** is shewn to them as an earnest of the return of the ancient System in its full extent. A Constitution is the desire of every thinking man in France. I am persuaded they have seen the bad effects of unlimited power in the two extremes of absolute and popular government too often and too recently not to be averse to placing it anywhere, and cannot (I think) be inclined to place it in the *same hands* who misused it before; and who would be likely to govern with a heavy hand in revenge for the persecution they have endured. There can be little doubt that there exists a party in France, and even in Paris itself, of the moderate kind, impatient under the present tyranny which puts their persons and property in such an irksome state of insecurity. This party might be induced to shew itself if support were near, and such support cannot be so quickly conveyed as by the *shortest route* and that on which there are the fewest barriers, viz. that above named.

Calais from its position does not seem to come into this line, or to be of any use as an insulated possession now that the Netherlands are evacuated. Dieppe and Havre I think would be valuable acquisitions. An army on the two banks of the River Seine, using that river as its line of communication, having its baggage, battering train and magazines afloat under the protection of gun-boats and consequently being unencumbered but with horses and forage might move with facility and be less liable to total discomfiture in case of failure, having a floating fortress to rally to.

I am persuaded that an expedition of this kind, if it did not succeed to the full extent of the object, might still do essential service; it would cut off one channel by which Paris is supplied with provisions, it would enable government to form a positive judgment of the real disposition of the people and finally in case of being obliged to fall back by the arrival of the northern army on the east bank of the Seine, the

* The flag of the deposed French monarchy.

(illegible) would afford our army a secure position with its
flanks towards the sea communicating on each side with its
floating Magazines by Carentan and La Hogue on the East,
and the little ports opposite Jersey on the west. Cherbourg
would by this position be cut off from the possibility of
receiving succour and as the high land behind the town
overlooks it, as Faron does Toulon, it must fall in the same
way; and thus, in case of ultimate relinquishment of the
enterprise, we should have destroyed the two ports of Havre
and Cherbourg, from whence we have otherwise everything
to apprehend if the enemy are left quietly at liberty to
realise their project of invading and 'revolutionising' this
country. I speak from local knowledge of the coasts and
ports in question, having examined the ground at leisure
during the peace when on a visit to the Duc d'Harcourt, then
Governor of Normandy, and I recommend his being consulted on the enterprise, his local knowledge and military
experience, together with his name and influence in the
country, would go a great way towards ensuring the success
of it. I beg to be understood to be very far from volunteering
it myself. I see my way clearly but I do not see my means.
Long legged frigates cannot approach the shore to co-
operate with or cover an army. Gun-boats alone can do it,
but it is not a boat with a gun that answers to my idea of a
gun-boat. I have acquitted my conscience towards my
country by having given my ideas distinctly to Lord St
Helens on the form of vessel I consider as adapted to this
service as well at home as in Holland, where the species
actually exists and requires only to be fitted. I have thus
enabled whoever may be destined for that service to act as
my peculiar experience would enable me, but I hope I may
stand excused from stepping forward myself, which I am
disinclined to do considering the little encouragement I meet
with for such voluntary exertions. Besides, no man can serve
in a situation of any degree of eminence without hurting his
private fortune, and I have unfortunately none to supply the
demand incident to such a situation. If I had I would most
willingly sacrifice that as I do my time and my health; these
with a daring spirit and as much military experience as I
could acquire by going wherever it was to be obtained, being
all I can call my own, I devote them to my country's service,
though I confess to you not so cheerfully as I have done

hitherto. I have suffered such pecuniary embarrassment and distress since my return from Toulon as makes me, though reluctantly, impeach my country's Justice; an Englishman never works the free horse to the utmost of his powers without seeing that he is well fed when he comes home, and yet collectively they can suffer an officer who has served them to the best of his ability to starve in their streets. I do not say this in any ill temper, I am ready to do what I am ordered as a military man ought to be, but when a man has suffered much and worked hard without having in the least mended his situation or even his prospects in life, his feelings must be wounded at seeing that he is working to little purpose. If a service which is denominated from the throne and acknowledged by Parliament of great national importance be left unrequited, what hope is there that any future service will be more considered? . . . I hope, my dear Sir, you will excuse the freedom with which I speak, but an honest man may, nay ought, to speak out to another.

Sir Sidney's resentful allusions in the above letter to his unrequited services between 1789 and 1794 are understandable, even though they are hardly justifiable. He had only himself to blame for it all and he can hardly have been surprised at the reaction of many of his brother officers to what they considered inexcusable conduct, unworthy of an 'officer and a gentleman'. It was, however, completely in character with his tempestuous nature and disposition to behave in such a way, and he was driven to it by his thirst for adventure and his passionate love of glory. While this cannot excuse him it does, perhaps, explain his behaviour.

The routine patrolling of the Channel during the long winter months Smith found very dull and wearisome but early in 1795 he had a welcome relief from it all. News had reached the Admiralty that a French fleet under Admiral Villaret de Joyeuse had sailed from Brest, and it became important to find out, if possible, its destination. H.M.S. *Diamond*, then serving with three other frigates under the command of Captain Sir John Warren, as Commodore, was selected by him to reconnoitre Brest harbour but Smith was warned, "Take care, Sir Sidney, to have no frigate-fighting!"

After completing the reconnaisance Smith sent the following report to the Commodore:

Diamond, at sea, January 4th, 1795.

Sir,

In pursuance of your orders, I this morning looked into the port of Brest, in his majesty's ship *Diamond*, under my command, in order to verify the intelligence of the enemy's fleet being at sea.

I went round the west point of Ushant yesterday, and the wind being easterly, I was obliged to work to windward between the shoals off Point St Mathew and the rocks to the southward, in order to come near enough to look into the road. We observed a large ship under French colours working in a-head, she took no notice of us, probably supposing that we were of her own nation from our making so free with the coast. I hoisted French colours, having previously disguised the figure of the ship, in order to favour such a deception. The tide of ebb coming strong out of the harbour, the enemy's ship anchored, and I accordingly, at sunset, anchored astern of her. I was in hopes when the flood made again, that she would have weighed, and proceeded up the passage, so that we might have done the same without approaching her so near as to risk the frustration of our object; but she continued to lie fast, and I was obliged either to relinquish the going close enough to the harbour to make my observations, or to alarm the coast by attacking her, or else to pass her silently, and thereby leave her in the channel of my retreat. I considered the occasion of my being detached from the squadron, as an object of sufficient national importance to justify all risks, and accordingly weighed, and passed her sufficiently near to observe by the light of the moon, that she was a line-of-battle ship.

As we proceeded, we saw two other ships at anchor, one of which was evidently a frigate: not being satisfied that I should be able to discern the anchorage plainly, when the day broke, from my present position, I was obliged to go between these ships and the Toulinguet rocks, observing the precaution in passing, to give all orders in a low tone of voice, that the enemy might not hear us speak English: they took no notice of us; and by daylight in the morning of this day, I had obtained a position from whence I could discern the anchorage of Brest, sufficiently distinct to ascertain that there were no men of war in the road, which is the usual anchorage.

N.B. The basin is not discoverable from without the fort.

I observed the wreck of a large ship on Mingan Island. It now became necessary to make the best of my way out of the passage; I accordingly altered my course for that purpose, taking a direction to re-pass the line-of-battle ship. A corvette, which was steering out in a parallel direction to us, was the first who took the alarm at this change of movement; she brought to, making signals, which communicated the alarm to the other two ships, and both hoisted their topsail yards immediately, and began getting under sail; my situation was now extremely critical. I saw, by the course the line-of-battle ship had taken, her intention to cut me off in my passage between her and the rocks, so that I could not effectuate it. There seemed no alternative but to remove their alarm, by a conduct that should bespeak ourselves unconcerned. I accordingly steered down directly within hail of this ship, which lay in my way between Basse Beuzec and the Trepieds. I could by this time see she was a disabled ship, pumping from leaks, with jury topmasts, and that some of her upper-deck ports were without guns; and to avoid being questioned in any way, that might embarrass me to answer, I began the conversation, in French, with the Captain, who was in the stern-gallery, accounting for my change of course, by saying, I observed his disabled state, and came down to him to know if I could render him any assistance; he answered, thanking me for the offer, but saying he had men enough, which indeed I could plainly perceive, as they were crowded on the gunwale and quarter, looking at our ship.

I could not but form hopes, from the disabled state of this ship, that I should be able to preserve my present position under her stern, so as to rake her repeatedly; and thus beginning an action with such advantages, as would be sufficient to ensure us a favourable issue to the contest. My guns were of course ready pointed, but I reflected that it was useless to fire, since I could not hope to secure the ship, and carry her off from the two others; and the execution of the service I was sent upon would be rendered totally abortive, by the unfavourable issue of so unequal a contest, as fighting the three together; the utmost then, that we could do, would be to give her a most destructive raking fire, and sail away; this, my men were both ready and eager for, but I over-ruled the proposition, considering the carnage must have been shocking, from the effect of our guns, double-loaded, enfilading a crowded ship within half a pistol-shot; and conceiving it both unmanly and treacherous to make such havoc, while speaking in friendly terms and offering our assistance. I trusted, therefore, that my country, though it might be benefited in a trifling degree by it, would gladly relinquish an advantage to be purchased at the expense of humanity, and the national character; and I hope, for these reasons, I shall stand justified in not having made use of the accidental advantage in my power for the moment. We parted, after much conversation, with mutual compliments; the French Captain telling me his ship's name was *Le Caton*, and I, in answer to his query, named my ship as one of the Norway squadron, which it was not likely he would know by sight. The other ships, observing we were spoken to by the *Caton*, discontinued the pursuit, and we passed the rocks unmolested.

I am Sir, etc.,
W. Sidney Smith

There is no evidence available of what Sir Sidney's superiors thought of this humane decision but it clearly shows that whatever his personal failings may have been his standards of honourable conduct in war were beyond reproach. This was again to be proved on other occasions.

Whatever the Sea Lords of the Admiralty might have thought, Smith was always sure of a fair and sympathetic hearing from Lord Spencer, the First Lord, whose patience was inexhaustible. Whether it was the report of some operation which Smith had just carried out, or a scheme for occupying the Seine with rowing gun-boats or a complaint about the conditions in which his men were serving, he never seems to have communicated through the usual channels but wrote direct to Spencer.

In one letter in which he drew the First Lord's attention to the terrible pain and misery which the wounded sailors under his command suffered through the shortage of ship's surgeons and the absence of any hospital ship he wrote, "It will certainly require all your energy to attack a form of office which coolly tells me a man must be sent into port to stop a bleeding artery." From some First Lords Sidney Smith would have received a rebuff, but not from Lord Spencer who promised to do all he could to improve these conditions. Nevertheless all this did not make him any more popular with his superiors.

But the elusive post-captain and his small flotilla were never idle. Up and down the coast they went, one day off Cherbourg, three days later off Le Havre, reconnoitring the main channel ports on the French coast and reporting on their defences, and on numerous occasions engaging French naval vessels in combat.

On 17th March 1796 Smith received information that a small squadron of armed vessels were sheltering in the small fortified harbour of Herqui, near Cap Fréhel. He lost no time in getting there in H.M.S. *Diamond*, accompanied by two other ships under his command and, although the channel leading to the port was narrow and difficult for navigation, as well as strongly defended, they sailed boldly in, bombarded the fortifications, landed and captured them and destroyed all the French ships. Smith's report to Evan Nepean, Secretary to the Admiralty, gives a graphic account of this raid.

To the Secretary of the Admiralty
> *Diamond*, off Cape Fréhel, March 18, 1796.

Having received information that the armed vessels, detached by the Prince of Bouillon, had chased a convoy, consisting of a corvette, two luggers, four brigs, and two sloops into Herqui, I proceeded off that port to reconnoitre their position, and found the channel very narrow and intricate. I succeeded, however, in gaining a knowledge of these points sufficient to determine me to attack them in the *Diamond*, without loss of time, and without waiting for the junction of any part of the squadron, lest the enemy should fortify themselves still further on our appearance.

Lieutenant M'Kinley, of the *Liberty* brig, and Lieutenant Gosset, of the *Aristocrat* lugger, joined me off the Cape, and, though not under my orders, very handsomely offered their services, which I accepted, as small vessels were essentially necessary in such an operation. The permanent fortification for the defence of the bay are two batteries on a high rocky promontory. We observed the enemy to be very busily employed in mounting a detached gun on a very command-ing point of the entrance. At one o'clock yesterday afternoon this gun opened upon us as we passed. The *Diamond*'s fire, however, silenced it in eleven minutes. The others opened on us as we came round the point, and, their commanding situation giving them a decided advantage over a ship in our position, I judged it necessary to adopt another mode of attack, and accordingly detached the marines and boarders to land behind the point, and take the batteries in the rear. As the boats approached the beach they met with a warm reception, and a temporary check from a body of troops drawn up to oppose their landing; the situation was critical, the ship being exposed to a most galling fire, and in intricate pilotage, with a considerable portion of her men thus detached. I pointed out to Lieutenant Pine the apparent practicability of climbing the precipice in front of the batteries, which he readily perceived, and, with an alacrity and bravery of which I have had many proofs in the course of our service together, he undertook and executed this hazardous service, landing immediately under the guns, and rendering himself master of them before the column of troops could regain the heights. The fire from the ship was directed to cover our men in this operation; it checked the enemy in their advancement and the re-embarkation was effected, as soon as the guns were spiked, without the loss of a man though we have to regret Lieutenant Carter of the marines being dangerously wounded on this occasion.

The enemy's guns, three 24-pounders, being silenced and rendered useless for the time, we proceeded to attack the corvette and the other armed vessels, which had by this time opened their fire on us, to cover the operation of hauling themselves on shore. The *Diamond* was anchored as close to the corvette as her draft of water would allow. The *Liberty* brig was able to approach near; and on this occasion I cannot omit to mention the very gallant and judicious manner in which Lieutenant M'Kinley, her commander, brought this vessel into action, profiting by her light draft of water to follow the corvette close. The enemy's fire soon slackened, and the crew being observed to be making for the shore, on seeing the English colours hoisted on the hill, I made the signal for the boats, manned and armed, to board, directing Lieutenant Gosset, in the lugger, to cover them. This service was executed by the party from the shore, under the direction of Lieutenant Pine, in a manner that does them infinite credit, and him every honour as a brave man and an able officer. The enemy's troops occupied the high projecting rocks all round the vessels, from whence they kept up an incessant fire of musquetry, and the utmost that could be effected at the moment was to set fire to the corvette (named *L'Etourdie*, of 16 guns, 12-pounders, on the main deck) and one of the merchant brigs; since, as the tide fell, the enemy pressed down on the sands close to the vessels; Lieutenant Pine, therefore, returned on board, having received a severe contusion on the breast from a musquet ball.

As the tide rose again, it became practicable to make a second attempt to burn the remaining vessels. Lieutenant Pearson was accordingly detached for that purpose with the boats, and I am happy to add his gallant exertions succeeded to the utmost of my hopes, notwithstanding the renewed and heavy fire of musquetry from the shore. This fire was returned with great spirit and evident good effect, and I was much pleased with the conduct of Lieutenant Gosset in the hired lugger, and Mr Knight in the *Diamond*'s launch, who covered the approach and retreat of the boats. The vessels were all burnt except an armed lugger, which kept up her fire to the last.

The wind and tide suiting at ten at night to come out of the harbour again, we weighed, and repassed the point of Herqui, from which we received a few shots, the enemy having found means to restore one of the guns to activity. Our loss, as appears by the enclosed return, is trifling, considering the nature of the enterprise, and the length of time we were exposed to the enemy's fire. Theirs, I am persuaded, must have been great, from the numbers within the range of our shot and shells. The conduct of every officer and man under my command meets with my warmest approbation; it would be superfluous to particularise any others than those I have named, suffice it to say, the characteristic bravery and activity of British seamen never were more conspicuous.

Lieutenant Pine will have the honour to present their lordships with the colours which he struck on the battery, and I beg leave to recommend him particularly to their lordships as a most meritorious officer.

W. Sidney Smith

Exactly a month later Sidney Smith was captured by the French, and the exploits of this Lion of the Sea, by which name he was known in the Republican Navy, were put to an end for just over two years.

The first news of this was conveyed to the Secretary of the Admiralty by the First Lieutenant of the *Diamond* in the following letter:

To the Secretary of the Admiralty

     Diamond, off Havre de Grace, April 19th 1796.

Sir,

  Please to communicate to my Lords Commissioners of the Admiralty, that Sir Sidney Smith, commander of his majesty's ship *Diamond*, was this morning captured and carried into Havre de Grace; he proceeded from the ship, on the 18th in the evening, with the boats manned and armed towards the pier of Havre, as I suppose to reconnoitre the enemy's strength in that port; I am informed that at two o'clock in the morning he boarded and captured a French national lugger, carrying eight guns, at the mouth of the harbour, but in attempting to bring her off he was driven up the Seine considerably above the town, the flood-tide then running strong, and there being little or no wind; in this situation he was discovered at daylight by the enemy, who immediately sent out and attacked him in the prize lugger, with four gun-boats, a large lugger, and a number of smaller vessels, also armed; the contest continued upwards of two hours, when he was obliged to surrender to the great superior force of the enemy; the launch, with Mr Goodall, midshipman, and one cutter with the greatest difficulty escaped through a heavy fire of the gun-boats. I have to regret that the situation was such as to render it perfectly impracticable for me to give any assistance with his majesty's ship *Diamond*, it being nearly calm, and not a sufficient draught of water to carry her so far up the river. Enclosed is a list of the officers and men who were left on board the prize lugger at the commencement of the action. As the service, already ordered by Captain Sir Sidney Smith, may be injured by the absence of the *Diamond*, I shall therefore proceed in quest of the next senior officer of the squadron for his further orders, which I hope will meet with their lordships' approbation.

       I am, etc.

       R. H. Pearson, First Lieut.

P.S. Since writing the above I have, through the channel of a fishing-boat, had communication with the commanding officer of Havre, who informs me Sir Sidney Smith, officers, and men, are all well, except Mr C. Beecroft, who was wounded in the hand and thigh.

A list of the officers and men who were on board the prize lugger at the commencement of the action.

Sir William Sidney Smith, K.S., Captain
Mr William Knight, Acting Lieutenant
Mr T. W. Wright
Mr R. L. Coulson
Mr Charles Beecroft
Mr J. F. Carroll
Mr James Boxer
Mr Edward Morris
Mr William Harvey
And twenty-four seamen.

R. H. Pearson, First Lieut.

Another and more detailed account of the capture of the French lugger and its unfortunate sequel was printed in the Annual Register for 1796 based on documents in possession of the Admiralty.

Advice was received at the Admiralty, brought by Lieutenant Crispe, of the cutter *Telemachus*, of the capture of the enterprising Sir Sidney Smith, commander of H.M.S. *Diamond*, on the coast of France, having, on the 18th instant, boarded and taken a lugger privateer belonging to the enemy, in Havre de Grace harbour, by the boats of his squadron, then on a reconnoitreing expedition; and the tide making strong into the harbour, she was driven above the French forts, which, the next morning, the 19th, discovering, at break of day, the lugger in two by a string of English boats, immediately made the signal of alarm, which collected together several gun-boats and other armed vessels, that attacked the lugger and British boats, when, after an obstinate resistance of two hours, Sir Sidney had the mortification of being obliged to surrender himself prisoner of war, with about sixteen of his people, and three officers with him in the lugger. The *Diamond* frigate is safe, but could afford her commander no assistance, there not being a breath of wind during the whole of this unfortunate transaction. We are happy to add, that only four British seamen were killed, and one officer and six seamen slightly wounded. The seamen were immediately thrown into prison on their landing, and Sir Sidney underwent a long examination before the French commandant, after which he was ordered to be conveyed under a strong escort to Paris.

The following were amongst the officers captured with Sir Sidney Smith: Messrs W. Moory, R. Kenyon, and R. Barrow; one of these was wounded. When the officers on board the *Diamond* heard of the disaster which had befallen their gallant commander, they sent a flag of truce into Havre, to inquire whether he was wounded, and entreating that he might be treated with kindness. The governor returned for answer that Sir Sidney was well, and that he should be treated with the utmost humanity and attention. The French, it appears, warped out another lugger, of superior force, against that captured by Sir Sidney Smith in Havre de Grace harbour, with which they engaged him for a considerable time with so much heavier metal, that rendered all his resistance ineffectual, and therefore compelled him to strike.

Lieutenant Pearson received a reply to the letter mentioned in the postscript of his letter to the Admiralty on the very next day and forwarded it direct to Lord Spencer with the following covering letter:

Lieutenant Pearson to Lord Spencer
> *Diamond*, off Beachy Head, 20th April 1796.

My Lord,

I have herewith enclosed you the answer to my letter of yesterday, to the commandant at Havre, by which your lordship will have the satisfaction to hear that Sir Sidney Smith is well; and I am informed by the master of the fishing-boat that he was last night ordered off to Rouen, most likely on his way to Paris; that being the report at Havre. Your lordship will see by my public letter, that I am about to join Captain Peyton, the next senior officer of the squadron, and wait his orders for my further proceedings; knowing by the information Sir S. Smith had received, that some of the frigates, corvettes, etc., now in the pier at Havre, were to sail these spring tides, I thought it most expedient for the good of the service, that the *Diamond* should not be taken from the squadron at this particular juncture of time, notwithstanding she is very much in want of every species

of stores, provisions, and water. Trusting that your lordship
will approve of my proceedings,

I remain with great respect, etc.

R. H. Pearson

P.S. Three frigates, three ship corvettes, besides brigs, etc.,
still are in the pier at Havre, with their sails bent, and
apparently ready for sea.

(Enclosure)

Barre, le 20 Germinal, an de la République Française.
Monsieur,
On vient de me remettre votre lettre de ce jour.

Mr Sidney Smith est prisonnier de guerre, et traité avec
tous les égards dus à son grade. Ses compagnons sont
également bien traités, et n'ont reçu aucunes blessures, à
l'exception du jeune élève William Beecroft, qui a été
blessé à la main et à la cuisse.

Soyez persuadé, monsieur, que vos frères d'armes
trouveront dans la générosité Française tous les soins dus à
leur état et à leur situation.

La Breteche

A Monsieur Richard Pearson,
1st Lieutenant sur la frégate Angloise
le Diamond, en mer.

It was generally expected that he would not remain in
French hands for long as it was the custom in those days for
belligerents to exchange prisoners of war of equal rank and
there were several French officers in England who could have
been released to make this possible, but it was not to be.

There were probably two main reasons for the decision of
the French authorities not to release Sidney Smith.

The Republicans had not forgotten Smith's destruction of
the fleet and arsenal at Toulon which they regarded as an
intolerable affront to the Republican Army. Almost exactly
144 years later the destruction of the French fleet at Mers-el-
Kebir and other ports to prevent it falling into wrong hands
produced a similar reaction in the French Navy and left a
bitterness which took years to subside.

Any reminder of the treason of Toulon, the 'ville infame'
which the Republican Convention had ordered to be destroyed
stone by stone, excited a feeling of vengeance.

On that occasion Napoleon called Smith *Capitaine de Brûlot*,

Captain of Arson, and when he was asked to explain his attempt to capture the *Vengeur* no one believed that he had not been attempting to set fire to Le Havre as he had done two years previously to Toulon.

At Toulon it is true that he was an officer on half-pay, but he still had a commission in the Royal Navy and had received written orders from Lord Hood to destroy the French fleet. There can be no doubt that what he did was not in violation of the laws and usages of war.

Smith defended himself against this accusation in a letter written to the 'Citizen Minister of the French Navy' after he had been in custody as a prisoner of war for seven months. The following is a translation from the original French:

Citizen Minister,

The official report which you made of Admiral Richery's successes proves that you admit the principle put forward in my letter of 26th June that it is "the usage of war to burn what cannot be taken" and encourages me to repeat my contention that I should not be punished any longer in solitary confinement for alleged intentions which, if they were true, could be legitimate.

Had Admiral Richery been captured by my compatriots, during or returning from his so well prepared and daringly executed expedition I ask whether you really think, in all good faith, that he would have been detained in solitary confinement in the Tower of London and punished by our government for having carried out the orders of his superiors with zeal and exactitude. . . . I ask you if you do not think that seven months of solitary confinement is not sufficient punishment for such an ordinary offence as that of doing one's duty well, and if you do not think that the honour of the army should be interested in ensuring that such hardship should not become common usage between our two countries.

This complaint also concerns the harsh way in which my secretary is also held and not allowed to see me. This can only add to the bitterness of my suffering.

I am,

Citizen Minister,

with respect,

Your innocent victim,

William Sidney Smith

In this letter Sidney Smith was alluding to the return of the French Admiral Richery who had recently returned to Rochefort after a cruise off Newfoundland where, in the space of two weeks, he had burnt or otherwise destroyed the British fishing fleets at St Pierre de Miquelon, Rose Blanche and other fishing ports taking or sinking more than eighty vessels.

Another reason why he was *non persona grata* with the Directory was that he was known to be on friendly terms with several French aristocrats who had managed to escape the guillotine but were, of course, antagonistic to the new Republican régime, and also in touch with a number of French *émigrés* against whom the Directors were conducting a reign of terror. One of these was none other than François de Tromelin, a wanted Royalist. Tromelin was actually on board the *Diamond* with Smith masquerading as his servant under the assumed name of John Bromley 'a native of Canada'.

These two, together with Smith's secretary Mr Wright, after they had been interrogated, were driven by *chaise* to Paris and confined in the Abbaye where, Smith wrote, he was led to a gloomy room, round which he cast his eye, and left there in charge of a single gendarme. It was from this, his first place of confinement, that Smith wrote a cheerful letter to his father giving a short account of the action which had ended with his capture.

Abbaye Prison, Paris, April 30th 1796.

Dear Father,

You, who know me, will not wonder when I tell you that I am in better health than usual from having nothing to fatigue me, and in excellent spirits, finding amusement in the novelty of my situation; the whole is like a very interesting play, "the characters, dresses, and scenery entirely new;" but whether tragedy or comedy, I cannot yet pronounce, as we are only at the third act. The first and second, although "not without the clash of arms and din of war", could not be called tragic, while there were so many merry faces on the stage; no lives were lost on either side, which is always a good thing in the round reckoning of humanity. I wish I could say there was no blood shed, but the grapeshot flew too thick for that to be possible. Those you know most of are not among the wounded. Our friends Wright, Boxer, Morris and Carrol are well. The end of the second act, when my brave fellows collected round me, on the enemy's closing on us, swearing to die fighting by me, was the most affecting and interesting scene I ever saw, of the many which have passed under my eye; the servants behaved admirably, and the boys acted like men. In this disposition were we, when the enemy, far superior in number, prepared to board us, sword in hand, refusing us quarter with insults and imprecations. Our firm posture checked them, and my harangue to their chief relented their fury and turned their resentment into admiration. It was acknowledged that we could not get away, and that further resistance would not avail, but we were determined to die with our arms in our hands, if they would not give us quarter, and this determination saved us. The menacing attitude of our enemy was instantly changed into that of cordial salutation; we met shaking hands, and I have since had every reason to thank the military part of those into whose power we are fallen, for very generous treatment. Separation and confinement is all we have to complain of, but the fortune of war is imperious, and I learn patience every day by the practice. Believe me, under all circumstances, Yours, etc. etc. etc.

W. Sidney Smith

This letter was followed, six days later, by another to the Secretary to the Admiral giving his first official account of the action.

Abbaye Prison, Paris, May 6th 1796.
Sir,

Although my successor in command will have announced my capture to you, I consider it my duty to acquaint my lords commissioners of the admiralty with the circumstances of that unfortunate event.

The *Vengeur* French lugger, having been very daring and very successful in her depredations on our trade, her capture became an object which it was my duty not to neglect, and I accordingly kept an anxious look-out for her. I found her on the 17th April at anchor in the inner road of Havre de Grace, and her situation being such as afforded a reasonable prospect of bringing her out, I determined to make the attempt. I was obliged to take on myself to command the boats destined to effect this service, detachment and sickness having deprived me of other officers, to whom such an enterprise could have been confided; we boarded her at half past two in the morning, and made prize of her after a short contest; unfortunately the enemy had cut the cable, on our attack, and the tide had driven the vessel into the river Seine, within Havre pier, before we had the complete possession and management of her; daylight discovered our situation to the enemy on shore, and immediately a large lugger, several gun-boats and small boats full of troops, were detached from the town to cut us off in our return,—there was very little wind; we, however, did our utmost to force our passage through them, making use of the prize's guns with considerable advantage at first. The enemy continued engaging us on the bow and quarter within half musket shot; we maintained this unequal combat for three quarters of an hour, and I have reason to be highly satisfied with the conduct of the brave officers and men with me, who exerted themselves to the utmost; it was, however, at length evident, that a moment's longer resistance would have been a useless sacrifice of the whole; and I thus found myself under the mortifying necessity of surrendering to the superior force of the assailants. . . . I have the honour to be, Sir, etc.

W. Sidney Smith

Evan Nepean, Esq., Secretary,
    Admiralty, London.

The news of Sidney Smith's capture was officially conveyed to the Minister of Marine and the Colonies in Paris by a letter, a copy of which was published in the *Gazette Nationale*, or *Moniteur Universal* on the very day on which the 'English incendiary' was locked up in the Abbaye.

At last we have got Sidney Smith, this English incendiary who burnt our ships at Toulon, the same man who has tried on several occasions to set fire to the buildings and shops in Le Havre and promised Pitt* to reduce our ports and our fleet to a heap of ashes. While his ship the *Diamond* was moored in the estuary after putting the *Vengeur* out of action she was attacked by a number of small vessels which had been sent to intercept her and obliged to surrender with her captain and crew. That Smith intended to set fire to the town is beyond doubt for a stick of sulphur was found in his possession similar to one which was discovered only a few months

---

* William Pitt, the Younger.

ago under one of our frigates under construction in the ship-
yard. This is to let you know that as we have not got in Havre
a severe enough prison in which to keep him we are sending
him under strong escort to Rouen pending the decision of
the justiciary in respect of all the attempts of this monster. I
understand that the Directory has just given orders for him
to be taken to Paris as an incendiary.

During the first few days of his imprisonment there was
nothing for poor Sir Sidney to do except peer out of the window
of his cell and look at the windows of the houses opposite. It
was not long before he realised that three women living there
were apparently taking a lively interest in the fate of the English
prisoner. These ladies, whom Smith had christened by the
names of the three muses, Thalia, Melpomene and Clio, by
means of an improvised system of 'deaf and dumb' signs, which
he soon learned to understand, communicated with him daily
and indicated that they were planning a means of escape for
him.

His jailers somehow became suspicious and he was soon
moved from the Abbaye to the Temple where life immediately
became much more tolerable, particularly as both Wright and
Tromelin had also been moved there and were now allowed to
see him.

Nor was this all. The Governor of the Temple, Monsieur
Boniface, proved to be a most reasonable man and took an
immediate liking to the distinguished inmate of his prison, as
did Madame Boniface, and it was not long before Smith was
allowed to go out during the day provided he said where he
could be found and promised to return by a certain hour. A
further request by Smith was also granted, and Tromelin was
released and went to England whence he subsequently returned to France in secret and played a notable part in his
'master's' escape. Meanwhile Madame Tromelin, who had
remained in Paris, was allowed to visit Smith in prison almost
daily and carried messages to and from her husband.

About this time another character came on the scene, Colonel
Phélypeaux, who was later to serve with Smith during the
defence of St Jean d'Acre.

This officer was in the French engineers and it was because
he, too, favoured the Royalist cause that he came to meet
Madame Tromelin. She told him about the handsome English

naval officer in the Temple prison and Phélypeaux immediately embarked on a plan to secure his escape.

There were many others in Paris, however, who were not so well disposed towards Sir Sidney. The incendiary 'Lion of the Sea' had, by this time, become almost legendary and many of those who enthusiastically supported the Revolutionary government were out for his blood. One of these was a French sailor who had been captured in March 1797 and a report about him was already in the files of the Admiralty.

Admiralty Office, May 5th 1798.

Denys Messant, French prisoner, taken in *La Bonne Citoyenne*, 10th of March 1797, lately confined at Porchester, being in company with a number of French officers at Petersfield, on their way to prison in consequence of the general orders given for reading the paroles, he heard one of them say to others who were near him, 'I shall very soon put an end to all this; we owe our present situation to that fellow, Sir Sidney Smith; I shall find the means of escape, which are not difficult, and when I get to France I will make my way to the Temple, and contrive to see him, under the pretence of having something to deliver from his friends in England; I will then put into his hands a small parcel of tea previously mixed with poison, and that will soon do its business. I have poisoned many, and it is not likely that I should fail with him.' He did not immediately notice the person of the man who made this speech, and being at night in a crowded inn, he could not ascertain it afterwards, and was also afraid to appear to make a particular inquiry.

This conversation had nearly escaped his memory, when he heard it revived at Porchester Castle, between two persons who were lying in a bed near him; but he was removed next morning to the prison-ship, and had not any opportunity of learning who the persons were that held such discourse; he was only one night at Porchester and arrived there very wet.

Meanwhile Bromley, who had by this time reached London, saw Pitt and Grenville and told them of the possibility of arranging Captain Smith's escape. He was given a sum of money, returned to Paris, and through his wife kept in touch with his friend in the Temple.

Many plans were discussed during the next few months by

the three conspirators, Phélypeaux, 'John Bromley' and his wife, Madame Tromelin, but all were judged to be too risky. By now, however, Smith had already been in prison for two years and he decided that something would have to be done soon or it might be too late.

The story of Sir Sidney's escape has been told many times, but the following version which is taken from the Naval Chronicle is thought by his family to be nearest the truth.

A forged order for his removal to another prison, properly stamped and signed by the Minister responsible for his custody, was obtained by means of a bribe and, on the day fixed for the escape, two men arrived at the Temple with this document, both dressed in military uniform. The Keeper having read the order and closely examined the Minister's signature sent for the Registrar of the prison and Smith was called from his cell to the Registrar's office. When he was informed of the contents of the order he pretended to be much concerned but one of the two officers informed him that no harm would come to him and that he would be very comfortable in the place to which he had orders to conduct the prisoner. The Registrar, however, insisted that an escort of at least six men must accompany Smith. The officer agreed but then said, "Captain, you are an officer; I am an officer also. Your parole will be enough. Give me that and no escort will be necessary." "Sir," Smith replied, "if that is sufficient I swear on the word of an officer to accompany you wherever you choose to take me." The gate was then opened and after an exchange of polite farewells the party left.

Outside the prison a cab was waiting. Phélypeaux was inside, and Tromelin on the box with the cabman. Smith got in and, after driving some distance, the cab stopped. Smith and Phélypeaux stepped out and mingled with the crowd and made their way to the house of a friend where they stayed the night. Next day they left via Rouen for Honfleur where they spent the night in a fisherman's hut, and eventually they embarked in a small fishing boat and rowed out to sea where the British frigate *Argo* sighted them and took them on board. In his report of the incident to the Admiralty her Commander, Captain Bowen, wrote, "I picked them up in a small fishing boat off Havre and safely landed them at Portsmouth."

As soon as he reached London, on 8th May 1798, Sir Sidney went straight to Lord Spencer, who was by this time First Lord, and was then received by the King. But the last thing he wanted was a quiet rest after his unpleasant experience in the Temple. He wished to go to sea again and it was not long before he was entrusted with an interesting and important mission which was, incidentally, to bring him into conflict with Lord St Vincent and Nelson, and which led up to the greatest triumph of his life, the defence of Acre.

5

MINISTER PLENIPOTENTIARY

In 1792, as described in an earlier chapter, a year before the burning of part of the French fleet at Toulon, Lord Grenville had sent Sidney Smith on a special mission to Constantinople, where his brother, Spencer Smith, was holding a diplomatic appointment, with the object of coming to some understanding with the Ottoman Government.

While he was there Sidney Smith wrote to Grenville and warned him that the French had designs on Egypt and on British trade in the Levant.

Shortly after Smith's escape from prison and his return to England Lord Grenville, who was then Foreign Secretary, wrote to Earl Spencer on the same subject and suggested that Nelson should keep an eye on the situation then developing in the Mediterranean and that a special squadron should be formed to deal with the French fleet off Alexandria. "The officer chosen to command such a squadron," Lord Grenville wrote, "should be Sir S. S., not out of partiality for him, but thinking that his name is better known to both Russians and Turks, and his character better suited to act with them, than many of the other officers whom, possibly, you would prefer for a Channel cruise!"

Lord Grenville did not immediately follow up the suggestion as he changed his opinion and thought that, perhaps, after all no such action need be taken.

On 3rd October, however, he wrote again to Spencer. "I think I have begun to alter my mind about Sir Sidney Smith, you must not laugh at me for the unstableness of my opinion, but I think that until the French are actually driven out of Egypt and the Archipelago, there still remains something to be done. . . ."

Within a few days Smith was appointed to command H.M.S. *Tigre*, a ship of eighty guns, which had been captured from the French in 1795, and on 21st October received the following order from the First Lord:

To put to sea without a moment's loss of time in the ship you command, and proceed with all possible despatch off Cadiz and, putting yourself under the command of the Earl of St Vincent, admiral of the Blue and commander-in-chief of his majesty's ships and vessels in the Mediterranean and along the coast of Portugal, follow his lordship's order for your further proceedings. In case the said admiral should not be off Cadiz when you arrive there, you are to go on to Gibraltar and put yourself under his orders, as above desired.

At the same time Sidney Smith received, direct from the Foreign Office and quite independently from the Admiralty, a commission appointing him "joint minister plenipotentiary" with his brother Spencer Smith at the Court of the Ottoman Emperor in Constantinople.

Sidney Smith's arrival had been announced in the following letter, dated 9th October 1798, which Spencer had written to Lord St Vincent:

The general view of the state of affairs in the Mediterranean, which was transmitted to you before the details of this action arrived here,* is in no respect altered by that event, as far as relates to its principle; and fortunately only rendered more easy of execution as to its detail. One great feature of this state of things is the emotion and sensation which has been excited in Turkey, and the vigorous declarations, at least, which have been drawn from the Porte. Of these, it appears to his Majesty's Ministers most urgent to make the most, and with a reference to the former habits of acquaintance which a residence at Constantinople has given him as well as his near connexion with our Minister there, it has been judged expedient to send out Sir Sidney Smith, who will very shortly wait upon your Lordship to put himself under your orders, and will communicate to you the instructions of which he is the bearer. His speedy arrival at the Dardanelles with these instructions you will immediately perceive to be of great consequence; and his ship having lately undergone a very thorough repair, will relieve any of those which may be in the Levant, in a state to render their stay in those seas less advisable. I am well aware that there may perhaps be some prejudices, derived from certain circumstances which have attended this officer's career

---

* This was Nelson's victory at Aboukir Bay.

through life, but from a long acquaintance with him personally, I think I can venture to assure your lordship, that added to his unquestioned character for courage and enterprise, he has a great many very good points about him, which those who are less acquainted with him are not sufficiently apprised of, and I have no doubt that you will find him a very useful instrument to be employed on any hazardous or difficult service, and that he will be perfectly under your guidance, as he ought to be. Should the arrangement of the force to remain for the present in the Levant, to co-operate with the Turks, lead to there being only one of two ships of two decks on that service, it may be most advisable that from the local and personal acquaintance Sir Sidney is possessed of with the Turkish officers, he should be the senior officer; but I have given him to understand, that if a large force should be thought necessary, his standing on the list will not admit of it, there being so many captains of distinguished merit who are his seniors.

It is clear from the terms of Lord Spencer's letter that he was not quite happy about the reception that Sir Sidney might receive on joining Lord St Vincent or quite sure that the new arrival would behave with modesty and discretion, two qualities which Sir Sidney entirely lacked.

It was, without doubt, an unusual arrangement but Spencer could hardly have expected that it would create such a commotion. The last paragraph of his letter to Lord St Vincent should have made it clear to anyone who took the trouble to read it that there was no intention of Sidney Smith being put in command of Lord Nelson in any circumstances whatsoever.

That Nelson failed to appreciate this was entirely Lord St Vincent's fault. He does not appear to have informed Nelson that Smith would be passing through the area of his command and a rather tactless letter from Smith to Nelson infuriated Nelson even more. The letter which Nelson wrote Lord St Vincent on 31st December 1798 speaks for itself:

My Dear Lord,

I do feel for I am a man, that it is impossible for me to serve in these seas with the squadron under a junior officer could I have thought it!—and from Earl Spencer! Never, never was I so astonished as your letter made me. As soon as I can get hold of Troubridge I shall send him to Egypt to endeavour to destroy the ships in Alexandria. If it can be done, Troubridge will do it. The Swedish Knight (Sir Sidney Smith) writes Sir William Hamilton that he shall go to Egypt, and take Captain Hood and his squadron under his command. The Knight forgets the respect due to his superior officer; he has no orders from you to take my ships away from my command; but it is all of a piece. Is it to be borne? Pray grant me your permission to retire, and I hope the *Vanguard* will be allowed to convey me and my friends, Sir William and Lady Hamilton, to England. God bless you, my dear Lord, and believe me your most affectionate friend,

Nelson

In reply to this letter, Lord St Vincent wrote to Nelson on the 17th January 1799:

I am not surprised at your feelings being outraged, at the bold attempt Sir Sidney Smith is making to wrest a part of your squadron from you. I have received much the same letter from him, as the one you describe to have been addressed to Sir William Hamilton; a copy of which, with my answer, you have enclosed, and orders for you to take him immediately under your command. I have informed Lord Spencer of all these proceedings, and sent him copies of the letters.

The ascendance this gentleman has over all His Majesty's Ministers is to me astonishing, and that they should have sent him out after the strong objection I made to him, in a private letter to Mr Nepean, passes my understanding. For the sake of your country, and the existence of its power in the Levant, moderate your feelings, and continue in your command. . . . The sensations you must have gone through before and since your departure from Naples, must have been very trying; nevertheless, I trust the greatness of your mind will keep up the body, and that you will not think of abandoning the Royal Family you have by your firmness and address preserved from the fate of their late Royal relations in France. Employ Sir Sidney in any manner you think proper: knowing your magnanimity, I am sure you will mortify him as little as possible, consistently with what is due to the great characters senior to him on the list, and his superiors in every sense of the word. God bless you, my dear Lord, be assured no man loves and esteems you more truly than your very affectionate, St. Vincent

This indignant letter from Lord St Vincent seems to have made Nelson feel much better, for on the very same day he wrote most politely to the unwelcome intruder.

To Captain Sir Sidney Smith, H.M. Ship *Tigre*.

Palermo, December 31st 1798.

Sir,

I have been honoured with your letter, from off Malta, with its several inclosures:—viz., an extract of a letter from Lord Grenville to John Spencer Smith, Esq., etc., "And his Majesty has been graciously pleased to direct that your brother, Sir Sidney Smith, shall proceed to Constantinople, with the 80 gun ship, *Le Tigre*. His instructions will enable him to take the command of such of his Majesty's ships as he may find in those seas, unless, by any unforeseen accident, it should happen that there should be among them any of his Majesty's Officers of superior rank; and he will be directed to act with such Force, in conjunction with the Russian and Ottoman Squadrons, for the defence of the Ottoman Empire, and for the annoyance of the Enemy in that quarter." Also an extract of another letter from Lord Grenville to yourself and brother. And Earl St Vincent having sent me an extract of a letter from Earl Spencer to him, saying that, for certain circumstances, you should be the Officer selected for the command of a small Squadron in the Levant Seas; and His Lordship having also informed me that Captain Miller was the officer of your choice, and desiring me to give you a Frigate, or a Sloop of War, will Captain Miller's arrival, you may rest assured that I shall most strictly comply with the instructions sent by Lord Grenville to your brother: also those of Earl Spencer and Earl St Vincent. For this purpose I must desire that you will lose no time in proceeding to Alexandria, to take upon you the command of the blockade, etc., which I shall direct to be delivered up to you; and, from my heart, I wish you every success. The united Squadrons of Turks and Russians, and of two sail of the line under your command, must be sufficient for the two ships *armés en flute*, under three Frigates, which, thank God, are all the enemy have left in those seas. I have the honour to be, Sir, your most obedient servant,

Nelson

Lord Spencer was clearly surprised at Nelson's violent

reaction to Sidney Smith's dual appointment. He wrote to say that there had obviously been a "very great misunderstanding" as there had never been any intention that Smith should consider himself a commander-in-chief or take even a single gunboat from the admiral's command without receiving orders to that effect. Sir Sidney had been sent to serve in the Mediterranean fleet not only under the command of the Admiral of the Blue but to remain subservient to every other officer in that fleet senior to him in rank.

Nevertheless, having regard to the fact that he was to work in close contact with the British representative at the Porte, and was well known to the majority of those most influential in Turkish public life, H.M. Government had thought it wise to give him the same diplomatic powers as his brother Spencer, to negotiate and conclude a treaty with the Turks.

This full explanation of the position by the First Lord appears to have pacified Nelson although he made it quite clear to Sir Sidney, in a letter written on 8th March 1799, that whenever he wrote to the Admiral he must indicate whether it was in his capacity as a naval officer or a plenipotentiary.

"Your situation as Joint Minister at the Porte," Nelson wrote, "makes it absolutely necessary that I should know who writes to me—therefore I must direct you, whenever you have ministerial affairs to communicate, that it is done jointly with your respectable brother, and not to mix naval business with the other, for what may be very proper for a representative of His Majesty, may be very subversive of that discipline of respect for the different ranks in our service. A representative may dictate to an Admiral, a Captain of a man-of-war would be censured for the same things, therefore you will see the propriety of my steering clear between the two situations.

I have sent you my orders, which your abilities as a sea officer will lead you to execute punctually. Not a ship more than the service requires shall be kept on any particular station, and that number must be left to my judgment, as an Admiral commanding the squadron detached by the commander-in-chief to the extent of the Black Sea. I shall of course keep up a proper communication with the Turkish and Russian Admirals, which no Captain of a man-of-war under my orders must interfere in."

This letter, as it was meant to do, left Sidney Smith in no possible doubt as to where he stood and, in order to make the position doubly clear, Nelson wrote a similar letter to Spencer Smith.

To do him justice, however, Sir Sidney had already tried to explain his unusual position to Nelson by letter as early as December 1798 and, immediately after his arrival at Constantinople, told him that the Ottoman treaty had been signed and what steps had already been taken to implement it.

To Admiral Lord Nelson, K.C.B.

Tigre, Constantinople, Jan. 24, 1799.

My Lord,

I did myself the honour of acquainting you, by my letter of the 11th of December, of my having been sent to this country, with the appointment of minister plenipotentiary, conjointly with my brother, Mr Spencer Smith, in addition to my naval rank, his majesty having judged it expedient for his service, that the officer who was destined to co-operate with the naval forces of this country should unite the two characters in his person, the better to preserve that good understanding which should subsist between allies. Our treaty of alliance was signed on the 5th instant, in the execution of which it is necessary that we should contribute our utmost endeavours towards restoring Egypt to the dominion of the Porte. You, my lord, have done much, very much towards it, even before we had incurred the positive obligation; but much is expected of us still, considering the infant state of their marine, and their absolute inability to equip any considerable naval force before the spring, when the grand expedition against Egypt is to sail from hence. They trust entirely to us for the complete blockade of Alexandria, and for co-operation with Djezzar Pasha, in *his attack*, in the mean time. Now it depends upon you, my lord, to say what means you can afford me to do this effectually, so as to preserve the advantages you have achieved for the cause. . . .

I have the honour to be etc.

W. Sidney Smith

With the signature of the treaty with the Turks the stage was now set for the campaign in Egypt which was to end with Napoleon's first great defeat.

6

ACRE

By December 1798 the French forces under Napoleon had subjugated much of lower Egypt and, during the course of the campaign, massacred thousands of its inhabitants. Napoleon then marched eastwards and turned north into Palestine, following much the same route as Allenby did 119 years later, capturing El Arish, Gaza, Ramleh and Jaffa. In Jaffa he put most of the garrison to the sword and the remainder, after being taken prisoner, were dealt with as described by one of his own officers:

> They were marched into the midst of a vast square, formed by French troops into which the silent column of victims was driven in fearful confusion, foreseeing their fate. They shed no tears, they uttered no cries, some who were wounded and could not march so fast as the rest were bayoneted on the way. The others were halted near a pool of stagnant dirty water, divided into small parties, marched in different directions and there fusilladed. . . . As our soldiers had exhausted their cartridges it was necessary to destroy those who still remained alive with the bayonet and the sword.

The treatment of French prisoners of war, however, by the Turks had been none too good, but on this being brought to the notice of Sir Sidney while he was in Constantinople he was able to intervene and better their conditions.

Meanwhile Djezzar Pasha, 'the butcher', who was governor of that part of Syria, with his headquarters at St Jean d'Acre, (generally known as Acre) had received the following from Napoleon:

> The provinces of Gaza, Ramleh and Jaffa are in my power. I have treated with generosity those of your troops who placed themselves at my discretion. I have been severe towards those who have violated the rights of war. I shall march in a few days to Acre.

As soon as Sir Sidney learnt of this threat he set sail in H.M.S. *Tigre* from Alexandria on 3rd March, together with the *Theseus* and a few smaller vessels which were all he possessed, and anchored in the Bay of Acre twelve days later.

No time was lost in putting Acre into a state of defence as the French were known to be not far away, and two days afterwards a force under General Kléber took Haifa where from Mount Carmel the tiny British fleet could be seen in the distance. It was not an easy job as the walls of Acre were in a state of decay, but under the direction of the French engineer Colonel Phélypeaux, who had helped Smith escape from the Temple, everything possible was done. The arrival of the British had a beneficial effect on the morale of the Turkish garrison which waited with some confidence for the French attack to begin.

Sir Sidney at once sent a situation report to Lord St Vincent in a letter written on 23rd March. In it Sir Sidney expressed his satisfaction at having arrived at St Jean d'Acre two days before Bonaparte made his appearance. The enemy's advance guard was discovered at the foot of Mount Carmel by the *Tigre*'s guard-boats, which, by their grape-shot, sent them precipitately up the Mount. They had musketry only; their cannon therefore was expected by sea, and a flotilla was soon discovered from the *Tigre* consisting of a corvette and nine sail of gun-vessels.

Our guns soon reached them and seven struck; the corvette containing Bonaparte's private property, and two small vessels escaped, and it was the first object to secure the prizes, without chasing further, their cargoes consisting of the battery train of artillery, ammunition, platforms, destined for the siege of Acre and much wanted for its defence. The boats were accordingly anchored off the town, manned from the ships and immediately employed in harassing the enemy's posts, impeding his approaches, and covering the ships boats. They had been constantly occupied in the services for the past five days and nights and such had been the zeal of the crews that they requested not to be relieved after many hours of excessive labour at their guns and oars.

Sir Sidney then expressed his sorrow that they had met with some losses but stated that the enemy's losses were much more severe. The result of the battle proved to be very encouraging to the Turkish troops and time was gained to allow for the arrival of reinforcements which were expected daily.

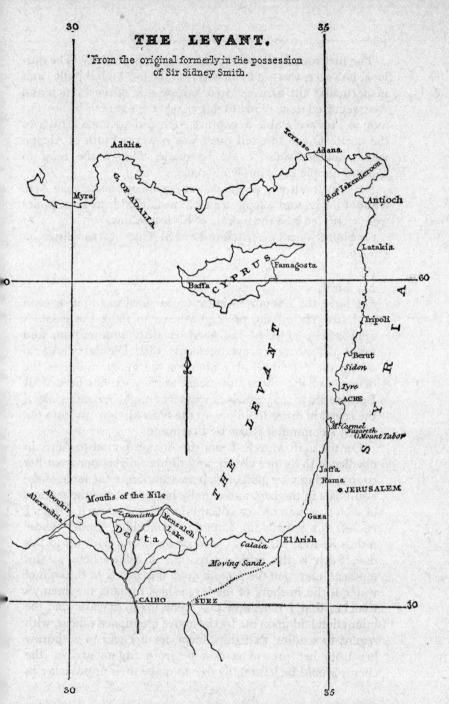

THE LEVANT.

'From the original formerly in the possession
of Sir Sidney Smith.

Reproduced from *The Life and Correspondence of Admiral Sir William Sidney Smith* by John
Barrow; London, Richard Bentley, 1848.

3*

The first round, therefore, had gone to Sir Sidney. The outlook, however, was not at all rosy. All the local inhabitants, and in particular the Druse,* were on the side of the French and were reported to be ready to put 15,000 men at their disposal as soon as they were able to capture Acre and advance further to the north. Once Acre fell there was nowhere south of Aleppo where another stand could be made. Thence the road to Constantinople lay completely open.

Nevertheless it was essential that Napoleon should take Acre without delay, and a long siege was unthinkable as his supplies were restricted and the morale of his troops low.

Sir Sidney's next despatch to Lord St Vincent was written on 4th April:

My Lord,

I have the honour to inform your lordship that as soon as I had placed the prize gun-boats to flank the enemy's approaches, supplied the garrison with ammunition, and made the necessary arrangements with Djezzar Pasha to secure the execution of a plan for the amelioration of the defences of the town, (fortifications they cannot be called) I proceeded to sea in quest of whatever might be coming along the coast, in order to follow up the blow already given to the enemy's communications by that route.

On the 24th March, I met the *Alliance* bound to Acre, in obedience to former orders, and did not divert her from her course, being very glad of such an addition to the force of the gun-boats in the bay, and equally happy to have the services of such a zealous officer as Captain Wilmot, at such a time. I enclose his journal to Captain Troubridge, under whose orders he was, which will account for his motions up to this day. Such is the critical situation of affairs here at this moment, and such the necessity of a ship of a light draught of water to lie in-shore of the large ships to flank the enemy's trenches that I must now take upon me to deviate from the injunction laid upon me by the above mentioned officer, with regard to sending that ship down, for if I was to withdraw her from her present station before a frigate arrives, the enemy would be left totally free to make their approaches in

* An independent tribe living mostly in the Lebanon and in the extreme north of Palestine.

any direction they pleased; whereas at present they are kept in check, on that side at least, by her well-directed fire. She fortunately rode out the equinoctial gales by being anchored in the undertow; the *Tigre* and *Theseus* clawed off shore by dint of carrying sail; but we are anxious for the fate of one of Buonaparte's transports, No. 1, which we captured on the 26th, and which separated from us before the gale came on; she was from Damietta, bound hither to the army, loaded with rice, bread, and flour, and the enemy must feel this loss in the proportion that we feel her cargo an acquisition to ourselves.

I am sorry to find no one of the measures agreed upon between the pasha and me, for the defence of the town, have been carried into execution, although Colonel Phélypeaux, an able officer of engineers, whom I left to superintend their execution, emphasised the necessity of them; the consequence of which is that the enemy has pushed one of his approaches, under cover of the garden wall of the aqueduct, actually into the town ditch, where he is mining the angle of a tower, that he has already battered in breach, and against which he at once placed scaling ladders; they were, however, too short, and the Turks did exert themselves so far, on this occasion, as to knock the assailants off their ladders into the ditch, where about forty of their bodies now lie; but if this mine is suffered to go on, there will be no occasion for scaling-ladders next time. I urged him strongly to make a *sortie*, and he begins to listen to the suggestion : what seems to have more effect on him, than anything is the idea I have thrown out, that if the enemy are suffered to come into the town I must, in my own defence, batter it down about their ears. He does not want for energy himself, but he has no second; and where there is nothing but a chief, with a multitude without subordinate officers, exertions that depend upon order cannot be expected. This accounts for two *sorties* he has made being unproductive of advantage; besides, Djezzar having been hitherto chiefly anxious to maintain his independence of the Porte, his heavy cannon are all pointed towards the sea, without any possibility of a land attack. He has, fortunately, a defence in two large English mortars mounted towards the land, which have been of the utmost use, but I am obliged to supply him with ammunition, which, with our constant firing single guns night and day on the enemy's workmen,

reduces our stock, and occasions me to request an immediate
supply of all kinds, particularly grenades and shells.

I have, etc.

W. S. Smith

Meanwhile there was a lull in the fighting as a violent gale
had sprung up and the *Tigre* and *Theseus* had to weigh anchor
and stand well off-shore until it had abated. When the British
fleet was able once more to approach the coast Sir Sidney found
that the enemy had profited by his enforced absence to push
their advance patrol right up to the ditch by the north-east
angle of the town wall where they proceeded to mine it.

The garrison decided to make a sortie in which British
marines and seamen were to force their way into the mine while
the Turkish troops attacked the enemy's trenches on both
flanks.

Sir Sidney, in a letter to Lord St Vincent, described the
operation:

The sally took place this morning just before day-light.
The impetuosity and noise of the Turks rendered the attempt
to surprise the enemy abortive, though in other respects they
did their part well. Lieutenant Wright, who commanded the
seamen-pioneers, notwithstanding he received two shot in his
right arm as he advanced, entered the mine with the pike-
men, and proceeded to the bottom of it, where he verified
its direction and destroyed all that could be destroyed, in its,
then state, by pulling down the supporters. Colonel Douglas,
to whom I had given the necessary step of rank, to enable him
to command the Turkish colonels, supported the seamen in
this desperate service with his usual gallantry, under the
increased fire of the enemy, bringing off Lieutenant Wright,
who had scarcely strength left to get out of the enemy's
trench, from which they were not dislodged, as also Mr
Janverin, midshipman of the *Tigre*, and the rest of the
wounded. The action altogether speaks for itself, and says
more than could be said by me in praise of all concerned . . .
our loss in wounded is twenty-three, among which is
Lieutenant Beatty of marines, slightly. The Turks brought in
above sixty heads, a greater number of muskets, and some
entrenching tools, much wanted in the garrison. A further
attack on the enemy's second parallel was not to be

attempted, without a greater number of regular troops; the return of the detachment was well covered by the *Theseus*'s fire, Captain Miller having taken an excellent position to that effect. The result of our day's work is, that *we have taught the besiegers to respect the enemy they have to deal with, so as to keep at a greater distance.* The apprehensions of the garrison are quieted as to the effect of the mine, which we have besides learnt how to countermine with advantage, and more time is gained for the arrival of the reinforcements daily expected.

I am, etc.

W. Sidney Smith

Realising that every day the likelihood of the garrison of Acre's being soon reinforced was increasing, Napoleon decided to step up the pressure. On 1st May a fourth attempt was made to carry the town by storm but like all the others it ended in failure. The presence off-shore of the *Tigre* and *Theseus* had convinced the French, on two previous occasions, that no attack could be made successfully within the range of the ship's guns. On 1st May, however, good fortune favoured them. A heavy gale the night before had blown up a heavy swell from the south-west and this continued all the following morning during which time Napoleon kept up a heavy bombardment of the town walls.

The attack, and its repulse with heavy losses to the French, was described in a letter written by Sir Sidney's private secretary to General E. Smith who was the Captain's uncle.

"At half-past 11 o'clock," he wrote, "we plainly discovered him (Napoleon) marching about 2,000 men from the camp to the trenches; a body of men sprang out from the inner lines and with six ladders boldly scrambled up a wall of upwards of thirty feet high backed by all the men in the trenches ready to follow them.

"The six men were instantly killed by the Turks upon the breach and, at the same time, the ships beginning their broadsides upon the trenches joined to the shells and musketry from the garrison, their repulse was bloody. At 4 o'clock we saw the unfortunate men march back to their camp in great disorder and I suppose much disheartened, for this is the most poignant of their disappointments.

"If the Turkish army from Rhodes and Macri would but make its appearance, as it might have done about three weeks

ago, since troops, ammunition, provisions and stores were embarked at the end of March, the business would soon be settled,
but until then we must confine ourselves to the defence of
the town which they will never get possession of *as long as we
are afloat.*"

Sir Sidney duly reported this success to the Admiral of the
Blue in a brief despatch in which he also announced the death of
his friend Colonel Phélypeaux, which was a great personal loss
to him. He also paid tribute to the Turkish garrison who had
behaved with great gallantry.

Apparently undaunted by the repulse of their attack on 1st
May the French made two further attempts next morning to
force the British fortifications but were again repulsed with
heavy loss, and Sir Sidney was able to report to the Admiralty
that his forces "had the satisfaction of finding themselves, on
the forty-sixth day of the siege, in a better state of defence than
they were on the first day the enemy opened their trenches . . .
and the garrison, having occasionally closed with the enemy in
several sorties, felt greater confidence that they would be able
to resist an assault for which they are prepared."

The long-awaited Turkish reinforcements had still not
arrived, however, and the French attacks increased in number
and ferocity. Sir Sidney reported to Lord St Vincent on 9th
May that the fortifications had been stormed "almost every
night" since the unsuccessful attack on the 1st May but that
on each occasion the enemy had been repulsed with heavy
losses.

At long last, on the fifty-first day of the siege, a fleet of
corvettes and transports, under the command of Hassan Bey,
made its appearance, and Napoleon, realising that a critical
moment in the battle had come, immediately ordered a strong
attack on the town, hoping to capture it before the Turkish
reinforcements could land.

"The constant fire of the besiegers was suddenly increased
tenfold," Sir Sidney wrote to Lord St Vincent. "Our flanking
fire from afloat was, as usual, plied to the utmost, but with less
effect than heretofore, as the enemy had thrown up epaulments
and traverses of sufficient thickness to protect them from it. The
guns that could be worked to the greatest advantage were a
French brass 18-pounder in the light-house castle, manned
from the *Theseus*, under the direction of Mr Scroder, master's
mate; and the last mounted 24-pounder, in the north ravelin,

manned from the *Tigre*, under the direction of Mr Jones,
midshipman. These guns, being within grape distance of the
head of the attacking column, added to the Turkish musketry,
did great execution; and I take this opportunity of recommend-
ing these two petty officers, whose indefatigable vigilance and
zeal merit my warmest praise.

"The *Tigre*'s two 68-pounder carronades, mounted in two
germes lying in the mole, and worked under the direction of
Mr Bray, carpenter of the *Tigre*, (one of the bravest and most
intelligent men I ever served with) threw shells into the centre
of this column with evident effect and checked it considerably;
still, however, the enemy gained ground, and made a lodgment
on the second story (sic) of the north-east tower, the upper part
being entirely battered down, and the ruins in the ditch forming
the ascent by which they mounted. Daylight shewed us the
French standard on the outer angle of the tower.

"The fire of the besieged was much slackened, in comparison
to that of the besiegers, and our flanking fire was become of less
effect, the enemy having covered themselves in this lodgment,
and in the approach to it, by two traverses across the ditch,
which they had constructed under the fire that had been opposed
to them during the whole of the night, and which were now seen
composed of sand bags, and *the bodies of their dead, built in with
them*, their bayonets alone being visible above them.*

"Hassan Bey's troops were in the boats, though as yet but
half way on shore; this was a most critical point of the contest,
and an effort was necessary to preserve the place for a short
time till their arrival. I accordingly landed the boats at the
mole, and took the crews up to the breach armed with pikes.
The enthusiastic gratitude of the Turks, men, women, and
children, at sight of such a reinforcement, at such a time, is not
to be described; many fugitives returned with us to the breach,
which we found defended by a few brave Turks, whose most
destructive missile weapons were heavy stones which, striking
the assailants on the head, overthrew the foremost down the
slope, and impeded the progress of the rest. A succession,
however, ascended to the assault; the heap of ruins between
the two parties serving as a breast-work for both, the muzzles
of their muskets touching, and the spearheads of the standards
locked.

"Djezzar Pasha, hearing that the English were on the breach,

* Like the *tranche des baionnettes* at Verdun.

quitted his station where, according to ancient Turkish custom, he was sitting to reward such as should bring him the heads of the enemy and distributing musket cartridges with his own hands. The energetic old man, coming behind us, pulled us down with violence, saying if any harm to his English friends happened all was lost.

"This amicable contest, as to who should defend the breach, occasioned a rush of Turks to the spot, and thus time was gained for the arrival of the first body of Hassan Bey's troops.

"I had now to combat the pasha's repugnance to admitting any troops, but his Albanians, into the garden of his seraglio, become a very important post, as occupying the *terre pleine* of the rampart. There were not above two hundred of the original thousand Albanians left alive. This was no time for debate, and I overruled his objections, by introducing the *Chifflick* regiment of a thousand men, armed with bayonets and disciplined after the European method, under Sultan Selim's own eye, and placed by his imperial majesty's express commands at my disposal. The garrison, animated by the appearance of such a reinforcement, was now all on foot, and there being con-sequently enough to defend the breach, I proposed to the pasha, to get rid of the object of his jealousy, to open his gates to let them make a sally, and take the assailants in flank. He readily complied, and I gave directions to the colonel to get possession of the enemy's third parallel, or nearest trench, and there fortify himself by shifting the parapet outwards. This order being clearly understood, the gates were opened, and the Turks rushed out; but they were not equal to such a movement, and were driven back to the town with loss. Mr Bray, however, as usual, protected the town gate efficaciously with grape from the 68-pounders. The *sortie* had this good effect, that it obliged the enemy to expose themselves above their parapet, so that our flanking fire brought down numbers of them, and drew their force from the breach, so that the small number remaining on the lodgment were killed or dispersed, by our few remaining hand grenades thrown by Mr Savage, midshipman of the *Theseus*. The enemy began a new breach, by an incessant fire directed to the southward of the lodgement, every shot knocking down whole sheets of a wall, much less solid than that of the tower, on which they had expended so much time and ammunition.

"The groups of generals and *aides-de-camp*, which the shells from the 68-pounders had frequently dispersed, were now re-assembled on Richard Coeur-de-Lion's mount. Buonaparte was distinguishable in the centre of the semi-circle; his gesticulation indicated a renewal of attack, and his despatching an *aide-de-camp* to the camp shewed that he waited only for a reinforcement. I gave directions for Hassan Bey's ships to take their station in the shoal water to the southward, and made the *Tigre* signal to weigh and join the *Theseus* to the northward.

"A little before sunset, a massive column appeared advancing to the breach with solemn step. The pasha's idea was not to defend the breach this time; but rather to let a certain number of the enemy in, and then close with them, according to the Turkish mode of war. The column thus mounted the breach unmolested, and descended from the rampart into the pasha's garden, where, in a very few minutes, the bravest and most advanced amongst them lay headless corpses, the sabre, with the addition of a dagger in the other hand, proving more than a match for the bayonet; the rest retreated precipitately, and the commanding officer, who was seen manfully encouraging his men to mount the breach, and whom we have since learnt to be General Lasne, was carried off wounded by a musket shot; General Rombaud was killed. Much confusion arose in the town, from the actual entry of the enemy, it having been impossible, nay impolitic, to give previous information to every body of the mode of defence adopted, lest the enemy should come to a knowledge of it, by means of their numerous emissaries.

"The English uniform, which had hitherto served as a rallying point for the old garrison, wherever it appeared, was now in the dusk mistaken for French, the newly arrived Turks not distinguishing between one hat and another in the crowd. Thus many a severe blow of a sabre was parried by our officers, among whom Colonel Douglas, Mr Ives, and Mr Jones, nearly lost their lives, as they were forcing their way through a torrent of fugitives. Calm was restored by the Pasha's exertions, aided by Mr Frotté, just arrived with Hassan Bey; and thus the contest of twenty-five hours ended, both parties being so fatigued as to be unable to move.

"Buonaparte will, no doubt, renew the attack, the breach being, as above described, perfectly practicable for fifty men abreast; indeed the town is not, nor ever has been, defensible, according to the rules of war; *but according to every other rule, it must and shall be defended; not that it is in itself worth defending, but we feel that it is by this breach Buonaparte means to march to further conquest.* 'Tis on the issue of this conflict, that depends the opinion of the multitude of spectators on the surrounding hills, who wait only to see how it ends to join the victor; and with such a reinforcement for the execution of his known projects, Constantinople and even Vienna must feel the shock.

"Be assured, my lord, the magnitude of our obligations does but increase the energy of our efforts, in the attempt to discharge our duty; and though we may and probably shall be overpowered, I can venture to say, that the French army will be so much further weakened, before it prevails, as to be little able to profit by its dear bought victory."

The French General Montholon describing the last few days of the abortive siege summed up the situation in these words:

In the circumstances what course was the general-in-chief to pursue? We heard from the Turks whom we captured that fresh reinforcements were on their way from Rhodes and these might render the success of the siege doubtful. So far distant as we were both from France and Egypt we could not afford to suffer fresh losses. The murder of our wounded at Jaffa and in the camp near Acre was 12,000 and the plague was in our hospitals. On the 20th May the siege was raised.

According to a report by Sir Sidney's private secretary, Keith, the number of Frenchmen killed was also extremely heavy. Eight generals, more than eighty of his best officers and about four thousand men.

"Nothing can surpass the bravery of the Turks in the four last attempts," Keith wrote, "they boldly rushed in on the republican bayonets, sabre in hand, cutting in pieces every bearer of them, with but little loss to themselves, as the French never had time to fire more than one round before they closed with them. Buonaparte has lost all his popularity and the confidence of his troops. They will all soon be destroyed one way or another, for the princes of the mountains, his only friends in the country, are all coming over to us, and have actually withdrawn from him all supplies."

For this Sir Sidney could claim all the credit. When it became clear that the siege of Acre was not going too well for the French he had written a circular letter to the princes and chiefs of the Christians of Mount Lebanon and to the sheiks of the Druse suggesting that they could help hold back the French invaders by cutting off all supplies. He also sent them a copy of Napoleon's proclamation in which he boasted of having over-thrown "all Christian Establishments" and called on them to "choose between the friendship of a Christian Knight and that of an unprincipled renegade".

This letter, Smith told Nelson, had just the effect that was intended. Two ambassadors from the chiefs and sheiks arrived with protestations of friendship and stated that several tribes-men in the mountains had already been arrested for carrying wine and gunpowder to the French camp. This ensured that "Buonaparte's career further northward would effectually be stopped by a warlike people inhabiting an impenetrable country".

Ten days after the siege was raised Sir Sidney sent a long despatch to Lord Nelson, the first since his arrival in the Bay of Acre. "The providence of Almighty God has been wonderfully manifested," he wrote, "in the defeat and precipitate retreat of the French army: the means we had of opposing its gigantic efforts against us being totally inadequate of themselves to the production of such a result."

Sidney Smith's personal triumph at Acre, for such it was, must have been a bitter pill for his many detractors in the British Navy to swallow and many of them did not hesitate to point out the "unusual modesty" of his final despatch to Nelson.

Lord St Vincent does not appear to have sent Smith any personal congratulations* but Nelson, to his credit, sent him a most generous letter, full of praise, though he could not resist the temptation, in the very last sentence, of harking back to their original bone of contention.

"The immense fatigue you have had," he wrote, "in defend-ing Acre against such a chosen army of French villains headed by that arch-villain Buonaparte, has never been exceeded, and the bravery shown by you and your brave companions is such as to merit every encomium which all the civilized world can bestow. As an individual, and as an Admiral, will you accept my feeble tribute of praise and admiration, and make them accept-able to all those under your command. . . . I hope Alexandria is long before this in your possession, and the final blow given to

---

* A few days after the siege of Acre was raised Lord St Vincent was, in fact, relieved of the Mediterranean command by Lord Keith.

Buonaparte. . . . Be assured, my dear Sir Sidney, of my perfect esteem and regard, and do not let anyone persuade you to the contrary. *But my character is that I will not suffer the smallest tittle of my command to be taken from me.*"

The news of Napoleon's defeat at Acre was received in London, and throughout the country, with great satisfaction, and honours and compliments were showered on Sir Sidney. He also received a letter from Lord Spencer.

"You will most probably," he wrote, "by the same conveyance which brings this letter, be officially informed of the great, and, I believe, unprecedented honour which has been paid you, by the thanks of the House of Commons for your services before Acre, which thanks I propose also to move in the House of Lords on the first day they sit after their present adjournment. I call this an unprecedented honour because I do not believe there is an instance of an officer of no higher rank than captain being mentioned in so pointed a manner in the King's speech as you have been, and thanked by Parliament. However, as you have thought fit to move out of the common and ordinary line of brilliant service it is very proper for us to move out of the usual practice of remuneration. I have the satisfaction of adding that it is not intended that the thanks should be barren of some substantial advantage, as it is in contemplation to bring forward a measure for granting you a pecuniary compensation, the exact mode or quantum of which is not fixed but I rather believe it will be a parliamentary pension of £500 a year."

The resolution thanking Sir Sidney for his "conspicuous skill and heroism" was moved by Mr Henry Dundas, then Secretary of State for War and the following is an extract from the report of his speech:

A twelvemonth had not elapsed since this country felt some apprehension on account of the probable destination of the French army in Egypt, an apprehension that was much allayed by the memorable and most glorious victory of Lord Nelson.* The power of that army had been still much further reduced by the efforts of Sir Sidney Smith, who, with a handful of men, surprised a whole nation, who were his spectators, with the brilliance of his triumph, contesting for sixty days with an enterprising and intrepid general at the head of his

* At Aboukir.

whole army. . . . He had heard that Sir Sidney Smith who had his difficulties, had sometimes been lightly spoken of by some persons; whoever they were, they were inconsiderate, and they might be left now to their inward shame, if they did not recant; be that as it might, the house, he was confident, agreed with him, that the conduct of Sir Sidney Smith for heroism, and intrepidity, and active exertion, was never surpassed on any occasion. He was glad of the opportunity he had to say this.

King George III, opening a new session of Parliament on 24th September, also mentioned Sir Sidney's defence of Acre: "The French expedition to Egypt," His Majesty said, "has continued to be productive of calamity and disgrace to our enemies, while its ultimate views against our eastern possessions have been utterly confounded. The desperate attempt which they have lately made to extricate themselves from their difficulties, has been defeated by the courage of the Turkish forces, directed by the skill, and animated by the heroism of a British officer, with a small portion of my naval force under his command; and the overthrow of that restless and perfidious power, who, instigated by the artifices, and deluded by the promises, of the French, had entered into their ambitious and destructive projects in India, has placed the British interests in that quarter in a state of solid and permanent security."

When, a week later, a vote of thanks was also moved in the House of Lords, Lord Spencer, Lord Hood and Lord Grenville all paid glowing tributes to Sir Sidney's conduct of the operation.

Earl Spencer said he had now to take notice of an exploit which had never been surpassed, and scarcely ever been equalled in the annals of history: he meant the defence of St Jean d'Acre, by Sir Sidney Smith. He had no occasion to impress upon their Lordships a higher sense than they already entertained of the brilliancy, utility, and distinction of an achievement, in which a General of great celebrity, and a veteran victorious army, were, after a desperate and obstinate engagement, which lasted almost without intermission for sixty days, not only repulsed, but totally defeated, by the gallantry and heroism of this British officer, and the small number of troops under his command. He owned that it was not customary, nor did he think it had any precedent in the proceedings of Parliament, that so high an honour should be conferred on long services, which might be performed by a force so inconsiderable in point of numbers; but the splendour of such an exploit, as defeating a veteran and well appointed Army, commanded by experienced generals, which already had overrun a great part of Europe, a fine portion of Africa, and attempted also the conquest of Asia, eclipsed all former examples, and should not be subjected to the rules of ordinary usage. He, therefore, in full confidence of universal approbation, moved the thanks of the house to Captain Sir William Sidney Smith, and the British seamen under his command, for their gallant and successful defence of St Jean d'Acre, against the desperate attacks of the French army under the command of General Bonaparte.

Lord Hood could not give a vote on the present occasion, without bearing his testimony to the skill and valour of Sir Sidney Smith, which had been so conspicuously and brilliantly exerted, when he had the honour and benefit of having him under his command. Had that officer been at the head of a more considerable force, there is every probability that not a Frenchman would have escaped. The nation must be sensible of the importance and benefits of the late achievement and, judging from his character and conduct, he made no doubt that even this was only an earnest of his future glory whenever an opportunity presented itself.

Lord Grenville said there never was a motion since he had a seat in that house to which he gave a more hearty concurrence and assent. The circumstance of so eminent a service having been performed, with so inconsiderable a force, was with him an additional reason for affording this testimony of public gratitude, and the highest honour that the house had in its power to confer. By this gallant and unprecedented resistance, we beheld the conqueror of Italy, the future Alexander, not only defeated and driven from the situation at which he had arrived, but also obliged to retreat in disorder and confusion to parts where it was not likely that he would find a shelter from the pursuit of British skill and intrepidity. How glorious must the whole appear when they looked to the contrast between the victor and vanquished. Bonaparte's progress, throughout the whole of his military career, was marked with every trait of cruelty and treachery. In defiance of every principle of humanity and of all the acknowledged rules of war, Sir Sidney

Smith had been long, with the most cool and cruel inflexibility, confined in a dungeon of the Temple, from which he was only rescued by his own address and intrepidity. But the French, by making him an exception from the general usages of war, had only manifested their sense of his value, and how much they were afraid of him. This hero, in the progress of events, was afterwards destined to oppose the enemy in a distant quarter, and, instead of indulging any sentiments of revenge or resentment against his former persecutors, indulged the natural feelings of his heart by interfering for, and saving the lives of, a number of French prisoners soon after this when, victorious in an obstinate contest, where he was but indifferently supported by the discipline of the native troops or means of defence in the fortifications of the fortress, he generously and humanely lent his protecting aid to a body of miserable and wounded Frenchmen, who implored his assistance, when the cruelty and obstinacy of their own general had devoted them to almost inevitable destruction.

Even Napoleon did not fail to pay a tribute to the naval captain but for whose generalship during the siege of Acre he might have been another Alexander the Great. While in exile on the island of St Helena, brooding bitterly over the past, the fallen Emperor of the French, referring to Sir Sidney, said, "that man made me miss my destiny."

7

EL ARISH

THE siege of Acre was over and Napoleon's advance to the north held up, but the French still had to be driven out of Egypt. Leaving all their artillery behind them they made for Jaffa and Damietta which Smith reached with his flotilla before the routed French forces could get there. He described the scene in a letter to Nelson.

"The enemy's vessels," he wrote, "being hurried to sea without seamen to navigate them, and the wounded being in want of every necessary, even water and provisions, they steered straight to His Majesty's ships, in full confidence of receiving the succours of humanity; in which they were not disappointed. . . . The utmost disorder has been manifested in the retreat and the whole track between Acre and Gaza is strewn with the dead bodies of those who have sunk under fatigue or the effect of slight wounds."

Notwithstanding this crushing defeat of Napoleon's armies the campaign in Egypt was by no means over, and on 10th July a large Turkish force from the island of Rhodes landed at Aboukir Bay, under cover of the guns of the British and Turkish fleets, occupied the fort and proceeded to take up a defensive position.

A fortnight later, however, Sir Sidney had to report, in a despatch to Nelson, the complete defeat by Napoleon of the 1st Ottoman Division, all of whom were killed or captured. But the French casualties were also heavy and led Smith to remark that a few more such victories would annihilate the French army.

Napoleon had already decided to leave Egypt before it was too late and this unexpected success at Aboukir gave him the opportunity of making his disappearance seem less dishonourable. Nevertheless, as Sir John Fortescue wrote in his *History of the British Army*, he did desert the troops under his command "like a thief in the night" but, had a British force been brought from Sicily, as Charles Stuart had suggested, to reinforce the

Turks "there was every reasonable probability that Bonaparte would have been defeated, his army and himself made prisoners and his reputation so far damaged that France would never have accepted him as her master".

When Napoleon made his escape by night from Alexandria in a small vessel which was, incidentally, nearly captured by H.M.S. *Theseus*, he left written orders to General Kléber to take over command. Kléber, realising that there was little or no chance of getting his troops safely back to France, entered into negotiations with the Grand Vizier for their evacuation, and the Convention of El Arish was signed on 24th January, 1800 under which the following was agreed between the two parties:

1. The French Army would retire with its arms, baggage and effects to Alexandria, Rosetta and Aboukir, there to be embarked and transported to France.

2. There was to be an armistice of three months to allow this to be done and the period would be duly extended, if necessary, until the embarkation could be completed.

3. The Turks agreed to make every endeavour to allow the French to make their way to the coast without being disturbed or molested.

4. Immediately after the ratification of the Convention, all Turks and other nationals who were subjects of the Sublime Porte and were imprisoned or otherwise detained in France or in the custody of the French in Egypt were to be freed and all French nationals detained in any of the cities or seaports of the Ottoman Empire were, similarly, to be set at liberty.

5. General Kléber was permitted to send news of the evacuation to his government and the Turks agreed to ensure safe conduct for the ship that was to carry this communication.

To sum up, the French forces with all its arms, supplies and stores together with all the French men-of-war and transport vessels at Alexandria would be allowed to return to France unmolested by the Allied Powers.

When Sir Sidney signified his agreement to the terms of this Convention he must have known how the news of it would be received by Lord Nelson. After taking over command in the Levant from Troubridge he had approved a form of passport intended to be used by any Frenchman wishing to go to Europe by sea. When one of these passports was shown by Troubridge to Nelson he wrote to Smith as follows:

> As this is in direct opposition to my opinion, which is never to suffer any one individual Frenchman to quit Egypt I must strictly charge and command you never to give any French ship or man leave to quit Egypt. And I must also desire that you will oppose by every means in your power any permission which may be attempted to be given by any foreigner, Admiral, General, or other person; and you will acquaint those persons that I shall not pay the smallest attention to any such passport after your notification, you are to put my orders in force not on any pretence to permit a single Frenchman to leave Egypt.

Nelson's views could hardly have been made more clear and Sir Sidney must have known that his approval of the Convention of El Arish was given in flagrant disobedience of his Admiral's orders, which were supported by H.M. Government and the Commander-in-Chief Lord Keith, who wrote the following letter to General Kléber as soon as he heard the news:

> Sir,
>
> I inform you that I have received positive orders from His Majesty not to consent to any capitulation with the French troops which you command in Egypt and Syria, at least unless they lay down their arms, surrender themselves prisoners of war, and deliver up all the ships and stores of the port of Alexander to the allied powers.
>
> In the event of this capitulation I cannot permit any of the troops to depart from France before they have been exchanged. I think it equally necessary to inform you, that all vessels having French troops on board with passports from others than authorised to grant them, will be forced by the officers of the ships which I command to remain in Alexandria: in short, that ships which shall be met returning to Europe with passports granted in consequence of a particular capitulation with one of the allied powers will be retained as prizes, and all individuals on board considered as prisoners of war.
>
> Keith

General Kléber's reaction to this ultimatum was swift and defiant. The contents of Lord Keith's letter were published in an Order of the Day, together with a stirring call to the French troops:

"Soldiers. We know how to reply to such insolence—by victories. Prepare for battle!"

One of the immediate effects of this apparent disavowal of the Convention by the British Commander-in-Chief was a crushing defeat of the Turks at the battle of Elhanka in which they lost 8,000 men.

Sir Sidney was, not unnaturally, greatly upset by the action taken by Lord Keith as he considered it as a breach of faith on the part of the British although, to do him justice, the Commander-in-Chief was not aware, when he wrote to General Kléber, that Lord Grenville had instructed Lord Elgin, the new British Ambassador at Constantinople, to allow the Convention to go on, though not in precisely the same terms as were first proposed, and had actually sent him a form of passport to be given to each ship carrying the French troops to Europe.

Smith felt strongly that he owed the French some explanation and he wrote at once to Citizen Poussielgue, Administrator-General of the Finances, who had been one of the French signatories to the Convention.

He told Poussielgue of the objections which his superiors had raised to the implementation of the Convention and suggested that a meeting should take place between the French representative and Lord Keith to discuss the whole matter.

Acting on this suggestion Citizen Poussielgue asked the British Admiral either to arrange a meeting between them or to allow him to go to France, so that the French Government might enter into negotiations with the British to bring the affair to a satisfactory conclusion.

"The lives of fifty thousand men," he wrote, "are at stake, who may be destroyed without any motive, since, according to the solemn treaty made with the English, Russians, and Turks, all hostilities had terminated." He regretted what appeared to him to be inexcusable behaviour, even for perfidious Albion, and told Lord Keith that when the Convention of El Arish was concluded "under the simple pledge of English good faith" the French never suspected that obstacles against it would be raised by "one of the most liberal" of all the powers with whom they had to treat.

Sir Sidney, too, appealed to Lord Keith to change his mind and stressed the impossibility "of revoking what had been

formally settled after a detailed discussion and mature delibera-
tion". Meanwhile he had also written home to Lord Spencer
expressing his annoyance that "his superiors at a distance",
meaning, of course, Lord Keith, had let down the man-on-the-
spot, namely himself. As "an honest man" he deprecated such
a breach of good faith.

By this time the British Cabinet had heard about the Convention and to say that they were displeased would be an
understatement. They were in two minds whether or not they
should repudiate it but on second thoughts decided that to do
so would be regarded everywhere as an unforgivable breach of
good faith. Lord Keith was, therefore, told that as the French
Commander-in-Chief in Egypt appeared to have treated
Sidney Smith as a person who had the authority to act as he
did, His Majesty, "from a scrupulous regard for the public
faith", judged it proper that Lord Keith should abstain from any
act inconsistent with the engagements to which Sir Sidney Smith
had erroneously given the sanction of His Majesty's name.

Having received the above instructions from his government
Lord Keith had no alternative but to climb down and on
25 April he replied to Poussielgue's letter.

"I have this day," he wrote, "received the letter which you
have done me the honour to write. I have to inform you that I
have given no orders or authority against the observance of the
Convention between the Grand Vizier and General Kléber,
having received no orders on this head from the King's
ministers. Accordingly I was of opinion that His Majesty should
take no part in it, but since the treaty has been concluded, His
Majesty, being desirous of showing his respect for his allies, I
have received instructions to allow a passage to the French
troops and have lost not a moment in sending to Egypt orders
to permit them to return to France without molestation. At the
same time I thought it my duty to my King, and those of his
allies whose States lie in the seas through which they are to
pass, to require that they should not return *en masse*, nor in
ships of war, nor in armed ships. . . . I have likewise asked of
General Kléber his word of honour that neither he nor his army
should commit any hostilities against the coalesced powers. . . ."
Lord Keith ended by telling Monsieur Poussielgue that he
would himself be given safe conduct to France.

After receipt of this conciliatory letter all would probably
have gone well had not Kléber been assassinated in Cairo about

two months later and been succeeded by General Menou. The new French Commander-in-Chief curtly refused to enter into further negotiations with Smith and insisted that any treaty to which he was prepared to be a party would have to be approved by "the Consuls who govern the French Republic". He was clearly not prepared to shoulder the responsibility himself. This whole incident, and the leading part which Sir Sidney had played in it, created a furore at home and was debated by both Houses of Parliament where he came in for much criticism. Nevertheless, in August he received a letter from Lord Spencer which largely exonerated him from any blame.

"I shall satisfy myself by saying in general," Lord Spencer wrote, "that your explanations and defence are so far completely satisfactory to my mind as to prove that you have throughout acted in the manner which to you appeared the best, and though I think you have been under an error with respect to the continuation of your power as a plenipotentiary (an error, by the way, into which I am not surprised that you were led by the communications from Lord Elgin) and though I also differ considerably with you in the opinion you seem to have formed of the probable result of the return of Kléber's army into France, I cannot help allowing that you acted upon very strong grounds, and that upon the whole, if it had been possible that we could have been in complete possession of all these grounds for the purpose of forming our determination on the subject, the Convention of El Arish would most probably have been carried into execution. . . . I think it would not be impossible for anyone not to allow that the policy of that Convention was such as to recommend its ratification."

Whatever else is said, there can be no doubt that if H.M. Government had been sensible enough to ratify the Convention immediately and without question a lot of time and trouble and many British lives would have been saved. Because of the delay caused by Lord Keith's first letter and the appointment of General Menou to succeed Kléber the campaign in Egypt was to run on desultorily for another eighteen months.

Towards the end of the summer of 1800 the British Cabinet decided to send a force under General Sir Ralph Abercromby, and Lord Keith wrote to let Sir Sidney know of this decision and ask him to give the benefit of his opinion on certain important matters in connection with this new expedition. "The long experience which you have had," Keith wrote, "the local

information which you have acquired and the extensive knowledge you must possess of the nature of the country, the coast,
the climate, as well as of the character and disposition of the
people with whom we are to deal" led him to take this step. Sir
Sidney was asked to suggest a rendezvous "where a fleet of at
least eighty or ninety sail" could be protected from all winds,
where it could be supplied with good water, fresh provisions,
vegetables and fruits—for an army, as Napoleon said, marches
on its stomach—and where there was comparative freedom
from disease. Finally he was asked to suggest a suitable place to
make a landing.

The British force landed in two parties, one under Sir John
Moore, of Corunna fame, and the other under Sir Ralph
Abercromby himself. On 21st March both these forces were
attacked by the French. Lord Keith's despatch to the Secretary
of the Admiralty reported heavy French losses, the death from
wounds of Abercromby, and the appointment of General Sir
John Hely-Hutchinson to succeed him.

Sir Sidney took an active part in the battle and, in his report
to Lord Keith, stated that the great losses which the French
had sustained "ought to make General Menou respect our
troops too much to risk a second attempt of the kind; at all
events we are prepared to receive him". He was himself slightly
wounded in the shoulder.

Hely-Hutchinson had not been in command very long before
trouble broke out between him and Smith. It was not the last
time that he was to wage war simultaneously against the enemy
and the British military command. On this occasion the campaign merely took the form of an exchange of rather pointed
letters in which Smith, as was not unusual, had the last word
and at considerable length.

Tigre, off Alexandria, 28th August 1801.

Dear Sir,

I have forborne to intrude on your time while active
operations were in train of progress. There being, however,
at this moment a truce, I profit by the interval of suspense,
to inform you of my intention of going to England as soon as
the French flag is hauled down in Alexandria, and to express
my wish to have an hour's conversation with you before I go.
Your letter (without date) received on the 2nd August, was
satisfactory as far as it went; and I can assure you, no man is

more ready than myself to accept a reasonable explanation of what appears to call for it, where a spirit of conciliation is manifest: but there is one weighty point to be discussed, which is of much importance to me, and which you may think of some to you, if you wish, as I am persuaded you do, to maintain your character for justice and liberality un-impeached.

It is well known that my sudden recall from the distinguished situation I had the honour to hold, under your orders, was brought about by a miserable intrigue of the Capitan Pasha. It is equally well known, that the British commander-in-chief of the army, instead of supporting his friend and coadjutor, for such I certainly then was, not only acquiesced to this Turkish policy taking effect, but contributed thereto. It may be well supposed, that those whom I had prevented from plundering the country, and massacring the inhabitants at Rosetta, and those whom I required to keep the faith with the beys, pledged in my hands, should wish to prevent such sort of interposition by complaining of 'interference', in order to remove me to a distance; but it was not to be expected that those who were in duty bound to further the salutary views of the British Government in that respect, should acquiesce thereto, and that at the precise time when I had brought things to a point, requiring nothing but one personal interview to claim the execution of the promises of which I was the depositary, in order to prevent the necessity of the strong remonstrances you acknowledge yourself to have been reduced to make to the vizier since, and, unfortunately, to very little effect, at such a late period of the business, as my letters from the beys inform me. I am still at a loss to know how you would have me answer them, and something I must say, for it is to me they look as having first engaged them to quit the French, under the guarantee of Sir Ralph Abercrombie.

Having said thus much on what regards the public, I beg leave to say a few distinct words on what regards myself personally. You have, by sending me afloat, deprived me of the only gratification I sought after three years' hard labour in this business; that of contributing my endeavours towards a successful end, or at least, of witnessing its termination on the spot. You have deprived me of the small share of credit I had a right to expect, in common with others of the same rank, whom you have specified, and thereby made it impossible for official notice to be taken of me, and excluded me from an army to which I felt proud to belong, and to which I shall ever feel myself warmly attached.

Unless *you now do me justice*, the only statement that will remain on record under your hand in the business is one of complaint, that the naval part of the army did not afford you assistance on your left flank at Rosetta: now, at that very time, I had created a flotilla on the Nile without the assistance of a single man of my brigade of seamen, which was kept inactive before Alexandria; while the want of force afloat was complained of, that flotilla, so created and introduced, was more than equal to anything that was or could be required of it; and I appeal to General Craddock, Colonel Spencer, and Lord Dalhousie, whose zealous exertions I endeavoured to second, as to the ground on which they testified their satisfaction to me at the time.

Now I am persuaded, in the general censure of the naval force, which your letter of the 27th of April conveyed to Lord Keith, you could not and did not mean me personally; yet, as being the officer immediately responsible on the spot, and so soon afterwards known to be recalled by your instigation, that censure must be supposed applicable to me, although, in fact, I was at the time in sufficient force to be able to go up the river and explore it in the teeth of the enemy, without waiting for the protection of the army. You will remember, I offered to proceed as much higher as you might require, in compliance with Lord Keith's optional order to me; and therefore, in justice, you ought to have recalled an unqualified censure; whereas, the naval force under my orders is not even mentioned in your official report of our having secured the important communication of the Rosetta branch of the Nile, notwithstanding a proportion of credit was handsomely attributed to us by Colonel Spencer, under whom I voluntarily placed myself, although my rank was not inferior to his.

On the appearance of your orders after the 21st, you may remember I thanked you (rather ironically to be sure) for having given the world a proof of your conviction that I was a man to work, whether I had any encouragement or not, as you afforded me work; at the same time I told you the case was different with regard to young officers seeking promotion,

and seamen, to whom civil words could not but be grateful:
you then promised me that you would write me a letter
expressive of your approbation; that letter is still to come;
and although I can well conceive the occupations which
pressed on your time and on your health, in the hot climate
of Cairo, may have been an obstacle to the execution of your
good intentions, I trust and hope that cause has ceased, and
that you will still express yourself with regard to the branch
of the service under my direction, in such a way as shall
remove all ground of discontent on that score; and that the
winding up of our Egyptian reports will, by doing everybody
justice, preclude the necessity of any body seeking redress for
an injury to their character which retards their promotion.

I am, sir, etc.

W. Sidney Smith

For Sir Sidney, however, the Egyptian campaign was soon to
be over. Cairo capitulated on 20th June and, by the middle of
August, Alexandria also fell. This was the final French reverse
and General Menou was allowed to evacuate Egypt upon
almost exactly the same terms as the Convention of El Arish in
January 1800. Sir Sidney has been criticised by Sir John
Fortescue for having no 'foresight or fixity of purpose'. Had his
advice only been taken then the Egyptian campaign would have
come to an equally satisfactory conclusion twenty months
earlier.

So, on the 5th September 1801, Sidney Smith and Sir Ralph
Abercromby's son, Colonel Abercromby, embarked at
Alexandria on H.M. Frigate *Carmen* with the final despatches
on the Egyptian Campaign. Although some of his superiors,
including Hely-Hutchinson were, doubtless, relieved to see the
end of him he was given a hearty send-off by the crew of the
Tigre, which he had commanded for nearly four years.

Not all the generals, however, were glad to see him go. One
of them, General Doyle, had written him a letter four months
earlier when Smith had been dismissed from his land command
by Hutchinson.

General C. J. Doyle to Sir Sidney Smith

Camp on the banks of the Nile, 29th April 1801.

My Dear Sir Sidney,

I cannot express how grieved I feel at your being called
away from us, at this most critical moment, when your

4

talents, your local knowledge, and above all, your *energy* would be so essential to our success. If I look upon you as a public man, deeply interested that the expedition should succeed, I consider your removal at this time as a national calamity; for, indisputably, the fate of Egypt, in which so many consequences are involved, will materially depend upon the combined movement against Rhamanie. Now, whatever other good qualities this army may possess, it cannot be denied but we are sadly deficient in promptitude and energy, at all times necessary in warfare, but peculiarly so against the enemy we have to cope with, and the baneful climate we must shortly expect to feel.

You have too long known my sentiments upon those subjects, to make it necessary for me to trouble you with them at present; indeed it has been always a source of pride to me, that our ideas have constantly been in unison as to the mode of carrying on the war; but as those have been, for the most part, diametrically opposite to the opinions of some of the *sober undertakers* of the army, I begin to give some credit to the idea of your being in a certain degree *mad*; and therefore, if you are no longer allowed to animate us by your example, do, for heaven's sake, *bite a few of us before you go; I should particularly recommend your sharpest fangs for our departmental folks*; as for myself, a slight scratch would answer, as I am considered already strongly tainted with the same calamity as yourself, zeal and madness being deemed synonymous terms!

God bless you, my dear fellow-sufferer, and continue you in your present state of madness, for your country's sake. I am always affectionately yours.

J. Doyle

8

THE ROCKET SHIPS

THE enthusiasm with which he was received on his arrival in England early in November and the congratulations showered upon him did much to make amends for the embarrassed feeling which Sir Sidney must have had when he came in for so much criticism for the part he had played in the negotiations which preceded the signing of the El Arish Convention.

Pitt, himself, cannot have felt quite happy about the way Sir Sidney had been treated for he sent for him, immediately after his return to London, and explained what had led the Cabinet to disavow the first treaty. Pitt said that they were not aware that Sir Sidney had any authority to act in such a way, but it is difficult to believe that the Cabinet were not aware of the powers bestowed upon him by Lords Grenville and Spencer when he was originally sent out to Constantinople on the special mission to the Sublime Porte. It is true that with Lord Elgin's appointment as ambassador to Turkey Smith's powers as a plenipotentiary were supposed to be at an end, but Lord Spencer had himself admitted when he wrote to Sir Sidney a year earlier that he was not surprised that Lord Elgin's correspondence with Smith had led him into the error that he still retained those powers.

Sir Sidney listened attentively to all that Pitt had to say but could not refrain from reminding the First Lord of the Treasury* that he had not signed any treaty himself: all he had done was to witness a treaty concluded between Turkey and the French Commander-in-Chief both of whom were fully competent so to do. Pitt appears to have accepted this explanation and ended the interview by congratulating Sir Sidney on his "skill, exertions and bravery".

Nevertheless, no honour was bestowed upon him by His Majesty but he was given the freedom of the City of London at the Guildhall when the City Chamberlain addressed him in these words:

* At that time the office of Prime Minister was not in existence.

Sir Sidney Smith,

I give you joy, in the name of the lord mayor, aldermen, and commons of the city of London, in common council assembled, and present you the thanks of the court for your gallant and successful defence of St Jean d'Acre, against the desperate attack of the French army under the command of General Buonaparte. And, as a further testimony of the sense the court entertains of your great display of valour on that occasion, I have the honour to present you with the freedom of the city, and this sword.

I will not, sir, attempt a panegyric upon an action to which the first oratorical powers in the most eloquent assemblies have been confessed unequal, but I cannot help exulting, on this happy occasion, at the vast acquisition national reputation has acquired by your conduct, at the head of a handful of Britons, in repulsing him who has been justly styled the Alexander of the day, surrounded by a host of conquerors, till then deemed invincible. By this splendid achievement you frustrated the designs of the foe on our East Indian territories, prevented the overthrow of the Ottoman power in Asia, the downfall of its throne in Europe, and prepared the way for that treaty of peace which, it is devoutly to be wished, may long preserve the tranquillity of the universe, and promote friendship and good-will among all nations. It must be highly gratifying to every lover of his country, that this event should have happened on the very spot, where a gallant English monarch formerly displayed such prodigies of valour, that a celebrated historian, recording his actions, struck with the stupendous instances of prowess displayed by that heroic prince, suddenly exclaimed, 'Am I writing history or romance?' Had, sir, that historian survived to have witnessed what has recently happened at St Jean d'Acre, he would have exultingly resigned his doubts, and generously have confessed, that actions, no less extraordinary than those performed by the gallant Coeur de Lion, have been achieved by Sir Sidney Smith.

To which Sir Sidney replied:

Sir,

Unconscious that I should have been thought worthy of being addressed by you on the part of the city of London, in terms of such high and unqualified approbation, I am but ill prepared for replying in a manner adequately to express the sentiments with which I am impressed. My confidence would be lessened, did I not feel that I was surrounded by friends who are dear to me, and whose approbation I am proud to have received. It shall be the object of my future life to merit the panegyric you have been pleased to pronounce in my favour. For the freedom of your city, with which you have honoured me, I return you my sincere thanks, and shall implicitly conform to all the obligations annexed to it. Above all, I accept this sword as the most honourable reward which could have been conferred on me. In peace it will be my proudest ornament, and in war I trust I shall be ever ready to draw it in defence of my country, and for the protection of the city of London.

He was also presented with a piece of plate by the Turkey Company, and the Levant Company voted him a gratuity of fifteen hundred pounds.

Negotiations between the English and French to end the war were by now in progress, however, and on 27 March 1802 the signing of the Treaty of Amiens ushered in a short uneasy peace which was to last for little more than a year. Nevertheless, Sir Sidney, faced with another spell of half-pay, looked round for some other way of satisfying his restless energy, and was approached by the Freemen of Rochester to stand as a parliamentary candidate for their borough. He accepted the invitation but in his election address made it quite clear that if he were duly elected he would not be content to sit in the House of Commons as a party hack.

To the Freemen of the City of Rochester

London, May 12 1802.

Gentlemen,

Invited in such flattering terms, by so large a portion of your respectable body, I cannot hesitate in avowing my determination to close with the offer that is made me, of becoming your representative in parliament at the next general election, should a majority declare in my favour, it being understood that the Hon. Henry Tufton declines.

The naval relations of your ancient city, placed, too, in the county of Kent, where my connexions lay—in short, every consideration I have given the subject, decides my preference, and fixes my resolution to avail myself of your favourable disposition towards me. I hope I do not stand in opposition to the well-founded claims of any other candidate: I am incapable of usurping the rights of any other gentleman; my expectations rest upon your kindness and my known public character, without intending offence or injury in any other quarter. *My political creed is the English constitution, my party the nation. Highly as I prize the honour of becoming your representative, I will not purchase even that, or any other distinction, by renouncing an atom of my independence;* and if anything in my professional career has tended to excite those sentiments in you, which create in me a corresponding feeling, I trust you will find that, in the exercise of a legislative function, I shall not forfeit any portion of your esteem. This I am sure of, that if you do me the honour to put this great trust into my hands, I will, to the best of my judgment, discharge it like an honest man.

I have the honour to be, Gentlemen,

Your faithful and devoted servant,

W. Sidney Smith

He was returned as Member for Rochester at the next election and took his seat at the opening of Parliament but it was not long before the opportunity arose for him to go, once more, to sea. There had been obvious signs for some time that the French were making further preparations for war, and on 12th March, a little more than two months before the declaration of war by England on 17 May, Sir Sidney was commissioned by the Admiralty to hoist his pennant on H.M.S. *Antelope*, a ship of 50 guns, then stationed at Sheerness. Seven months later he received the following orders from Lord Keith, then in command of the North Sea fleet:

As the enemy have made, and are still making, extensive preparations at the port of Flushing and in the River Scheldt for the invasion of this country it has become highly necessary that their operations should be watchfully attended to and every exertion made for preventing and defeating their hostile designs. Placing full confidence in the address, judgment, industry and activity you will exercise in the conduct of this service you are directed to take under your orders the ships and vessels named in the margin* and all such others as may be placed under your direction.

Sir Sidney was also instructed to take up the most convenient

* Eight vessels were named.

station near the Scheldt and to work in co-operation with the fleet stationed at Yarmouth under Rear-Admiral Thornborough and another squadron at Helvoet.

This kind of assignment was not to Smith's liking. He preferred something more exciting. Cruising about in the North Sea and the Straits of Dover was a dull business after Acre and the only occasion on which it looked as though he might bring off a coup against the French ended in failure.

On 17th May a French flotilla was lying at anchor off Ostend and Sir Sidney decided to cut off another small fleet of French ships based on the port of Flushing and prevent the two from joining up with each other. This attempt failed owing to a shortage of gun-boats, the only kind of craft which alone could successfully act against the enemy in such shallow waters. Sir Sidney sent a report of this action to Lord Keith. He told the Admiral that he had received information that the French were preparing to set sail from both these ports and that on 17th May he had the satisfaction of seeing the Flushing flotilla of some 59 ships cruising close to the coast in the direction of Ostend and had decided to "bring them to action".

He gave orders to pursue the French and engage them.

"Captains Hancock and Mason," he wrote, "went into action and Captain Broughton worked up to the centre of the enemy's line as near as the shoal water would allow, while the *Antelope* (Sir Sidney's flag-ship) tried to cut the van off from Ostend. Unfortunately our gun-boats were not in sight, having, as I understood since, devoted their attention to preventing the Ostend division from moving westward. The enemy, however, then attempted to get back to Flushing, but when harassed by the *Cruiser* and the *Rattler* and the wind coming more easterly against them they were obliged to run the gauntlet to the westward keeping close to the shore under the protection of the coastal batteries. Meanwhile the *Antelope* had manœuvred herself into a position from which she was able to bring her broadside to bear on the leading schooners before they could reach the shelter of Ostend harbour."

Although the objective of this operation was not achieved several French ships were driven ashore and the French suffered heavy casualties. It was shortly after this unsuccessful action that Sir Sidney's health gave out and, on his doctor's advice he obtained sick leave and was succeeded in command by Sir Home Popham.

He quickly regained his health, however, and was soon on the warpath again and began plans for a projected attack on Boulogne with a fleet of ships, designed by himself, armed with explosives invented by a Mr Congreve.

Lord Castlereagh, who in May 1805 had been appointed Secretary-of-State for War and Colonies in the second Pitt administration, became interested in this project which was discussed in a lengthy correspondence between him, Sir Sidney, and Lord Keith.

Sir Sidney Smith to Lord Keith
Antelope, off Etaples, 29 Sept. 1805.

My Lord,

I have waited till I had an opportunity of inspecting the enemy's position closely, before I ventured to answer your lordship's letter of the 24th instant, calling upon me, by direction of the Lords Commissioners of the Admiralty, to state what fire and explosion vessels I might require for the service on which I am employed; and I now beg to leave to say, as the enemy appear to have stationed an advanced guard (in two lines) of gun-vessels superior in number and weight of metal to the force of that description under my orders, independent of the reinforcement that can be brought out any day at half tide, it becomes necessary to adopt some other mode of attack than cannonade, towards rendering their position in the road untenable, since, so long as they remain there, it is impossible for any inferior force to approach either the harbour, or even the neighbouring coast, without being completely checked, and kept at such distance as to preclude the occupation of the near position required for subsequent operations against the flotilla in the harbour, which latter we see in such close contact with each other, as to ensure the rapid spreading of flames, if once fire was communicated to any part of the line, or rather forest-like assemblage of masts.

Such is the nature of the local tide in Boulogne Bay and harbour's mouth, and such the precaution taken, by placing a sunk net between the pier-heads, that no explosion or fire-vessel, sent at random, could ever penetrate thereon, or under the surface of the water; but these vessels may be used, with reasonable hope of success, against the advanced vessels outside. At any rate, they should be shown their liability to this mode of attack by occasional explosions amongst them; and, provided there were some instances of grappling, (which I am persuaded, from the spirit of enterprise I have the satisfaction to observe among the officers and petty officers under my orders, there would be) it would probably occasion them to withdraw and keep within the harbour. I therefore request that such fire and explosion vessels as can be appropriated to this service may be sent (in succession, as they are ready) to join me at Dungeness.

I am etc.
W. Sidney Smith

Sir Sidney's recommendations, however, were considered by Lord Keith to be too revolutionary and he wrote the following letter in reply, in a vain attempt to damp Smith's ardour.

Lord Keith to Sir Sidney Smith
Edgar, off Ramsgate, October 3 1805.

Sir,

I have received your letter of the 29th ult., on the subject of the mode of attacking the enemy's flotilla at Boulogne, and requesting that such fire and explosion vessels as can be appropriated to this service may be sent in succession, as they are ready, to join you at Dungeness.

It has been the constant practice of the enemy, for these last two years, to keep a force in Boulogne Roads, in fine weather and east winds, varying from fifty to one hundred vessels, as an advance guard, and to cover the beach opposite the basin, but I am not of opinion that such a force is at all equal to that under your orders.

Whatever mode of attack you may determine upon will be duly weighed when communicated to me, and carried into execution, as soon as I receive orders from the Lords Commissioners of the Admiralty to that effect. But experience has convinced me that any attempt to dislodge a few brigs from the Roads will be attended with no good consequences, even although it succeeded; as they would resume their station the next tide, as has always been the case heretofore, whilst the risk, on our part, is considerable, and the expense great and certain.

At the time the attempt was made to burn the flotilla last year, there were in Boulogne Roads 150 sail; and, although the night was fine, the duty well performed, and the alarm considerable, the damage sustained by the enemy was small, and the expense on our part great.

I have to add that the orders of the French admiral are that no vessel is to have more than two feet of water under her keel at low water, from which you will see the almost impossibility of getting fire and explosion vessels inside or even alongside of them, while they are moored in small numbers in open order along the shore, which they always are, and as, in the moment of danger, they can be almost instantaneously hauled on shore, and the vessels got afloat again the next rising tide. It is therefore doubtful if any of them would be destroyed with the expenditure of all the fire and explosion vessels we have prepared; but, in a crowded state, (such must be the case previous to any attempt to invade this country) I think that I can venture to assure my superiors, that so prepared, I could destroy many, and create much confusion among the whole.

The fire vessels now prepared, as well as the mortar boats and gun-boats, are not of a description to enable them to ride at Dungeness at this season of the year, nor in Boulogne Roads, except in fine weather and an off-shore wind.

I have the honour etc.

Keith

As Lord Castlereagh, however, appeared to have less conservative ideas about the effectiveness of rocket ships, Sir Sidney, who could not be brushed aside so easily and was endowed with considerable powers of persuasion, wrote again to the Secretary of State for War and Colonies complaining that red tape in the Department of Naval Ordnance was preventing him from getting essential supplies, but he received a not very encouraging reply.

Sir Sidney Smith to Lord Castlereagh
Antelope, at anchor in Boulogne outer Road.
soi-disant Imperial Battery, S.E. 1/4 E., 5,200 yards.
Undated

My Dear Lord,

We did not make much progress after I despatched my last letter, for want of wind. The breeze did not come till six yesterday evening, when the squadron stood in, and the

Antelope anchored abreast the centre of their line, a gunshot and a half from them, their numbers being twenty-nine brigs and a galliot. The enemy reinforced their vessels with numbers of men, and have a line of long, swift-rowing pinnaces, as guard-boats, between and in front of them, our vessels not having been able to take their stations, from baffling winds and the heavy sailing of the gun-brigs, till today. I could only establish our counter-line of guard-boats, and try to send carcasses* among them in the night. Our vicinity occasioned them to fire at they knew not what, on one of their line firing at one of ours, who got too near in; except that one, we have not had occasion to return a shot; they even fired musketry at nothing. Mr Robinson having prepared carcasses, and having volunteered his active services, and Captain Secomb his, I sent them away with eight galleys: the sea ran so great, that they filled, and nothing but the cork kept them up; they could not reach the enemy's line, whose expectations were thus disappointed as well as our own.

Congreve is busy getting his apparatus in order; but there is no use in firing rockets at random in the air at their line, and they occupy the point from which alone we can reach the basin. I have tried four rockets from *Sagittarius* horizontally to ricochet on and from under water; they go some distance, and rise or fire after having been under water: two had shells, both of which went some seconds under water with great velocity, as we could see by the fire through the water—they then burst under water. We shall improve upon this. In short, my dear lord, we are at work in earnest, and will do all that can be done, but we must have the tools we ask for now, or we shall not be able to vary our modes of attack as they vary theirs of defence. They are now passing ropes from brig to brig, and placing intermediate boats. Their instructions we know to be, in case one is boarded, to run below decks, and hoist a light from thence, when the next vessels on each side are to fire volleys of musketry on the decks of the one attacked. We must get at them from underneath, as we cannot from above; but get at them we will, if it can be done

---

* A 'carcass' was a special iron shell used for incendiary purposes. It was filled with a composition of saltpetre, sulphur, resin, turpentine, antimony and tallow. The shell had three vents through which the flame emerged. On occasions, carcasses were equipped with pistol barrels, fitted to discharge their bullets at various times.

anyhow. I send a demand for advance stores which would preclude the necessity and danger of loading carcasses on board ship. The storekeeper has told me he is not allowed to give any particular squadron any extra thing; I must, therefore, refer the enclosed to the Ordnance in London!!! through your lordship.

I am, etc.
W. Sidney Smith

Lord Castlereagh to Sir Sidney Smith

Downing Street, October 21, 1805.

My Dear Sir,

The success of Mr Francis's experiment* gives me great confidence in our means of annoying the enemy in their ports, with little comparative risk to ourselves. I am anxious to hear of the destruction of the Boulogne flotilla, if it was only for the purpose of liberating you for more important enterprises. I should be glad to hear when you calculate upon making the attempt. I cannot, upon reflection, wish you to risk much at present for the Imperial Battery. If it was in one of our harbours, if ten times stronger, I should encourage you to the attempt. If invasion at this moment was the order of the day, I should think it worth attacking, in order to expose the enemy's flotilla, when issuing from their port, more completely to our assault; but, under present circumstances, trusting to your rocket launches approaching near enough, notwithstanding this impediment, I am averse to your exposing your squadron, or—what I value not less— yourself, for an object which you could not maintain under the fire of the enemy's batteries, and of which you could make no use. The advantage of its conquest must, under any circumstances, be of the negative description; and at present they do not seem to be required.

I am, etc.
Castlereagh

The Secretary of State for War's apparent cooling-off, however, did not discourage Sir Sidney and he made yet another attempt, three weeks later, to get his own way, still, however, without success.

* Francis and Congreve were both working, under Smith's command, on the design and construction of rocket ships.

Sir Sidney Smith to Lord Castlereagh
Dover, November 8, 1805.

My Dear Lord,

The enclosed correspondence speaks for itself.* I wish it may be more intelligible, and appear less contradictory to your lordship than it is to me. I may take the bombs to be spectators of an imperfect bombardment from two row boats, who roll so much, that no precision can be expected from them; it is a *novel mode of warfare* to expect to annoy the enemy without being within reach to be annoyed in a degree in turn. I am here urging forward the preparations to complete the launches: everything Mr Congreve asks I give him immediately; the moon is too light for Lord Keith's suggestion of going in the dark at present. I shall go the moment Mr Congreve announces himself to be ready; we must go in with the flood, and out again with the ebb; so that part of the Minute requiring us to fire at low water is impracticable; we can fire at half ebb, which may be better than when the flood is returning to float the vessels.

I profited by the Gazette to animate our people, and to remove some of the terror that had been assiduously and artfully instilled into them. Alas, poor Lord Nelson! I grieve on every account.

Your lordship's faithful and obedient servant,
W. Sidney Smith

Lord Castlereagh to Sir Sidney Smith
Downing Street, November 14, 1805.

My Dear Sir,

I return the correspondence with Lord Keith. As his lordship seems to have waved his objection to your having the means of strengthening your general bombardment, it is unnecessary for me to take any steps on this point. As opposed to the enemy's batteries, I consider the presence of the bomb-vessels of no importance, with a view of distracting the enemy's attention by keeping up a fire upon the basin: after the rockets have been discharged their assistance may be material. I am aware that force may be necessary to dispose of the enemy: my hopes of success, however, rest more upon an approach effected by surprise, and I trust you

* This was a reference to a number of letters which had been exchanged between Lord Keith and Sir Sidney.

will prefer this game, although I know your natural gallantry would rather prefer the direct attack.

I shall reply to your letter upon the Nile etc., tomorrow. With my cordial congratulations on the late glorious achievements of your profession and upon your promotion.*

I am, etc.
Castlereagh

But it was a letter from Mr Francis written to Lord Castlereagh on 26th November which eventually turned the scales. The Secretary of State for War relented and it was decided to send Smith 1,500 rockets, together with the necessary supplementary stores sufficient for 10 ships.

Mr Francis to Lord Castlereagh

Dover, November 26, 1805.

My Lord,

In addition to my letter of yesterday, I have the honour to send you some thoughts on the mode to be pursued in attacking the fleet in the inner Roads of Brest. It is similar to one I delivered to Mr Pitt last year; but, having now more experience in the use of the carcasses, there is at present a greater certainty of success.

Since writing your lordship, I have had a conversation with Sir Sidney on system; he likes my plan, but thinks his squadron should consist of more ships than I have mentioned, not for my particular use, but for his security, in all cases. Of this I do not pretend to judge, but, my lord, *I give it to you as my decided opinion, founded on calm reflection and a knowledge of the immense powers of the engines to be used,* that the Brest and other fleets of the enemy which lie in open ports may be destroyed by pursuing the plan here proposed. The attainment of such an object surmounts all smaller considerations; and, in this work, if Sir Sidney wishes two or three ships extraordinary to accompany him, they may perhaps be as well with him, as lying in the Downs during the winter doing nothing.

What I beg of Lord Barham is good boats, and sufficient of them well manned; and I hope his lordship will see the necessity of our having them, as our whole business is boat-work; good boats, well manned, and in unusual numbers, make themselves respected. My lord, letters which I write you on this subject are for you, Lord Barham, and Mr Pitt

---

* Sir Sidney had, at last, been promoted to Rear-Admiral on 9th November.

only; for perhaps my ideas of system and the mode of acting may not be the opinion of other men. My wish is to do that which is right, and offend no one.

I have the honour, etc.

Robert Francis

Memorandum for an equipment of rocket boats to be sent out with Sir Sidney Smith

December 20, 1805.

It is proposed to send 1,500 rockets and ten sets of frames, with stores etc. complete for ten boats. The rockets and necessary apparatus are in readiness, and it only requires, to complete the outfit, that two small brigs should be either hired or purchased, to convey the stores, and act as tenders. Mr Bray has, by Sir Sidney Smith's orders, found two suitable vessels in the River, which are either to be hired or sold.

It is further requisite that some officer of the navy should be appointed exclusively to this service. I therefore beg leave to recommend Mr William Perkins, an old lieutenant in the navy, who volunteered in the late business off Boulogne. This officer was on board the *Antelope* on that occasion, and Sir Sidney would approve of his appointment, as he is perfectly master of the service, and very zealous for its success.

William Congreve

So at last Sir Sidney got his precious rockets, though too late for him to prove the value of them, for three weeks later he hoisted his flag on H.M.S. *Pompée* and received orders to proceed to the Mediterranean and place himself under the command of Vice-Admiral Lord Collingwood.

9

THE DELICATE INVESTIGATION

IT WAS at this stage of his career that Sir Sidney became involved in a public scandal without parallel in English history. "I will never marry," the Prince of Wales said to Lord Malmesbury. He did not think that he was suited to a marriage of convenience; and who would contradict him? In the end it was only the combination of overwhelming debts and the need for a legitimate grandchild to George III which drove him into a marriage which had, from the outset, little chance of success.

Although his future bride appears to have been moderately good-looking there was little else to commend her. Her mother, the Princess Augusta, an elder sister of the King, was a coarse woman with a vulgar mind, and the daughter's underclothes were said to be as filthy as her mother's follies. "I knew," wrote Lord Malmesbury, though he did not explain how he got the information, "that she wore coarse petticoats, coarse shifts and thread stockings, and these were never well washed or changed often enough." Nor was that all. There was madness on both sides of the family.

There may have been some excuse, therefore, for the Prince being fuddled at the wedding on 8th April 1795 and worse after, though not too drunk to be unable to consummate the marriage, for in nine months almost to the day Princess Charlotte was born. From that moment the marriage was at an end, for the Prince withdrew from his wife's presence though they lived under the same roof until the autumn when he returned to Mrs Fitzherbert to whom he had been married since 1786.

The Princess went to live at Montague House in Blackheath and attracted considerable popular sympathy, owing to the profligate life of her husband which had become a public scandal. It is scarcely surprising that, deserted by her husband for his mistress-wife, the Princess sought her pleasures elsewhere and in 1806, owing to her many indiscretions, a Commission of twenty-three Privy Councillors was appointed, on the Prince's suggestion, to conduct an inquiry into her conduct. This became known as the 'Delicate Investigation'.*

During the year 1802 Sir Sidney was a frequent visitor to the royal house at Blackheath as, also, was Lord Hood and Sir John Douglas, an old service friend of the Rear-Admiral and a near neighbour of the Princess of Wales; and it was while Sir Sidney was staying with the Douglases that he first became friendly with her.

A number of witnesses, all members of the Princess's domestic staff, testified, before the Commission, to Sir Sidney's frequent visits, but there was little in their evidence of a really compromising nature.

One of them, Robert Bidgood, who had been in the Prince of Wales's service for twenty-three years before he went to the Princess in 1798, stated that it was early in 1802 when he first saw Sir Sidney at Montague House. It was while the Admiral was staying with Sir John and Lady Douglas and all three frequently lunched or supped there. Sometimes Sir Sidney stayed very late. One day Bidgood saw him in the "Blue Room" about eleven a.m., which was two hours earlier than they ever "expected to see company", and he asked the servants why they had not let him know that Sir Sidney was there. The footman said that no one had let him in. There was a private door to the park by which he might have entered if he had a key to it, and he could, in that event, have got into the Blue Room without any of the servants knowing it.

Another witness before the Commission was William Cole, who had been in the service of the Princess ever since her marriage. He had observed her "too familiar" with Sir Sidney. One day, in February 1802, the Princess had ordered some sandwiches and as he carried them into the blue room he saw Sir Sidney there. Cole was surprised to see him and came to the conclusion that he must have come in from the park, for had he come in from Blackheath he would have had to pass through the room where Cole was waiting. After Cole had left the room he returned later and saw Sir Sidney sitting very close to the Princess on the sofa. Both of them "looked a little confused".

Samuel Roberts, a footman, stated that the Admiral was a

* The Commission was composed of Lord Erskine, who was Lord Chancellor, Lord Grenville, First Lord of the Treasury; Lord Spencer, Secretary of State; and Lord Ellenborough, Chief Justice of the King's Bench.

frequent visitor but Roberts had never seen him alone with the Princess nor had he ever stayed later than eleven p.m. Another servant, named Robert Stikeman, stated that at one time Sir Sidney came two or three times a week to Montague House, particularly when the Princess was redecorating some of the rooms in Turkish style, and she consulted him about the new décor. Sometimes he stayed alone with her until eleven p.m., and he had seen them sitting together on the same sofa in the Blue Room.

The house-steward, however, who told the Commission that Sir Sidney was a frequent visitor to Montague House in 1802 with Sir John and Lady Douglas, said that he never had any suspicion of the Princess acting improperly with him or with "any other gentleman". Similar evidence, also, was given by Charlotte Sander who had known the Princess since she was eleven years old and had come to England with her from Brunswick. She frequently saw Sir Sidney at Montague House and she had known him stay there until two a.m. but she had never seen him alone with her mistress late at night nor had she noticed any "familiarity" between them.

There was really very little to go on and the most serious allegation made against the Princess, namely that she had given birth to an illegitimate child in 1802, was declared by the Commissioners to be a complete and unjustified fabrication. "That child," they stated, "was, beyond all doubt, born in the Brownlow Street Hospital, on 11th July 1802, of the body of Sophia Austin, and was brought to the Princess's house in the month of November following."

With regard to the other allegations, however, of the indiscreet behaviour of the Princess the Commissioners were not so specific.

Although they did not mention Sir Sidney by name they stated that there was no reason to doubt the veracity of witnesses like Bidgood and Cole but the "precise bearing and effect of such evidence" was not for them to decide and it was left to "His Majesty's wisdom".

The Princess of Wales, however, was not prepared to take these allegations lying down, and in a letter to her father-in-law the King, she dealt with the evidence implicating her and Sir Sidney at considerable length. She did not attempt to deny that he had been a frequent visitor to Montague House during 1802 but she trusted that it would not imply a confession of guilt to admit that his conversation, his account of the various and extraordinary events, and heroic achievements in which he had been concerned amused and interested her, and the circumstance of his living for so long with his friends, Sir John and Lady Douglas, in Blackheath gave the opportunity of his increasing his acquaintance with her.

"It happened also that about this time," she wrote, "I fitted up, as your Majesty may have observed, one of the rooms in my house after the fashion of a Turkish tent. Sir Sidney furnished me with a pattern for it, in a drawing of the tent of Murat Bey, which he had brought over with him from Egypt." Of course she had sat upon the same sofa as Sir Sidney and, for that matter, with other gentlemen but, she wrote, "I trust that I should not be called upon to account for what corner of a sofa I sat upon four years ago, and how close Sir Sidney was sitting to me. I can only solemnly aver to your Majesty that my conscience supplies me with the fullest means of confidently assuring you that I never permitted him to sit on any sofa with me in any manner which in my own judgment was in the slightest degree offensive to the strictest propriety and decorum."

It had all been a storm in a teacup and the old King would have liked to dismiss the whole affair as such, but he appears to have felt that had he done so it might leave his profligate son open to still more criticism. In his reply to the Princess's long and fervent appeal, while stating unequivocally that the allegations regarding her pregnancy had been proved to be without foundation, he stated that there had appeared circumstances of conduct which he never could regard but with serious concern. "The elevated rank which the Princess holds in this country," he wrote, "and the relation in which she stands to His Majesty and the royal family, must always deeply involve both the interests of the State and the personal feelings of the King, in the propriety and correctness of her conduct."

Sir Sidney was a striking personality and a great conversationalist, and the graphic accounts of his campaigns must have brightened up the unfortunate Princess's enforced loneliness. From what others have said of him the gallant Admiral's exploits would have lost no glamour in the telling, but once he had opened his mouth it is unlikely that he would have stopped to do anything more sinister.

10

ITALY AND SICILY

THE new mission for which Sir Sidney had been specially selected, at the suggestion of Lord Nelson, only a few weeks before Nelson lost his life at Trafalgar, was of such a special nature that no orders were issued to him on the subject by the Admiralty. Instead, he was personally briefed by Pitt. The only account of this still in existence is contained in a memorandum written by Sir Sidney himself. When Nelson made the suggestion it was intended that he should be in command of the operation and that Smith should serve under his command in the Mediterranean. That his choice should have fallen upon Sir Sidney showed how greatly Nelson's opinion of Smith had changed since the days when both of them were serving under the command of Lord St Vincent. How these two would have got on together had Nelson's tragic and premature death not changed the whole position can only be a matter for conjecture but it is evident that he thought Sir Sidney was the right man for the job.

According to Sir Sidney's own account he was "solicited by the late Lord Nelson and proposed by his lordship to Mr Pitt for the particular service of executing the promise made by Great Britain to Austria, at the time of the renewal of the alliance with that power, that a British naval force should be appropriated and employed to act offensively on the coasts of Italy in such a manner as to operate as a powerful diversion in that quarter, and so as to prevent the occurrence of similar events to those which had driven the King of the two Sicilies from Naples in the former war; at any rate to secure the island of Sicily to that sovereign."

This proposed plan of operation was confidently communicated to Smith by Pitt as a secret to be carefully kept among those who were to be employed in it. Pitt further explained, Sir Sidney wrote, that the object of the expedition was to restore to King Ferdinand the sovereignty of the two Sicilies, and especially the Kingdom of Naples, of which he had been dispossessed by Bonaparte, whose revolutionary armies were overrunning a great part of Europe including the coasts and islands of Italy.

Nevertheless, it now seems clear, from a private letter written after this interview, that Pitt, who died very shortly afterwards, was far too ill to have gone into the matter in such great detail as described by Smith in the above statement.*

Sir Sidney, however, seems to have realised that with the death of Nelson the nature of the whole expedition might well be changed, for Collingwood regarded the hero of Acre with a somewhat jaundiced eye and did not approve of his rocket-ship tactics.

"As a general rule of warfare," Collingwood had written, "they (explosion ships and sky rockets) are unworthy of the English, for their operations chiefly affect laborious individuals who know nothing of war but its miseries. Besides, it is worthy of consideration that the Spaniards are nowhere so vulnerable as we are at Gibraltar. If they should be goaded to retaliation, with very little activity on their part Gibraltar Bay would not be a safe place to live in for one night."

Just before he left England Smith wrote to his friend Mr Windham, soon to become Secretary of State for War and told the Minister of his misgivings. "Surely," he wrote, "Lord Nelson's death ought not to operate so very disadvantageously to us as to change our system into a simple and passive one of defence when active operations towards destroying the enemy's means of annoying us and our allies are so much more efficacious to that end."

Sir Sidney's apprehensions, however, were not without foundation for Collingwood was personally completely out of sympathy with the whole project of regaining possession of Sicily for the King and Queen of Naples.

"When they possessed it," he wrote to Mr Elliott, the British Ambassador, "with all the resources of the country at their command, with the (professed, at least) loyalty of an armed people, and the army of the allies at their head, it was abandoned as untenable; and now that the country is disarmed, and every person supposed to be yet attached to their Prince removed from it, and the enemy possessing every place of strength, on what foundation can the hope of success be built? Let her beware of counsels which I suspect are of French origin,

* See *The War in the Mediterranean* by Piers Mackesy, p. 122.

and of the people from whom they come. Whatever can diffuse the limited resources of Sicily, or distract her counsellors, is favourable to the enemy and can be suspected to come from them."*

Meanwhile Sir Sidney, aboard the *Pompée*, had arrived off Cadiz and joined Collingwood who had already received instructions to prepare a squadron to be placed under the Rear Admiral's orders to carry out his special mission.

Three other ships the *Excellent*, *Athénienne* and *Intrepid* had already been dispatched to Palermo and Smith was given the following orders to join them and take them under his command:

By the Rt Hon. Cuthbert Lord Collingwood Vice-Admiral of the Red, and Commander in Chief of His Majesty's ships and vessels employed and to be employed in the Mediterranean.

MOST SECRET

You are hereby required and directed to take under Convoy all such vessels (transports or trades) as are now at Gibraltar, and bound to Sicily or Malta, and proceeding without loss of time in His Majesty's ship the *Pompée* to Palermo in the Island of Sicily—take under your orders the squadron of His Majesty's ships employed upon the coasts of that Island, and Naples, list of which is herewith enclosed.

It being of the utmost importance that the Island of Sicily should not fall into the hands of the enemy, but be defended against any assault that may be made on it, you are to station the ships in such positions as will most effectually prevent their landing, and getting a footing in any part of it, and will give the most perfect protection to that part of His Sicilian Majesty's dominions.

Gen. Sir James Craig is at present with his army in the Garrison of Messina, where the transports also are, with the lively *Ambuscade* and *Aurora* for their protection and from this point a very vigilant look out must be kept on the operations, and the movements which the enemy will probably make from Naples, and the Coast of Calabria or from the Adriatic. As the Port of Messina is not at all seasons of the year a convenient place for a great number of ships to lay in safety I have proposed to Mr Elliot, that another harbour (either that of Augusta or Syracuse which on viewing them you should be of opinion is best suited to the convenience of a fleet)

* See Lord Collingwood's *Correspondence and Memoirs,* p. 240.

should be put in possession of the British army for the more
secure defence of the Island against the enemy and of
ensuring it to the Navy, in case there should be any change
in the state of affairs in that Island, or the Sicilian Court
should be induced by the threats or promises to pursue
another system of politicks. On this subject you will consult
with Mr Elliot His Majesty's Minister at the Court of Naples
and Gen. Sir James Craig the commander-in-chief of the
army, in order that the consent of His Sicilian Majesty may
be obtained to a measure which I consider of high importance, and the sooner it is done the better.

Should it however happen that the King of Naples, either
by treaty or promise from the French of favourable conditions, consents to the admission of the enemy's troops into
Sicily you must hold in mind that it is not His Majesty's
interest that they should be allowed to enter it or suffer to
occupy any part of the Island, but to be expelled and driven
out of a station so necessary to the security of His Majesty's
interests, notwithstanding any remonstrance which the King
of Naples may make on the subject, and whenever the conduct of the Court of Naples shall indicate an intention
favourable to the enemy you are to enter and to occupy any
port which may be necessary to the Service whether his
Sicilian Majesty shall approve of it or not.

In all operations which may be necessary for effecting this
purpose you are to act in counsel with Mr Elliot His Majesty's
Ambassador and in counsel and co-operation with His
Majesty's chief of his Majesty's forces maintaining with them
a constant and confidential correspondence, they must be
privy to your most secret movements and I beg strongly to
impress on your mind to maintaining the utmost harmony
with the army, and inculcating into the minds of the Officers
under your orders the same as a first principle in all operations and that they manifest this disposition with every act
of kindness. Vice-Admiral Sinivian commands the Russian
squadron at Corfu with consists of 9 or 10 sail of the line.
I do not know what co-operation may be expected from him,
but should hope that the Adriatic will be an object of his
attention, with the force he has he may certainly prevent any
progress being made by the French in that quarter, but I
would not depend on the part he may take, and have some
time since directed Captain Dunbar, an officer well

acquainted in that sea, with a small squadron, to a discovery and any interruption of any Enterprise which may be on foot there by the enemy.

On the 1st of May the convoy is to sail from Malta for Gibraltar and England, and I have directed the charge of it to be given to Captain Dundas of the *Naiad* if the *Excellent* cannot be immediately spared, and would have the *Bittern* also attached to it as far as Gibraltar.

I enclose to you an order for Captain Sotheron of the *Excellent* to join me in that ship at this rendezvous which you will please deliver to him, as I intend that ship should go to England soon, and if she can be spared from the Service immediately, I would have Captain Sotheron charged with the convoy together with the before mentioned ship.

Collingwood

Given aboard the *Queen*
Off Cadiz, 26 March 1806
To: Sir W. Sidney Smith, Bt.,
Rear Admiral of the Blue
etc. etc. etc. *Pompée*

Sir Sidney lost no time in carrying out these orders, and on 24 May sent the following letter to his Commander-in-Chief reporting the events of the first three weeks after his arrival at Palermo.

Sir Sidney Smith to Lord Collingwood
Pompée, at anchor off Scalea, May 24 1806.

My Lord,

I arrived at Palermo in the *Pompée* on the 21st of last month, and took on me the command of the squadron your lordship has done me the honour to place under my orders. I found things in the state that may be well imagined, on the government being displaced from its capital, with the loss of one of the two kingdoms, and the dispersion of the army assembled in Calabria. The judicious arrangement made by Captain Sotheron of the ships under his orders, and the position of the British army under Sir John Stuart at Messina, had, however, prevented further mischief. I had the satisfaction of learning that Gaeta still held out, although as yet without succour, from a mistaken idea, much too prevalent, that the progress of the French armies is irresistible.

It was my first care to see that the necessary supplies should be safely conveyed to the governor; and I had the inexpressible satisfaction of conveying the most essential articles to Gaeta, and of communicating to his serene highness the governor (on the breach battery, which he never quits) the assurance of further support to any extent within my power, for the maintenance of that important fortress, hitherto so long preserved by his intrepidity and example. Things wore a new aspect immediately on the arrival of the ammunition. The redoubled fire of the enemy with red-hot shot into the Mole (being answered with redoubled vigour) did not prevent the landing of everything we had brought, together with four of the *Excellent*'s lower-deck-guns, to answer this galling fire, which bore directly on the landing-place.

A second convoy, with the *Intrepid*, placed the garrison beyond the immediate want of anything essential; and the enemy, from advancing his nearest approaches within two hundred and fifty yards, was reduced to the defensive in a degree, dreading one of those sorties which the Prince of Hesse had already shewn him his garrison was equal to, and which was become a much safer operation, now that the flanking fire of eight Neapolitan gun-boats I had brought with me, in addition to four his highness had already used successfully, would cover it even to the rear of the enemy's trenches. Arrangements were put in train for this purpose, and, according to a wise suggestion of his serene highness, measures were taken for the embarkation of a small party from the garrison, to land in the rear of the enemy's batteries to the northward.

I confided the execution of the naval part of this arrangement to Captain Richardson, of his majesty's ship *Juno*, putting the Neapolitan frigate and gun-boats under his orders. His serene highness possessing the experience of European warfare, and a most firm mind, having no occasion for further aid on the spot, I felt I could quit the garrison without apprehension for its safety in such hands, with the present means of defence, and that I could best co-operate with him, by drawing some of the attacking force off for the defence of Naples.

I accordingly proceeded thither with the line-of-battle ships named in the margin.* The enemy's apprehension of

* *Pompée, Excellent, Athénienne, Intrepid.*

attack occasioned them to convey some of the battering train from the trenches before Gaeta to Naples. The city was illuminated on account of Joeseph Buonaparte proclaiming himself King of the Two Sicilies! The junction of the *Eagle* made us five sail of the line, and it would have been easy for their fire to have interrupted this ceremony and show of festivity, but I considered that the unfortunate inhabitants had evil enough on them; that the restoration of the capital to its lawful sovereign, and its fugitive inhabitants, would be no gratification, if it should be found a heap of ruins, ashes, and bones; and that, as I had no force to land and keep order, in case of the French army retiring to the fortresses, I should leave an opulent city a prey to the licentious part of the community, who would not fail to profit by the confusion the flames would occasion. Not a gun, therefore, was fired; but no such consideration operated on my mind, to prevent me dislodging the French garrison from the island of Capri, which, from its situation, protecting the coasting communication southward, was a great object for the enemy to keep, and by so much more, one for me to wrest from him.

I accordingly summoned the French commandant to surrender: on his non-acquiescence, I directed Captain Rowley, in his Majesty's ship *Eagle*, to cover the landing of marines and boats' crews, and caused an attack to be made under his orders. That brave officer placed his ship judiciously, nor did he open his fire till she was secured, and his distance marked by the effect of the enemy's musketry on his quarter-deck, where the first lieutenant, James Crawley, fell wounded, and a seaman was killed: Captain Rowley regretted much the services of that meritorious officer in such a critical moment. He has since recovered.

The short duration of an hour's fire from both decks of the *Eagle* (between nine and ten o'clock) with that of two Neapolitan mortar-boats, under an active officer, Lieutenant Rivera, drove the enemy from the vineyards within their walls. The marines were landed, and gallantly led by Captain Bunce; the seamen in like manner, under Lieutenant Morrell of the *Eagle*, and Lieutenant Redding of the *Pompée*, mounted the steps, for such was their road, headed by the officers nearest to the narrow pass, by which alone they could ascend. Lieutenant Carrol had thus an opportunity of particularly distinguishing himself. Captain Stannus, commanding the *Athénienne*'s marines, gallantly pressing forward, gained the heights; and the French commandant fell by his hand: this event being known, the enemy beat a parley; a letter from the second-in-command claimed the terms offered; but being dated on the 12th, after midnight, some difficulty occurred, my limitation as to time being precise; but, on the assurance that the drum beat before twelve, the capitulation annexed was signed, and the garrison allowed to march out, and pass over to Naples with every honour of war, after the interment of their former brave commander with due respect.

We thus became masters of this important post. The enemy not having been allowed time to bring two pieces of heavy cannon with their ammunition to Capri, the boat containing them, together with a boat loaded with timber for the construction of gun-boats at Castelamare, took refuge at Maffa, on the main-land opposite to the island, where the guard had hauled the whole upon the beach. I detached the two mortar-boats and a Gaeta privateer, under the orders of Lieutenants Falivane and Rivera, to bring them off, sending only Mr Williams, midshipman of the *Pompée*, from the squadron, on purpose to let the Neapolitans have the credit of the action, which they fairly obtained; for, after dislodging the enemy from a strong tower, they not only brought off the boats and two thirty-five pounders, but the powder (twenty barrels) from the magazine of the tower, before the enemy assembled in force.

The projected sorties took place on the 13th and 15th, in the morning, in a manner to reflect the highest credit on the part of the garrison and naval force employed. The covering fire from the fleet was judiciously directed by Captains Richardson and Vicuna, whose conduct on this whole service merits my warmest approbation. I enclose Captain Richardson's two letters, as best detailing these affairs, and a list of the killed and wounded on the 12th.

On the 19th ult., the boats of the *Pompée*, under Lieutenant Beecroft, brought out a merchant-vessel from Scalvitra, near Salerno, although protected by a heavy fire of musketry. That officer and Mr Sterling distinguished themselves much. The enemy are endeavouring to establish a land-carriage thence to Naples.

On the 23rd, obtaining intelligence that the enemy had

two thirty-six pounders in a small vessel on the beach at Scalea, I sent the *Pompée*'s boats in for them. But the French troops were too well posted in the houses of the town, for them to succeed without the cover of the ship. I accordingly stood in with the *Pompée*, sent a message to the inhabitants to withdraw, which being done, a few of the *Pompée*'s lower-deck guns cleared the town and neighbouring hills, while the launch, commanded by Lieutenant Mouray-Lion, with Lieutenant Oats of the marines, and Mr Williams, drove the French, with their armed adherents, from the guns, and took possession of the castle and of them. Finding, on my landing, that the tower was tenable against any force the enemy could bring against me from the nearest garrison in a given time, I took post with the marines, and under cover of their position, by the extreme exertions of Lieutenant Carrol, Mr Ives, master, and the petty officers and boat's crews, the guns were conveyed to the *Pompée*, with twenty-two barrels of powder.

I have the honour to be, etc.

W. Sidney Smith

Enclosed with the above letter were copies of the 'summons to surrender' which Smith sent to the Commandant of the French troops on Capri and his reply.

To the Commandant of the French troops at Capri

On board his Majesty's ship *La Pompée*, May 11, 1806.

Sir,

Before I make a regular attack, which must necessarily reduce an insulated and irregular fortress without works, I have thought proper, according to the custom of war, to summon you to evacuate the post which you occupy. If you refuse, I inform you that you will be forced to yield upon terms more or less favourable, according to the degree of force and time which you may oblige me to employ to reduce you to this extremity. Thus, sir, you see that the terms of the surrender of the post depend upon yourself *to-day*; in the hope of an answer which will spare blood on both sides.

I have the honour to be, etc.

W. Sidney Smith

The Commandant of Capri to Rear-Admiral Sir Sidney Smith

Capri, May 11 1806.

I received, sir, your letter dated this day, and for answer I have to observe to you, that a true soldier does not surrender till he has tried his force with that which attacks him. You are, sir, too good and brave a soldier to blame me if I do not accept your polite invitation.

                    I have the honour to be, etc.
                         Chervet, Capt. 101st Regt.

Collingwood's orders were that every possible means should be taken to defend Sicily and Calabria. Sir Sidney Smith, not unreasonably, considered that if British forces were landed on the coast of Calabria the peasants would rise *en masse* against the French. Sir John Stuart, the same General Stuart who had been in Egypt when Smith was there, apparently shared this view and offered to supply a large force to effect such a landing. Smith agreed and immediately sailed for Palermo to ensure the co-operation of Queen Maria-Carolina, for it was she who wore the trousers in the Neapolitan Court. Sir John Moore's opinion of this formidable woman appears in his diary for 7th January 1807:

"The Queen," he wrote, "is generally called clever; she is active, meddling and intriguing. She has assumed so much of the character of a man as to make her unamiable as a woman. The late Empress Catherine of Russia is, perhaps, her model. She has, like her, a lover, but with this difference—that Catherine rewarded the lover with titles and riches but was not governed by him. The Queen of Naples has placed hers in an employment for which he has no capacity, is influenced by him and, as he is a Frenchman, it is more than suspected that she is betrayed by him. The truth is that she is not clever, except in conversation and intrigue. She is violent, wicked, with a most perverted understanding, led by her passions and seldom influenced by reason. She is attached to nobody except so far as they can be of use to her. She gives her confidence, however, to all who flatter her and enter into her views, and by these she is led. She is quite incapable of discretion in affairs, though never happy but when dabbling in them. Her passion at present is to return to Naples and she will not listen to any obstacles which oppose it, but would sacrifice every man in Sicily in the attempt, though if the force now here were once annihilated she can have no hope of ever seeing another formed for her protection."

Sir John Stuart gave his reasons for suggesting a descent on

Calabria in a despatch which he sent to the War Office. Early
in June 1806, Sir John wrote, Sir Sidney arrived at Messina
in the *Pompée* and in the course of their first meeting asked for
some troops to be put at his disposal to make raids on the
Neapolitan coast for the purpose of spiking guns and destroying coastal batteries. Sir John refused this request as the
objects appeared to him too trivial but himself agreed to undertake an operation upon a larger scale which might promise a
more permanent advantage. While Sir Sidney was in Palermo
seeing the King and Queen to arrange the assistance and co-
operation of all the military and naval resources of the country
Sir John got together all the stores and supplies which would be
required and secretly loaded them on to the transports at
Messina.

Sir Sidney was kept fully informed of all this and Stuart
naturally expected that Smith would keep in touch with him
but more than five weeks elapsed before he received any news,
Then, at last, a letter arrived from Smith written from Palermo
on 26 June.

"The King," Smith wrote, "is with us. He was delighted to
hear of your being disposed, as you are, to activity. In a private
audience he begged me to speak plainly on that head to him
saying he had been led to believe your letters to others were in
a different tone."

This letter, which contained very little else of any interest,
can hardly be said to have been very helpful, and Sir Sidney
took great pains not to let Stuart know much about what had
really been happening. On his arrival at Palermo his charm and
his vanity had made an immediate impression on their
Majesties, and particularly on the Queen, who invested him
with unlimited powers, on land and sea, to command any
Neapolitan troops without having to refer back to General
Stuart, and as Sir John Fortescue wrote this "accession to his
importance inflated his conceit to bursting point".

Meanwhile, annoyed at having received no news from Sir
Sidney, Stuart had written to him on 23rd June and the two
letters must have crossed each other.

Sir John Stuart to Rear-Admiral Sir Sidney Smith
                                        Messina, 23 June 1806
My Dear Sir Sidney,
    I have been much disappointed at not having had the

pleasure of hearing from you since your arrival at Palermo on the subject of our discussions previous to your departure from hence as my arrangements for the objects we had in view have been interrupted altogether from that circumstance.

I have continued to receive constant and reiterated tokens of the disposition of our friends in Calabria to shake off the yoke of their present tyranny could any succour offer itself, while on the other hand their oppressors are studious to avail themselves of the absence of that succour to fix their authority more firmly. This morning a considerable body of the peasantry flew hither from Baganara to avoid the forced levy which is now being carried into effect, and by which it is the intention of the enemy to send off such numbers as may be collected successively after the 30th towards the northern frontier of the Kingdom. Their endeavours at the same time are unremitting to fortify the opposite coast and thus to prepare the facility of future enterprise upon this country.

Under these circumstances I have determined upon the immediate execution of the plan upon which we reciprocally agreed before our separation. We have been invited. We have been entreated in humble supplication to shew ourselves. Majesty itself has condescended to recommend the object to our attention, and I trust that the issue of a second conflict will prove to General Reynier, if he ventures to put it to the test, that we are as much superior to his boasted legions on terra firma as his countrymen have found and acknowledged us (or rather you) upon the waters.

St Euphemia I before mentioned to you had been the point of our observations. In every view it is the most favourable for our landing. No opposition is I believe to be apprehended. At least I am informed there are no preparations there for resistance. Our movements will begin from hence on the 27th and should I not hear from you or see your protecting flag with us before that period I shall commit myself to the escort and assistance of your representative Capt. Fellowes who tells me he has your full and kind deputation to concur with me in all objects of service.

etc. etc. etc.
J. Stuart

Sir John kept to his schedule, and on the afternoon of 30th June the main body of his force anchored in the Gulf of St

Euphemia. Six days later General Reynier, who was in command of the French forces in southern Italy based on Reggio, marched to meet the British and drive them back into the sea, and took up a position near the village Maida on the plain of Euphemia. His forces numbered 4,000 infantry and about two squadrons of cavalry but he expected any day to receive strong reinforcements.

Meanwhile Sir Sidney had been cruising up and down the Italian coast and Sir John received a letter from him on 4th July while his army was moving forward to meet the French. This letter had been written on 2nd July and in it the Admiral explained, with some embarrassment how it came about that the King of Naples had invested him with such full powers. Sir Sidney's squadron had only just reached the bay of St Euphemia two days after General Stuart had landed.

Sir Sidney Smith to Sir John Stuart
   dated: *Pompée*, off Cape Matturano, July 2, 1806.
My Dear Sir John,

  The *Pompée* was on her way to join you, in the hope of her flanking fire being of use, in case of the enemy attacking the army in its position, as described by Capt. Hoste, which Capt. Fellowes informed me their movements indicated: but the arrival of a second boat, with the contradiction of that information from Capt. Fellowes, and your distinct and satisfactory letter expressing yourself not to be in immediate need of naval co-operation, beyond what Capt. Fellowes' zeal and ability has furnished you and looking rather to the favourable effect of the alarm I may be able to excite at Gaeta, and the bay of Naples, I found myself at liberty to lay the ships head northward, to form a junction with the principal part of the Naval force so employed. I wish much to have been of immediate use to you, in your present manly, and I will venture to say, glorious undertaking; but you will have seen by the Prince of Hesse's letters to me, that he was so near a capitulation, that I had reason to apprehend the worst effect from the contre coup on your operation, by the enemy's being able to concentrate their whole force in Calabria. I therefore thought it incumbent on me to force through all obstacles that lay in the way of that important fortress being duly relieved, as earnestly required by the Prince of Hesse. The discussions relative to this measure in

5

which there were differences of opinion; the difficulty I found in disposing of a single division of gun-boats, without a circuitous solicitation; and the absolute independence of the naval resources of the country from those who were to conduct that force in action occasioned me to insist on a more extended and liberal scale of acting, in that respect; the difficulties lay with the departments only, there were none in the minds of the King, Queen or Sir John Acton. Thus all parties uniting in the principle of placing unlimited confidence in the commander of the force immediately menacing Naples, where all ideas concentrated, *I found myself suddenly, by the King's decision, and positive orders*, vested with full powers to act on the spot, as he could himself, in case of any opening for the recovery of the Seat of Government, by insurrection, of which there is much probability, and that, without interregnum or confusion from the absence of authority. The Dispatch from Acton, and the Royal Decree of the 28th in conformity thereto, gave much more extensive powers than I imagined. For it, of course, never entered into my head to expect authority in some of the branches therein specified, when I was only requiring a right of decision on naval movements, without reference to a distant authority, and an authorization to speak in the King's name to his subjects, who had applied to me wherever I came on the coast, in order that I might direct or restrain their impetuosity. When the decree appeared, it immediately struck Mr Elliot and me that, as it was worded, it might interfere with you and the Prince of Hesse, and under that idea I thought I owed it to you to remove any difficulty you might feel as to using the King's name authoritatively, when that might be the only means of guiding or goading the masses which, it was thought, might hesitate, if not be disinclined, to receive a foreign impulse without it.

I am delighted you have found no difficulty of that sort, and I augur most favourably of all you tell me. I should, however, have thought myself highly culpable, if, foreseeing such a possible difficulty, I had not done what depended on me to obviate it, by rendering your signature as valid as my own, on the official document which had emanated from the Royal authority, for the direction of his subjects in arms, which might hoist or join the Royal Standard. I am thus precise in the detail of the progress of this business from its origin; the conclusion of which was not made known to Mr Elliot or me, or even to Acton, till it was promulgated in the form you see it. I am thus prolix in laying my Motives before you, to prove to you that I had not the smallest idea of pointing out a line of conduct to you, who are, fortunately for the Royal Cause at the head of an independent branch of the service; lest you should suppose me wanting in delicacy to you, when in fact, it was a sense of what was due to you, in every respect, that made me hand over to you, what had been placed in my name generally, on account of the great facility of my intercourse with all points of the coast, and the menacing position of the force under my orders, as bearing on Naples in a way that might encourage the numerous adherents of the Royal Cause, to hoist the standard there, when the French army should be weakened by the greatest part of their force being withdrawn to oppose you.

I now take my leave of the subject, with the assurance of my perfect acquiescence in the principle you assert of not being amenable to any other authority, than that from whence you have the commission you bear to command the King's forces. It is the one I act upon as distinctly as yourself. No other impulse but that, and the conviction of what is right to be done, can, of course, have any weight on the mind of an officer, and being agreed on both these points, we shall pull together for the good cause. Now as there is no necessity of reference to a distance when all authorities are concentrated in the scene of action; whatever you wish of me within my sphere, limited or extended as it may be, you know will be done the moment you express that wish, or that I, from the general conformity of our sentiments may imagine it. And I am so perfectly persuaded of the same disposition on your part, that I have no reserve towards you, being with the most sincere regards,

Sidney Smith

It was no understatement when Sir Sidney described himself as being prolix, for he was as long-winded on paper as he was in speech; and it is hardly surprising that he received a curt though dignified reply. When he disembarked, Sir John wrote, he had made his views and intentions clear to the inhabitants in his capacity of commander-in-chief of a British army. He had landed in Calabria to assist them. For this purpose he needed no orders from the King of Naples nor did he consider himself under the orders of anyone other than his own King. He would, nevertheless, take care not to offend King Ferdinand by his conduct or his language but he proposed to act quite independently of the Court of Palermo.

"The population of this Province," he continued, "are resorting to me in great numbers and while they continue to obey my directions, and render me the services I have required, I shall take it upon myself to enlist them and give them my promised allowances. But this I have not prevented them from knowing, is not an Act of Bounty from their own Sovereign, but from mine, the great and powerful friend and ally of the former."

The real sting, however, was in the last paragraph:

"As I gave you full and early intimation of my intended movements," he wrote, "I can only regret that I had not your personal presence with us at our début. From your representative, however, Captain Fellowes, and from every part of the Naval Department under his direction, I have met with the most zealous promptitude and ability in forwarding my views for the public service."

Sir John also made it clear, in a despatch which he sent to the War Office after the Battle of Maida, that the above incidents had somewhat shaken his confidence in Sir Sidney. "I must regret to say," he wrote, "I was left with difficulty to reconcile the present proceedings of Sir Sidney with those attributes of candour, of disinterested zeal, and of honest exemption from any impulse of selfish motives which, until the occurrences of the present service, had been generally believed by the army to have been his generous characteristics."

On receipt of this despatch the whole circumstances were considered by the Cabinet and it was decided that the Secretary of State for War, William Windham, should convey his displeasure to Sir Sidney via the Admiralty, and the following minute was written by Lord Grenville to Windham agreeing that this should be done but suggesting that the reprimand should not be too severe.

Lord Grenville to William Windham

September 9, 1806.

PRIVATE

I certainly have every reason to agree with you in the wish

of making the censure on Sir Sidney Smith as mild as possible, nor would I on any account urge you to a decision on the subject before you have given yourself time to consider the papers before us, which, I am sorry to say, are such as to have impressed my mind with the absolute necessity, on grounds of public duty, of our expressing a decided, tho' mild, disapprobation of the following points:

1. His having, without the concurrence of the King's Minister in Sicily, accepted a commission from that Government.
2. His having taken upon himself the command or direction (call it which we will) of an insurrection in Calabria destined to co-operate with a body of British troops under the command of a British General, in whom that direction ought, as far as it was fit to be assumed by any British officer, *exclusively* to have been vested.
3. The issuing, and his acting under, the proclamation of the Court of Sicily, such as we have actually received, and are not therefore at liberty to doubt of its existence; or of its having been directly remonstrated against by the King's Minister in Sicily.

All these facts appear to be but too well established by Elliot's letter to Fox, by the copy of Sir Sidney's letters inclosed in that to Fox, and by the copy of the proclamation itself, transmitted to Lord Howick by Lord Collingwood.

But the censure may certainly be so worded as to attach only on the facts *supposing them to be such as they now appear.*

In point of form, there can, I think, be no doubt that this, which is matter of general and political direction, ought to issue from the Secretary of State thro' the Admiralty, and not from the latter in the first instance.

The strength of Sir John Stuart's forces on the eve of the Battle of Maida was almost identical to Reynier's, except that he had no cavalry. Had the French General only sat tight, the British, on Sir John's own admission, could have made no impression on him, but he foolishly decided to advance and, having crossed the river that lay between them, he debouched on to the open plain.

Of the fighting which then ensued Sir John has given a vivid description. As the French troops approached the British line and came within musket range a few rounds were fired but then "as if by mutual agreement the firing was suspended and in close compact order and awful silence they advanced towards each other until their bayonets began to cross". The French then broke and began to flee from the field of battle, but, as they did so, were mown down in large numbers, leaving behind 700 dead, 1,000 wounded and an equal number of prisoners. Total British casualties, killed and wounded, were not more than 330.

This defeat was a disaster for the French and one of Reynier's officers wrote, "*Avec nos bonnes troupes, et à forces égales, être défaits, détruits en si peu de minutes, cela ne c'est point vu depuis la révolution.*"

"The action, though sharp," wrote General Bunbury, who was Stuart's Chief-of-Staff, "had not been of long duration, and by midday our soldiers were resting on their arms, gasping with heat and thirst, and watching through the dust, with disappointed eyes, the rapid retreat of the French column. Our ammunition was nearly spent, there was no water for the men, save on the right, and every step we might advance led us further away from our supplies of every sort. Reference was made to Sir John Stuart, and he then gave orders that the army, except the Light Infantry Brigade, which was far away on the hills of Maida, should return to the beach for repose, and food, and supplies of ammunition."

The Chief-of-Staff, however, was not impressed with the part played before and during the battle by his general.

"In truth," he wrote, "he seemed to be rather a spectator than a person much, or *the* person *most*, interested in the result of the conflict. He formed no plan, declared no intention, and scarcely troubled himself to give an order. Perfectly regardless of personal danger, he was cantering about, indulging himself in little pleasantries as was his wont, and he launched forth with particular glee when a Sicilian marquis, whom he had brought with him as an extra aide-de-camp, betook himself to shelter from fire behind a haystack. But after the charge of the Light Infantry, and the utter rout of the French left wing, a change of spirit came over the spirit of Sir John. Still he dawdled about, breaking into passionate exclamations. 'Begad, I never saw anything so glorious as this! There was nothing in Egypt to equal it! It's the finest thing I ever witnessed!' From that moment he was an altered man with full visions of coming greatness. As I found that I could get no orders from him I made it my business to go round to the leaders of our several brigades, to give them what information I could and supply them with their wants."

When the victorious British force reached the beaches they found Sir Sidney already there aboard his flagship anchored close to the shore. He came ashore to congratulate Stuart although as General Bunbury said, "there was no great love between them." Smith invited Stuart to spend the night on board the *Pompée* and, after some hesitation, he accepted, taking his Chief-of-Staff and his aides-de-camp with him.

While they were waiting for the Admiral's launch to take them alongside the *Pompée* an amusing incident took place which Bunbury described in his diary. "While sitting on the beach we were amused by an alerte attended by laughable circumstances. Permission had been given that the men of each brigade in turn might refresh themselves by bathing in the sea. While the Grenadiers and Inniskillings were in the water, a staff officer came galloping in from the front, crying aloud that the enemy's cavalry were coming down. In a moment the troops sprang to arms and formed line, and Cole's brawny brigade rushing out of the sea and throwing their belts over their shoulders, grasped their muskets and drew up in line, without attempting to put on an article of clothing. The alarm was utterly groundless : a great dust and an imperfect view of a herd of scampering buffaloes had conjured up a vision of French *chasseurs* in this noodle of an officer."

That night, on board his flagship, Sir Sidney entertained Stuart and his staff with lavish hospitality and bored them for hours with his account of the siege of Acre, not omitting the part which he had played in it. He was good enough to tell the General that he had expected the British to be defeated and that he had, for that reason, decided to run the *Apollo* ashore broadside on to cover their retreat. It might, perhaps, have been more useful if Sir John and his host had discussed how best to exploit the victory but, if Bunbury is to be believed, no Council of War was held and Sir Sidney "closed the evening by taking one of the many shawls with which his cabin was hung and instructing Sir John in the art of wreathing it, and putting on the turban after the fashion of the most refined Turkish ladies."

According to General Stuart, however, he and Sir Sidney did find time to discuss the future and it was suggested that Smith should cruise northwards as "everything to the southward was in the power of the enemy," and when the General left the *Pompée* next morning he fully expected that this would, in fact, be done.

The Battle of Maida, however, though a resounding and encouraging victory over Reynier's army proved to be barren of any strategic result. Instead of cruising northward to Gaeta Sir Sidney went in the opposite direction. Gaeta had been gallantly holding out against the French for more than six months and the garrison there had been pinning down a considerable part of the enemy's forces. It would have been much better if Stuart and Smith had gone to its relief, but they did nothing of the kind. Stuart marched southwards "preparatory to returning to Sicily" and Sir Sidney attacked the insignificant fortress of Scylla on the Straits of Messina. This action on the part of the two British commanders has been discussed and criticised by a large number of military historians and General Bunbury had very definite views about it.

"If our Admiral and our General," he wrote, "instead of spending all the evening of the 4th July talking about Turkish ladies and Greek girls, had concerted and acted immediately on a vigorous plan of operations, the results might have marked our victory at Maida as a feat productive of an important change in the great war of European nations."

Gaeta did not surrender to the French until 18th July and if only Sir Sidney had arrived there by the 14th, as he could easily have done, he would probably have been able to save the fortress.

And what about Sir John? Bunbury has suggested that with some 5,000 Neapolitan reinforcements which were available Reynier's line of retreat could easily have been cut off, in which event, instead of finding rest and safety at Cassano, Reynier would have been forced "to pursue his weary way", harassed by the Calabrian guerilla forces along the coast of the Adriatic towards Taranto, while the other French Commander, cut off from the main body, would have had to continue his retreat to Salerno.

Still assuming that Gaeta had been saved, General Bunbury continued, Sir John's next appearance might have been at Capri, or, better still, at Ischia which he might then have taken with as much ease as he did afterwards in 1809. The capital, Naples, would then have been in a ferment, the strength of the English expedition and the extent of the insurrection would have been exaggerated and "all the hot passions of the south would have been at work". The revolt would have become widespread and it would have been all the more formidable because the news of their decisive defeat at Maida had gone round and destroyed the legend of French invincibility.

In such circumstances what could Marshal Masséna have done? So long as his army was pinned down before Gaeta, Bunbury argued, its influence over public opinion in Naples would have been inconsiderable and the presence of an increasing British army, by this time numbering 13,000, would have been a constant threat and menace to King Joseph.

It might well be asked whether such a threat could have produced any beneficial results, and what influence it could have had on the fortunes of war? Would not French reinforcements have poured in from the north of Italy to beat off any British attack on Naples? Bunbury thought that it might have had a considerable effect on events outside Italy.

"It so happened, though we did not know it at the time," he wrote, "that considerable reinforcements could not have been spared to Masséna. Our commanders were ignorant of the state of political affairs. They knew, indeed, that Russia was again at war with France, but they did not know that Prussia and Spain were on the eve of breaking into open hostility. Successes in Italy and the spreading of revolts against the French might have had a great effect on the councils of Austria, particularly a few months later when Napoleon withdrew his army to the Vistula after the sanguinary battles of Pultusk and Golymin and retired from the destructive conflict of Eylau."*

All this speculation, however, depended upon the assumption that Sir Sidney would have succeeded in relieving Gaeta, had he, in fact, decided to go there, but he did not. He preferred, as he had done before and was to do subsequently, acting on his own; but on this occasion his predilection for being a lone wolf may well have had unfortunate results.†

Meanwhile General Fox had arrived at Messina with reinforcements and orders to take over command from Sir John Stuart, and when Sir Sidney heard what to him was welcome news he wrote the following letter.

---

* The Russians fought a drawn battle with the French at Eylau in February 1807.
† The wandering Admiral was something of a Will o' the Wisp. This often meant, in the days when there was no wireless communication between ships, that when it was important to get in touch with him he was not easily available. A statement of the disposition of the ships near Sicily contained the name of H.M.S. *Aurora* as being employed "in search of Sir Sidney Smith".

Sir Sidney Smith to General Fox
                    Pompée, Policastra Bay, August 5, 1806.
Dear Sir,

I have the honour to acknowledge the receipt of two letters from you, written on your arrival at Messina, announcing that event. I shall have the same pleasure in meeting your wishes, in every thing wherein the powers of the two services combined can be applied with advantage against the enemy, such as I have hitherto had in complying with, and endeavouring to anticipate, those of Sir John Stuart.

I have left, and shall always leave, at least one of the few frigates under my orders, near head-quarters, that her captain may carry through the details of any service that may be required of the smaller vessels, co-operating with the army and protecting the transports therewith; and likewise a proper force to protect any detachment, you may please to make, to annoy any part of the enemy's coast; or to afford succour and protection to the armed inhabitants of Calabria, who are successfully resisting the attempts of the French to re-establish their government in the Calabrias, which was completely overthrown by the effects of the signal victory obtained by the British army under Sir John Stuart on the 4th ult.

I have been occupied in endeavouring to give such a direction to their zeal and enthusiasm, as to ensure this result, so much to be wished for the safety of Sicily. The passes in this bordering province of Basilicala being considered by military men as defensible, and as having been lost very improperly by the Neapolitan army in its retreat, I have thought I could not serve the British army better, than in engaging the chiefs of the *massi*,* in correspondence with me, to devote their attention and force to this object, supporting them by ammunition and money, as far as my resources went. Arms I had none but our own to give them; and, considering the necessity of keeping the line of battle ships complete and collected, in readiness to oppose any naval operation the enemy may attempt, I have not ventured to detach many men from the ships. A few regular troops are absolutely necessary to give consistence and connexion to the mass. . . .

Since the detachment from the Maisters transport took the fort of Sopri, and intercepted the convoy from Naples at

* The Calabrian guerilla forces.

Lauria, the three first-named of these chiefs have disputed the ground, with various success, in many sharp but of course irregular conflicts. The posts of Rocca Gloriosa and Casalnuovo have been won and lost. The ardour of Stoduti, the younger, occasioned him to commit himself and get beaten in the valley of Diano; the result of this was that Major Necco's position at Lago Negro was forced yesterday by General Gardanne's column, said to be about three thousand men, marching to relieve Reynier and *invade Sicily*. Their confidence is according to their numbers and their numbers according to their pay.

If you agree with me, that the ultimate defence of Sicily depends on keeping the theatre of war at this distance from it, you will send arms, ammunition, money, light artillery, and at least one thousand troops of the line, to this quarter. Had the regiment in Sicily, which I had reason to hope was disposable, from Sir John Stuart's having consented to their embarkation, been at Lago Negro yesterday, we should not have lost the post, such is the ground. It is recoverable. The peasantry of Sorracca cut a detachment, sent to Capri, to pieces last night: I send you two survivors, prisoners, to interrogate. I have a division of gun-boats in Capri to meet the column I see coming over the mountain: another division yesterday dislodged the party that came without cannon to occupy Policastro, and now keeps it clear. I have a station for gun-boats at Palinuro, from whence I annoy an extent of coast to Salerno; from thence the Capri division takes up the question, and co-operates with the insurgents.

Colonel Lowe will have communicated the facilities that quarter offers for this mode of warfare. I shall be glad to learn, that this officer is authorised by you to act on the information he receives. I shall most readily and gladly co-operate with him, or any other you may delegate the power to, in anything you may direct; and I earnestly call upon you to tell me distinctly, whether I am right in my idea that these operations aid and cover the army in Calabria and Sicily, by thus occupying and diminishing the enemy's force here: if so, you will no doubt support and direct them according to your views, when I shall feel myself more at liberty to extend mine to other quarters.

At present, I feel that I am stemming a torrent which it would be criminal in me to let rush on, though the pressure is heavy; for if the passes between here and Cosenza are not disputed, we shall again be reduced to the defensive in the Straits of Messina, and Scylla perhaps be attacked before it is rebuilt; and I must candidly tell you that my naval means, limited and restricted as they are, with a very inadequate rowing force, cannot with certainty oppose the passage of a rowing force in a calm, considering the shortness of the distance, and the strength and set of the current. I beg you will communicate your wishes to me here; they shall be obeyed as commands with alacrity.

I have the honour to be, etc.
W. Sidney Smith

From his reply to Sir Sidney, written three days later, it appears that Fox did not think much of the Admiral's ideas about continuing the campaign in Calabria. He thought that a landing there, unless it was made with more troops than could readily be spared would be "very hazardous" and that the advantages to be gained would not justify the risk. He was convinced that if the enemy were really determined to regain Calabria it could not be prevented, but he felt confident that with the assistance of the Navy Sicily could be held. A second letter from Sir Sidney, written on 10th August, informing Fox that Major Necco's Calabrian corps, harassed, famished and without pay, had deserted, did nothing but confirm the General's opinion.

"The late alarm of the enemy," he wrote in a letter to Smith, "intending to advance into Lower Calabria, has been attended by the most dreadful consequences. Almost all the *capi di massi* immediately fled in the greatest confusion. The latter, since their first panic has been got over, have given in to every latitude of horror and excess, murdering and plundering every person of property, and making the whole country desolate.

In fact, I am fully convinced that no confidence nor dependence can be placed upon these people, and that our interference in the country is only giving opportunity to the lawless and vicious, to oppress and plunder the better sort of inhabitants; and encouraging a disposition to revolt, that will not in any way assist our cause, and bring upon them a tenfold vengeance from the French government.

I have for some time past directed that no more arms nor

ammunition should be distributed among them. It only leads the inhabitants to do mischief, and to plunder and oppress the more peaceable; and causes dreadful individual mischief, without doing any general good.

The defence of the island of Sicily is the great object of our naval and military force; and expending our means among the *banditti* of Calabria, I fear will not very effectually answer this end. If I might be allowed to give an opinion, I should think our purposes would be more effectually answered, by the gun-boats and other vessels, appropriated by you for that service, doing their utmost to prevent the enemy from sending their supplies coastways, without interfering in any way with the inhabitants or interior of the country; and I most strongly recommend that no more arms nor ammunition be given to them from the ships.

The enemy have no guns nor warlike stores there at this moment; and I trust, by means of our naval force, you will be able to prevent their getting any by sea. Thus we may keep our post secure, without encouraging, at an enormous expense, a sort of predatory civil war, which cannot answer any general good purpose, though fraught with individual mischief and barbarity.

As, from the variety of services at present, and likely soon to be afoot, that may require our transports, I must request you will, as soon as possible, send here the vessels named in the margin,* to remain here at my disposal. You have, no doubt, retained such transports as you judged necessary for the naval division; and those above mentioned, that I selected for the troops and the military service, I hope will be sent here with as little delay as possible.

I shall at all times be happy to communicate with you, and be much obliged to you for your information that you are good enough to send me respecting Calabria; and if I find the population can be organised, or directed to any useful purpose, I shall be willing to give them such support as may be judged expedient; but I must most earnestly request, that you will not encourage or make promises to the *capi*, or leaders of the *massi*, as this may only tend to counteract the measures I find it necessary to adopt.

As to Sir John Moore, he has, no doubt fully, explained my sentiments and views when he saw you on board the

* *The Crown, Ellice, Symmetry, John and Robert, William,* and *Comet.*

Pompée. I shall add nothing further, than to urge the absolute necessity of the sending the above-mentioned transports here immediately.

I have the honour to be, etc.

W. R. Fox

Sir Sidney, however, who had not been sorry when General Fox arrived to take over the chief command from Stuart, did not last the course very long. The new Commander-in-Chief found it no less difficult to work with the Admiral than Stuart had done, and in Sir John Moore* he found an invaluable ally for he, too, had a low opinion of the Calabrians, and of Sidney Smith.

Six days before Fox wrote the above letter to Sir Sidney, he had received a letter from Sir John. "It will be necessary," Moore wrote, "for you to express your sentiments much more decidedly if you wish him to discontinue his interference in Calabria, where in his imagination he is directing the operation of armies, but where in reality he is only encouraging murder and rapine, and keeping up amongst that unhappy people, whom we have no intention to support, a spirit of revolt which will bring upon them the more severe vengeance of the French Government. As long as Sir Sidney had money he distributed it profusely, and now, with as little judgment, he is distributing arms, ammunition and provisions. Transports are employed all along the coast with orders to receive and victual all the men, women and children who apply to them, to re-land them in Calabria or carry them to whatever part of Sicily they direct. . . . It will be necessary for you to send him a list of the transports, stating names and number, which you wish to be left at Messina subject to your call."

Meanwhile, according to an entry in Sir John Moore's diary, Fox had written home about Sir Sidney "stating the impossibility of acting in concert with him," and on 25 January 1807 the Admiral received instructions from the Admiralty to proceed to Malta, where he was to place himself under the command of Lord Collingwood who would give him further orders.

Notwithstanding the many criticisms about the conduct of

---

* Although General Fox was nominally in command of the British forces in this area, Sir John Moore had been sent out by the British Government as *Supremo.*

the campaign in Southern Italy it had not, by any means, been barren of results. Piers Mackesy, in his book, *The War in the Mediterranean*, summed it up very fairly. "In spite of the Admiral and of the wretched disputes with which the year ended, it had been a successful campaign. Stuart's counter-stroke had destroyed Reynier's laborious preparations to cross the Straits, and put it out of Joseph's power to attack Sicily that year. The army of Naples had lost heavily. Stuart had put four thousand troops out of action; Gaeta, sustained by Sir Sidney, had cost Joseph another two thousand, and many more were destroyed by the guerillas. Masséna's army was committed to a campaign in the Calabrias which cost many lives by battle and sickness as it dragged into the winter. At the beginning of August nine thousand of Joseph's army were sick, and two months later, after the reconquest of Upper Calabria, a quarter of Masséna's corps in the Calabrias were in the hospitals. The deaths from sickness during the year rose to three thousand eight hundred. The first year of the French occupation must have cost the enemy eleven or twelve thousand dead and wounded. . . . The lesson of Maida had been learnt. Henceforth the French would beware of lending a flank to the British general. By demonstrating the power of a small army off the Italian coast, Stuart and Smith had forced Napoleon to keep large forces in his brother's kingdom. Whilst the British army remained in Sicily, Naples was not secure; and, instead of providing free peacetime quarters for the Imperial armies, it became a permanent military burden to the enemy."

When he arrived off Malta, on the 3rd February 1807, Sir Sidney wrote to Lord Collingwood acknowledging his orders and giving the latest information about the Calabrian campaign:

I enclose, for your lordship's information, the latest reports I have received of the state of the unsuccessful war which the Calabrese are reduced to carry on for want of the support and direction which might enable them to prevail against the dispirited troops that are feebly attacking them. Scylla will at all events remain to us, should Amantea fall, as no army can attack that peninsula without naval co-operation, similar to that which reduced it in July, with any possibility of success. Cotrone has the royal flag of Ferdinand IV flying there, but with a feeble garrison, and that supposed to be not well affected, since they have been left to their fate without supplies.

I thus take my leave of this service with the conscious certainty that I have acted from the purest motives for the common cause against the cruel and rapacious foe we have had to do with, on the general principle of pursuing a beaten and flying enemy and to assist a known friend in view. I have given every support to the British army in my power, paying every deference to his Majesty's plenipotentiary and the commander-in-chief, although they did not agree with me in the application of the general principle, which is, and I trust will remain, that on which his Majesty's service habitually acts.

Having regard to the rather contrary opinions of Sir Sidney's activities held by the army commanders the above self-eulogy may seem a little overdone, but he always had a good conceit of himself and was never backward in coming forward, as the final paragraph of his letter shows.

"I am happy to lay before your lordship," he wrote, "the enclosed flattering testimonial from the Court of Palermo, which has not fallen a prey to the enemy as it was expected to have done, had the theatre of war been allowed to reach the shores of Sicily, which I defended by keeping it at a distance. On this ground, I beg leave, through your lordship, to request his Majesty's Secretary of State to lay before the King his Sicilian Majesty's gracious offer to me of the Order of St Ferdinand, as granted to my ever lamented predecessor in that local service, Lord Nelson, in order that I may obtain his Majesty's gracious permission to accept and wear the same."

When King Ferdinand wrote to Sir Sidney bestowing on him the Order of the Grand Cross of St Ferdinand and of Merit the Queen also wrote:

My very worthy and dear Admiral,

I cannot find expressions sufficiently strong to convey the painful feeling which your departure, so unforeseen, has caused, both to me and to my whole family, I can only say that you are accompanied by our most sincere good wishes, and most particularly on my part, by the gratitude which will cease only with my life, for all that you have done for us,

and for what you *would* moreover have done for us if everything had not been thwarted and your zeal and enterprise
cramped. May you be as happy as my heart prays for, and
may you continue by fresh laurels to augment your own
glory and the number of the envious. I still cherish the hope
of seeing you again in better times, and of giving you proof of
those sentiments which, at the present moment, I cannot
express; but you will find, in all times and places (whatever
may be the fate reserved for us) our hearts gratefully attached
to you, even unto the grave.

Pray make my sincere compliments to the Captain and to
all the officers of *La Pompée*, as well as my good wishes for
their happiness. Assure them of the pain with which I witness
their departure.

Sir Sidney was highly pleased with the Queen's demonstra-
tion of admiration and affection but it cannot have impressed
Lord Collingwood much, for he had as poor an opinion of Sicily
in general as he had of Her Majesty and all the Sicilian
aristocracy whom he met on a visit to Palermo just after Smith
had left. Referring to Queen Charlotte he said, "such a
depravity of manners should never have been found perched
upon a throne, from whence should issue the bright example of
all that is good and great." The more he saw of the princesses
and duchesses of Sicily, he said, "the more I bless my stars that
I was born in England and have a darling wife who is not a
princess." Sicily itself had "divided councils, a King who ought
to rule and a Queen who will, no army for its defence, no
revenue except to support their gaieties, and a people who,
having nothing beyond their daily earnings, are indifferent as
to who rules them."

Nevertheless he must have forwarded Sir Sidney's request to
be allowed to accept the honour which Ferdinand had offered,
for two weeks later permission for him to accept and wear the
Grand Cross of the Order was published in the London Gazette.

II

THE DARDANELLES

THE first order that Sir Sidney received from the Admiralty which was the reason for his leaving Southern Italy was to sail at once in the *Pompée* to Plymouth Sound from which base he was, once again, to be employed in operations on the Channel coast. Almost immediately, however, this was changed, and the *Pompée* was ordered to join a squadron under the command of Sir John Duckworth and to sail to the Dardanelles on a special mission.

Sir Sidney had already been approached by Charles Arbuthnot, then British Minister at Constantinople. Arbuthnot had written to the Admiral four months earlier when he was still cruising up and down the coast of Calabria.

"I don't know whether you will be able to send any ships up," he wrote, "but I am certain that their presence is become very necessary. France has produced such a panic that the Porte is wholly alienated from us; and the most vigorous measures alone can now preserve our interests in this part of the world. Under the supposition that you may send some ships to cruise as far as the Dardanelles I shall take care to send a letter to our consul at that place directed to the commanding naval officer who may happen to ask for it and that letter shall contain all the information that I may have it in my power to communicate." Although it was but a forlorn hope, Arbuthnot thought that if the British navy could show the flag in that part of the world it might dissuade the Turks from entering into an alliance with the French and, at the same time, serve to maintain our lines of communication with Russia.

With this private covering letter a copy of another letter was enclosed referring to a previous letter which Arbuthnot had written some weeks earlier and which had not been received by Smith up to the time when he had been given his new orders by Collingwood.

Mr Arbuthnot to Sir Sidney Smith
   Buyukderé, on the Bosphorus, September 27, 1806.
Sir,

On the 3rd of this month I wrote to you, by the way of Corfu, to inform you that the conduct of the Porte towards England and Russia was become very suspicious, and that I thought the presence of a couple of line-of-battle ships at the Dardanelles would be extremely desirable.

Since the departure of that letter, we have had still more reason to be dissatisfied with the Porte; for, although the professions of friendship still continue, we know from undoubted authority that France has made proposals of an alliance with this government, which, though not perhaps yet agreed to, have most certainly not been rejected.

In making privately these proposals to the Porte, France accompanied them with a public notification (a copy of which is in my possession) that the continuation of the alliance with England and Russia, and the passage of Russian ships of war, or even of Russian transports, through the Bosphorus, would be considered as an act of hostility against herself, and that the French troops now collected in Dalmatia would immediately be ordered to cross the Ottoman Empire on their way to the Dniester, where the Russian army is assembled.

Instead of declaring to General Sebastiani that the treaties with England and Russia could not be violated, the Porte has delivered a note in answer to his, in which it is acknowledged that the passage of Russian ships by the Bosphorus (which, it must be observed, is a right ceded to Russia by the treaty renewed some months since) occasions great inconvenience to this government, and that the court of Petersburg has been and will again be desired to discontinue that practice.

A note has accordingly been presented this day to the Russian minister, in which the above demand is made. It was delivered just at the moment when that minister received orders from Petersburg, to declare, that, unless the deposed hospodars were reinstated (the details respecting which I communicated to you in my former letter) and unless the passage through the Bosphorus was consented to and confirmed, he was to quit this residence with the whole of his mission, and merely to leave one of his dragomans to act for the moment as chargé d'affaires. On his departure he was also ordered to write to the general commanding on the frontier, and to the admiral in the Black Sea, to whom eventual orders would be given from Petersburg.

As the whole extent of this state of things could not have been exactly foreseen by his majesty's ministers, I am naturally without instructions how to act, and am consequently in no small degree embarrassed.

As however the union between the two courts of London and Petersburg is, if possible, more intimate than ever; as the refusal to renew the treaty with England is alleged in the dispatches from Petersburg as one of the emperor's motives for recalling his mission; as that refusal has been occasioned by the ascendency of French influence; and as nothing but the strict alliance which had existed between Great Britain and the Porte could have induced his majesty to send an ambassador to this country; I have, in consideration of all these circumstances, determined to take the responsibility upon myself of supporting the representations which are now to be made by the Russian minister. It is my intention, therefore, to inform the Porte, that, unless the just demands of Russia are complied with, I shall take it as a proof that the sultan has abandoned his ancient system; and not conceiving it as consistent with the dignity of his majesty that his representative should witness all the marks of condescension for his enemies—incompatible as they are with the treaty still existing between this country and England—I should, in that case, follow the example of my Russian colleague, and appoint a chargé d'affaires for the transaction of the current business.

These declarations to the Porte we intend making immediately. It would have been very satisfactory for me if I could have informed you of the effect produced by them. But as the Porte is at all times slow and dilatory; as I think that this government has entered too far into connexions with France to be either willing, or perhaps indeed able now to retract; and as whatever may be the result or the measures we are taking, a British naval force, either to awe or to defend, seems now to be indispensable; I have, therefore, on these accounts, thought it of extreme importance that not a moment should be lost in apprising you of the situation of affairs, and I have consequently determined to send off his

majesty's sloop, the *Rose*, that you may have the means of
acting according to your judgment, or according to the
instructions which you may previously have received from
Lord Collingwood.

You are so well acquainted with the nature of this government that I need not endeavour to impress you with the
advantages to be derived from the appearance of a British
force in the Archipelago. You see that our sole and most
faithful ally will in all probability be very shortly engaged
in hostilities with the Porte; and from what I have written to
you, you will learn that the offence committed against us
(for I ought to inform you that at one time the Porte had
most earnestly besought his majesty to renew the treaty) has
been one of the causes which has induced the emperor to
withdraw his mission. It will therefore, I think, be as evident
to you as it is to me, that in some way or other our government cannot well avoid to resent the conduct of the Porte;
and should this notion be well founded, we should derive
incalculable benefit from the presence of a small squadron,
which would be in readiness to execute any orders which
might afterwards arrive from England. But the determination
on this subject must remain with you. I have given you a full
insight into the state of our affairs, and, as far as my opinion
can have weight, I declare freely that, should it be left to
your discretion, you will render a most essential service in
proving to the Porte that we are prepared and determined to
resent any injury which the counsels of France may cause
to be committed against us.

It is also necessary for me to let you know that although,
in the event of a non-compliance with the demand of Russia,
it would be my determination not to continue the exercise
of my functions as ambassador, I should still, however, think
it prudent not to quit the country until an answer to the
dispatches I shall now write has been received from England.
I should appoint a chargé d'affaires to be the ostensible
transactor of business; but under the plea (and indeed the
real one) of not having the means at present of removing my
family, I should remain here to observe what was going on.
By this I should enable his majesty's government, in case
my conduct were disapproved, to send out another ambassador to replace me; and, at any rate, whether my conduct
be approved or otherwise, I shall, by continuing on the spot,

be able to direct the person whom I shall appoint to do the business.

You will, therefore, have the goodness to direct your answer to me, and I need scarcely say that I shall look for it with much impatience.

I have the honour to be, etc.

Charles Arbuthnot

P.S. Upon further consideration I have determined not to appoint a chargé d'affaires, but to content myself with declaring to the Porte, that I do not conceive it possible for his majesty to allow his ambassador to remain here. The Russian minister is naturally very anxious that I should go to the same lengths as he does; and if I were fully authorised to take that step, our chance of success would certainly be far greater.

The Turks fear nothing but our fleets, but they will not believe us to be in earnest. On this account, and I really think that on this account alone, they have ventured to insult Russia. If you can possibly send some ships to the Dardanelles you will undeceive them. We owe it to Russia.

C.A.

In order fully to understand the importance which Her Majesty's Government attached to this expedition it is necessary to know the written orders which Duckworth received from Collingwood and which are set out in full below.

Copy of the Orders to Sir John Duckworth, to proceed to the Dardanelles, dated 13*th January,* 1807.

Some late proceedings on the part of the Turkish government, indicating the increasing influence of the French in their councils, and a disposition in the Porte to abandon the alliance which has happily subsisted between that government and his majesty, inducing a conduct on their part which it would be inconsistent with the dignity of his majesty's crown to submit to, have determined the king to adopt such prompt and decisive measures as are suitable to the occasion.

On the other hand, the last accounts, of date the 13th October last, from his majesty's ambassador at Constantinople, stated as the matters of difference to have been amicably adjusted; yet, as recent events may have an effect unfavourable to his majesty's interests, it is necessary that a squadron, under the command of a judicious and skilful officer, should proceed to Constantinople, to be ready to act with vigour and promptitude, as circumstances and the state of affairs on his arrival may make necessary.

You are hereby required and directed to take under your orders the ships named in the margin,* which you are to collect as you arrive at the stations and ports where they are; and, having completed the provisions and water for four months at Gibraltar, proceed as expeditiously as possible to the Straits of Constantinople, and there take such a position as will enable you to execute the following instructions:

On your arrival at Constantinople, you are to communicate with his majesty's ambassador as soon as possible, sending him the accompanying despatches, and consulting with him on the measures necessary to be taken.

Should the subject of difference have been amicably settled between the Turkish court and the British ambassador, as was stated in the last accounts from him, the relations of amity are to be maintained; should, however, the reverse be the case, or should the representations which Mr Arbuthnot is instructed to make to the Turkish government fail of their effect, you are to act offensively against Constantinople. But as, from a barbarous practice of the Turkish government, it may happen that the ambassador and the persons of his suite are forcibly detained, in such case, before you proceed to any actual hostility, you are to demand and insist on the release of that minister and suite, together with all those who belong to and compose part of the British factory; and in the event of the demand not being complied with, you are to proceed to measures of hostility against the town. If Mr Arbuthnot shall not have been forcibly detained, or, having been detained, should be released in consequence of your requisition, you are then to communicate and consult with that minister on the measures proper to be pursued, and govern yourself in your further proceedings by such communications.

Should the result of your communications with Mr Arbuthnot determine, and he inform you that it is his opinion that hostilities should commence, having previously taken all possible precautions for the safety of that minister and the

* At Palermo, the *Pompée*, Rear-Admiral Sir Sidney Smith, and in the Archipelago, under the orders of Rear-Admiral Sir Thomas Louis, *Canopus*, *Thunderer*, *Standard*, *Endymion*, *Active*, *Nautilus*, *Delight*, *Royal George*, *Windsor Castle*, *Repulse*, *Ajax*.

persons attached to his mission, and having disposed the squadron under your orders in such stations as may compel compliance, you are to demand the surrender of the Turkish fleet, together with a supply of naval stores from the arsenal, sufficient for its complete equipment, which demand you are to accompany with a menace of immediate destruction of the town.

At this crisis, should any negotiation on the subject be proposed by the Turkish government, as such proposition will probably be to gain time for preparing for their resistance, or securing their ships, I would recommend that no negotiation should be continued more than half an hour; and, in the event of an absolute refusal, you are either to cannonade the town, or attack the fleet, wherever it may be, holding it in mind that the getting the possession, and, next to that, the destruction of the Turkish fleet, is the object of the first consideration. On the adoption of hostilities, the communication of that decision to the commander-in-chief of the British army in Sicily, and the officers commanding the squadron on the coast of that island, must be as prompt and immediate as possible, sent by a fast-sailing vessel; and, the more to insure this important communication, a duplicate should follow in a very few days, orders having been sent to General Fox to detach five thousand men for the purpose of taking possession of Alexandria, as soon as he is informed that hostilities have commenced; which armament you must regard as acting within the sphere of your co-operation, and be prepared to give all the assistance to it that is in your power.

When hostilities have been entered upon in that quarter, it will be of the first importance to possess a naval station in the Archipelago. The island of Milo, from the situation and the excellence of its harbour, presents itself as best calculated for preserving the communication in the Archipelago, and such as will certainly be necessary in the Morea. In proceeding up the Archipelago, pilots are procured at Milo, and when you are there for that purpose it will be a favourable opportunity for you to examine how far the possessing yourself of it is practicable, and what force will be necessary to maintain it, and make such communications to General Fox on this subject, and a request for such troops, as may be wanted to possess it.

His majesty's ship *Glatton* is stationed in the Bay of Smyrna for the purpose of receiving on board the persons and property of the factory resident there, whenever circumstances make it necessary for them to embark; and as this will depend upon the operations at Constantinople, you will give Captain Leccombe and the factors timely notice for their security.

Having thus detailed particularly the situation of affairs at the Porte, and what are the instructions of his majesty in the event of a war with Turkey, yet, in a service of this nature, many circumstances will doubtless occur which cannot be foreseen, and can only be provided for by an intelligent mind upon the spot; in your ability a resource will be found for every contingency; and in your zeal for his majesty's service, a security that, for the full execution of these instructions, whatever is practicable will be done.

The force which is appointed for this service is greater than the original intention, as it was expected the Russians from Corfu would be ready to co-operate with you; but as its success depends upon the promptness with which it is executed, I have judged it proper (that no delay may arise from their squadron not joining) to increase your force by two ships. I have, however, written to Vice-Admiral Sercovies to request him to detach four ships, with orders to put themselves under your command; and that you may be possessed of all the force that can be applied to the important service under your immediate direction, you are hereby authorised to call from the coast of Sicily whatever can be spared from the perfect security of that island, as well as the despatch vessels at Malta; but as little more naval force is at Sicily than is absolutely necessary for its defence, and the convoy which may be wanted for the troops, a strict regard must be had that that island is not left in a weak state of defence. While employed on this service you must take every opportunity of communicating to me your proceedings in as full detail as possible, transmitting to me by such opportunities the general return and state of the squadron.

In the event of your finding a pacific and friendly disposition in the Porte, so that the squadron under your orders is not required in hostile operations there, you are to detach a flag-officer with such number of ships as are not wanted, which detachment being made up to five ships of the line from those at Sicily, you will proceed direct off Toulon, endeavouring to fall in with any squadron of ships the enemy may have put to sea thence. Not finding the enemy at sea, those ships attached to the service of Sicily are to return to their stations, and the flag-officer with the others are to proceed and join me at this rendezvous.

I enclose for your information copies of the orders delivered to Rear-Admiral Sir Thomas Louis, and Captain Leccombe of the *Glatton*. Given on board the *Ocean* off Cadiz.

Collingwood

No time was lost in carrying out these orders, and before seven weeks had passed Sir Sidney had attacked a Turkish squadron in the Dardanelles off Point Pesquies burning eleven ships and capturing two. This victory he duly reported to Duckworth in a letter from H.M.S. *Pompée*. Sir John had been present when the attack began but as the coast intervened after he had passed Point Pesquies he was unable to see how the battle had developed and Smith therefore considered it necessary to give him a full description.

"The Turks," Sir Sidney wrote, "fought desperately, like men determined to defend themselves and their ships as long as they could; but the superiority of our fire, within musket shot, obliged them in half an hour to run on shore on Point Pesquies, or Nagura Burun. As the redoubt on the point continued to fire, also as the ships kept their colours up, and the part of their crews which had deserted them remained armed on the beach, while a considerable body of Asiatic troops, both horse and foot, appeared on the hills, it was necessary to make an arrangement for boarding them, with some precaution; at the same time, that it was of consequence to press them closely before they recovered from the impression and effect of our cannonade. A few shells from the *Pompée* dispersed the Asiatics, and convinced them that we commanded the ground within our reach, and that they could not protect the green standard they had hoisted, which I caused to be brought off by Lieutenant Oates, of the *Pompée*'s marines, that they might not rally there again.

"The *Standard*'s guns bearing best on the frigates on shore, I sent the *Thunderer*'s boats to that ship, to be employed with her own, under the direction of Captain Harvey, making the signal to him to destroy the enemy's ships in the N.E. The

Active's signal having been previously made to follow and destroy a frigate, which had cut her cable to get from under the *Thunderer*'s and *Pompée*'s fire, and ran on shore on the European side in the N.W.; at the same time Lieutenant Beecroft, of the *Pompée*, was detached to take possession of the line-of-battle ship, on which the *Thunderer*'s and *Pompeé*'s guns could still bear, under the protection likewise of the *Repulse*, which you had considerately sent to my aid; that officer brought me the captain and second captain, the latter of whom was wounded, also the flag of the rear-admiral who had escaped on shore, which I shall have the honour of presenting to you.

"The whole of the Turks were landed, in pursuance of your orders, including the wounded, with due attention to the sufferings of our misguided opponents, as I must call them, for the term *enemy* does not seem applicable, considering their evident good disposition towards us nationally. The ship was then set on fire by the *Repulse*'s and *Pompée*'s boats, and completely destroyed.

"Captain Harvey, in making his report to me of the conduct of the boat's crews under the command of Lieutenants Carter, Waller, and Colby, of his majesty's ship *Thunderer*, and of the marines employed with them to board and burn the frigates and corvettes, under the command of Captain Nicolls, speaks in strong terms of the gallantry and ability of them all. The latter, whom I have long known to be an intelligent and enterprising officer, after destroying the frigate bearing the flag of the Captain Pasha, which is preserved to be presented to you, sir, landed; and profiting by the consternation of the Turks from the explosions on all sides of them, the effects of which occasioned no small risk to him, with Lieutenants Fenmore, Boileau, and the whole party, Captain Nicolls entered the redoubt (the Turks retreating as he approached), set fire to the gabions, and spiked the guns, thirty-one in number, eight of which are brass, carrying immensely large marble balls.

"As, however, the expected explosion of the line-of-battle ship made it impossible for the boats to stay long enough to destroy them effectually with their carriages, or to level the parapets, the wicker of the gabions being too green to burn, I have directed Lieutenants Carroll and Arabin, of his majesty's ship *Pompée*, and Lieutenant Laurie of the marines, to continue on that service with the Turkish corvette and one gun-boat, which you will observe by the return were not destroyed, and to act under the protection and direction of Captain Mowbray, of his majesty's ship *Active*, whose name I cannot mention without expressing how highly satisfied I am with the able and gallant manner in which he executed my orders to stick to the frigate, with which he was more particularly engaged, and to destroy her.

"Captain Talbot placed his ship admirably well in support of the *Pompée*, thereby raking the line-of-battle ship and the frigate we were engaged with, when I made his signal to anchor, as the *Pompée* had previously done, under the directions I gave for that purpose to Captain Dacres, which were promptly and able executed; Mr Ives, the master, applying his local knowledge and experience, as I had a right to expect from his long tried abilities, while Lieutenant Smith made my signals to the squadron in rapid succession and with precision. Captain Harvey merits my entire approbation for placing the *Standard* in the manner he did, and for completing the destruction of the others. Much as I must regret the loss of the *Ajax*, as a most efficient ship in my division, I have felt that loss to be in a great degree balanced by the presence of my gallant friend, Captain Blackwood, and the surviving officers and men, whose zeal, in their voluntary exertions on this occasion, does them the highest credit. In short, all the captains, officers, and men concerned, merit that I should mention them in high terms to you, sir, as their leader, whose example we humbly endeavoured to follow. The signal success that has attended the general exertion under your direction speaks more forcibly than words.

I have the honour to be, etc.

W. Sidney Smith"

Duckworth was delighted with the outcome of this action and on this occasion Sir Sidney came in for unstinted praise in the despatch which was sent to Collingwood. Sir John described how Smith with his 'rear division' had closed in with such effect that in half an hour the Turks, who were lying at anchor off the Point, in half an hour had all cut their cables to run on shore. Sir Sidney's next objective was to destroy them and he did not take long to do it. In less than four hours all the Turkish ships had been blown up with the exception of a small corvette and a gun-boat which were purposely spared. The British losses were slight. "It is with peculiar pleasure," Duckworth wrote, "that I embrace the opportunity, which has been at this time afforded, of bearing testimony to the zeal and distinguished ability of Sir Sidney Smith. The manner in which he executed the service entrusted to him was worthy of the reputation which he has long since so justly and so generously established."

Little more than this, however, was accomplished, and after hanging about off Constantinople for a further three weeks, during which time the Turks made several attacks on his fleet, Duckworth retreated through the Straits suffering heavily from the coastal batteries during the passage.

The expedition to the Dardanelles, therefore, was not a success and it completely failed in its object, which was to intimidate the Turks. It is true, however, that the force placed under Duckworth's command was inadequate for the task entrusted to him but it is doubtful whether he would have done much better in any event. The choice of Duckworth to command the expedition was a bad one, and it should have fallen on Sir Sidney whose experience of that kind of operation was exceptional. The reason why Collingwood did not give him command was, doubtless, a personal one, for Smith had made many enemies in the Mediterranean theatre of war, particularly among those in his own service.

Had Sir Sidney been in command there is reason to think that the expedition might have had a very different result. A mutual friend of both himself and General Sebastiani, who was in command of the Turkish forces stationed in Constantinople, strongly held this view.

"The same jealous feeling," he said, "which followed poor Sir Sidney everywhere all through his service appears to have been conspicuous on this occasion. Had he commanded this expedition, as ought to have been the case, the result would most certainly have been very different. His name alone would have acted like a charm upon the Turks by whom he was respected and beloved. The moral influence, which he possessed over them to such an extraordinary degree was here thrown away by the then councils of England, and the greatest fault of all was, perhaps, that of placing the naval force under direction, as it were, of the diplomatic agent. The fleet ought not to have passed the Dardanelles until diplomatic measures had been exhausted and the object should then have been Constantinople, and the action against it one of direct hostility."

After Admiral Duckworth had passed through the Dardanelles back to comparative safety he wrote a long despatch to Lord Collingwood explaining, among other things, the reasons for his decision to retreat without attacking Constantinople. He felt confident it would require no argument to convince his lordship of the utter impracticability of the British force making any impression on the Turks as the whole coastline was thick with batteries. Twelve large and powerful Turkish men-of-war were in readiness for battle, filled with troops. In Constantinople itself there were at least two hundred thousand troops all ready for action. With the batteries alone, Duckworth said, he could have coped, or with the ships had it been possible to tempt them out to sea, but he was sure that Lord Collingwood would understand that "after combating the opposition which the resources of an empire had been employed many weeks in preparing we should have been in no state to have defended ourselves against them, and then repass the Dardanelles".

Sir Sidney, however, never publicly complained and his only contribution to the discussion was a Memorandum, entitled 'Naval Poetry'* which he forwarded to his brother Charles with the following letter:

Sir Sidney Smith to Charles Douglas Smith, Esq.
            Pompée, off the Island of Tenedos, March 11, 1807.
Dear Charles,

I have written at length to my uncle, to Spencer, and to Lord Grenville, as I could seize moments in the midst of my occupations, amongst which, the throwing in the hints my experience dictates to prevent things going from bad to worse, has been an unceasing one, though I fear a thankless office. However, a sense of duty makes me act conscientiously, and my motives are not doubted by those who do not follow the advice or take the early warnings I have given. It is poor consolation to me, to see that the result sometimes justifies my predictions; it is painful to see so much within our reach, while our means of realising any object are inapplicable, notwithstanding their apparent magnitude; it is painful to look back and see our ascendency in these countries lost, by the political experiment of sending new diplomatic men, who (whatever their talents) had to buy their local experience, and during their noviciate were totally in the hands of a dragoman, who, if not in the French interest, was in that of the Turks, which, becoming blended latterly by the march

* See page 160.

of the Russians into Moldavia and Wallachia, enabled Buonaparte to induce the Turks to see their safety in the success of the French arms, and not to listen to the counsel of the British ambassador, who could no longer speak as an ally, after the expiration of our treaty, which was, as you know, signed by Spencer and me (the two plenipotentiaries) on the 6th of January 1799. The Turks are wrong in their calculation after all, for they have more to fear from French pretended friendship, than from the passage of Russian troops through two provinces, that hardly belonged to them. *I am quite sure that I could have made them see this*, if I had been allowed to open a collateral intercourse with those, who could have over-ruled the cry of the fanatic junto and mob by our aid. The latter will be the victims in the end. *Quem Deus vult perdere prius dementat*, you will have said on the first knowledge you had of this rupture; the sultan knows better; but the ecclesiastical and juridical bodies being in one, and having a veto on every thing, he cannot act as sound policy dictates. Spencer will explain all this to you, and agree with me in the advice I sent the poor sultan by his confidential messenger, Isaac Bey Vizier, to employ the three fleets combined to chastise his rabble, and guard his capital against the French. I am convinced he personally was sorry to see us go. I wrote to Spencer on our passage down, to my uncle, and Lord Grenville since. I trust you are in communication; the whole is a series.

Yours affectionately,
W. S. Smith

N.B. Killed going up and down, twenty-two; wounded ditto, one hundred and ninety. Some valuable lives lost in a hap-hazard, hand-over-head boat expedition, to turn a few Turks out of the Prince's Islands, more than I lost in disarming all Calabria, and yet I am criticised for pretending to be something of a general! I ought not to omit to say, for your satisfaction, that your son Thurlow proved himself to be of a good breed, by steady clear-headed conduct in the situation I entrusted to him, of signal lieutenant with me on the poop, where we could see round us and *know* the worst.

Yours etc.
W. S. Smith

Memorandum

'Naval Poetry'

On the 14th of February, 1807, a squadron of his majesty's ships consisting of the *Ajax, Canopus, Repulse, Standard, Pompée, Thunderer, Active, Windsor Castle, Lucifer*, and *Meteor* * bombs, commanded by Vice-Admiral Sir John Duckworth, K.B., in the *Royal George*, also the *Endymion* frigate, which had brought his majesty's ambassador from Constantinople, and afterwards was the medium of intercourse by flag of truce, assembled at the anchorage between Tenedos and Troy. The *Ajax* was unfortunately burnt by accident on the 14th, and on the 19th the remaining ships forced the passage of the Dardanelles, burning by their way the Turkish squadron commanded by the Captain Pasha which attempted to oppose their passage. On this occasion some conversation occurred as to the lines in "Moore's Almanac," for 1807, as applicable to existing circumstances, viz. "April, about this time the Turkish emperor dies, or it may be he hides his head, his people are tumultuous, let him save his life if he can, I give him fair warning of it." This almanac being put into the hands of an officer in the squadron,† he returned it with the following lines:

Ajax, alas! devouring flames destroy
His ashes left before the walls of Troy;
Canopus led the way, 'twixt "neighb'ring strands"
Of Helespontus, thronged with Turkish bands.
Dreading Repulse the Turks dared not assail;
The British Standard turned the crescent pale:
On Caesar's allies Pompée vengeance wreaks,
And rushing in the midst their line he breaks;
While showers of deadly bolts the Thunderer hurled,
The anchor goes, again the sails are furled:
Whilse Asia trembles with explosion dire,
An Active torch in Europe kindleth fire.
The Pasha's fleet in fragments on the coast,
Propontis now doth bear the British host;
Its dread approach each Turkish heart appals,
Lo! Windsor Castle's at Byzantium's walls.

* *Ajax, Canopus, Standard, Thunderer, Lucifer, Repulse, Pompée, Windsor Castle, Meteor, Active* and *Endymion* were all British men-of-war.
† The officer was, of course, Sir Sidney himself.

Grim Lucifer his brimstone doth prepare,
Whilst fiery Meteor glows to dart in air;
Th' astonished Turks, who ne'er beheld the like,
Fear Royal George a final blow should strike;
Mercy they beg: Endymion stands between,
The hand of power to mercy still doth lean:
A truce requested, and obtain'd they break,
Loud tumult Sultan Selim's throne doth shake;
His empire's fate a thread alone doth bear,
Suspended hangs the blow of death in air;
'Tis not yet time, saith Moore, the spell to break
That Greece doth shackle: 'tis not time to take
Revenge on Europe's scourge, Mahommed's race:
A greater scourge for them his lines would trace,
The curse of hell, the greatest, man hath seen
'Tis Buonaparte's friendship he doth mean.

W.S.S.

When he reached Malta Duckworth found orders from
Collingwood waiting for him to hand over the squadron to
Rear-Admiral Louis and proceed immediately to Spithead.
Sir Sidney arrived back in England only a fortnight later, struck
his flag and went, on half-pay, to Bath to take the waters.

12

MISSION TO PORTUGAL

SIR SIDNEY did not remain unemployed for long, however, and on 12th November, having hoisted his flag again on H.M.S. *Hibernia*, he set sail, this time for a secret destination, Portugal.

Napoleon, determined to exploit his control over the Iberian peninsular to the full, had decided to carry the war into Portugal. Shortly after war was declared, the Prince-Regent in Lisbon, who was a weak character, in an attempt to appease the French, signed a proclamation ordering the detention of those British subjects who still remained in the country and the confiscation of their property. Lord Strangford, our ambassador at the Portuguese Court, having protested vigorously without success, hauled down the Embassy flag and joined the British squadron which had just arrived at the mouth of the Tagus under Smith's command. A total blockade of the river was then begun.

This had the desired effect, and Lord Strangford returned to the Portuguese capital where he was soon able to persuade the Prince-Regent that the wisest course would be to leave Lisbon immediately, with as much of the Portuguese fleet as he could muster, and sail to Brazil. The British Ambassador then wrote the following letter to Sir Sidney and next day sent a full report to George Canning, the Foreign Secretary.

Lord Strangford to Sir Sidney Smith
Lisbon, November 28th, 1807, at night.
Sir,
I am to inform you that a great and rapid change has taken place in the conduct of the Portuguese government, and that preparations are actually in *bona fide* making, with due alacrity, for the execution of those articles of the convention which relate to the disposal of the Portuguese navy. The prince-regent and all the royal family are embarked and propose to sail instantly, as a French army is within nine leagues of Lisbon. Time will not admit of your entry into the

Tagus for the purpose of co-operating in the preparations necessary for the removal of the Portuguese fleet, as you will probably receive this letter after his royal highness has already passed the Bar. And it is on this ground that his royal highness does not acquiesce in the preliminary surrender of the forts of St Julian and the Bugio.

Every vessel belonging to the Portuguese marine, whether royal or commercial, is engaged and prepared to accompany his royal highness. It is utterly inexpedient to throw any unnecessary difficulties in the way of his royal highness's departure or to raise any question that might be avoided, for I am convinced that so great is the discontent of the people, and so strong the consequent alarm of his royal highness, that all depends on the support and encouragement which he may receive from us, and of which I have given him the most frank and unequivocal assurance.

> I have the honour to be, etc.
> Strangford

Lord Strangford's letter to Mr Canning was dated 29th November and was written on board the *Hibernia*, off the Tagus.

Lord Strangford to Mr Canning
> *Hibernia*, off the Tagus, November 29, 1807.

Sir,

I have the honour of announcing to you that the Prince-Regent of Portugal has effected the wise and magnanimous purpose of retiring from a kingdom which he could no longer retain, except as the vassal of France; and that his royal highness and family, accompanied by most of his ships of war and by a multitude of his faithful subjects and adherents, have this day departed from Lisbon, and are now on their way to the Brazils, under the escort of a British fleet.

This grand and memorable event is not to be attributed only to the sudden alarm excited by the appearance of a French army within the frontiers of Portugal. It has been the genuine result of the system of persevering confidence and moderation adopted by his majesty towards that country: for the ultimate success of which I had, in a manner, rendered myself responsible; and, which, in obedience to your instructions, I had uniformly continued to support, even under appearances of the most discouraging nature. I had frequently and distinctly stated to the cabinet of Lisbon, that, in agreeing not to resent the exclusion of British commerce from the ports of Portugal, his majesty had exhausted the means of forbearance; that in making that concession to the peculiar circumstances of the prince-regent's situation, his majesty had done all that friendship and the remembrance of ancient alliance could justly require; but that a single step beyond the line of modified hostility, thus most reluctantly consented to, must necessarily lead to the extremity of actual war.

The prince-regent, however, suffered himself for a moment to forget that, in the present state of Europe, no country could be permitted to be an enemy to England with impunity; and that however much his majesty might be disposed to make allowance for the deficiency of the means possessed by Portugal of resistance to the power of France, neither his own dignity, nor the interests of his people, would permit his majesty to accept an excuse for a compliance with the full extent of her unprincipled demands.

On the 8th instant, his royal highness was induced to sign an order for the detention of the few British subjects, and of the inconsiderable portion of British property which yet remained at Lisbon. On the publication of this order I caused the arms of England to be removed from the gates of my residence, demanded my passports, presented a final remonstrance against the recent conduct of the court of Lisbon, and proceeded to the squadron commanded by Sir Sidney Smith, which arrived off the coast of Portugal some days after I had received my passports, and which I joined on the 17th instant.

I immediately suggested to Sir Sidney Smith the expediency of establishing the most rigorous blockade at the mouth of the Tagus; and I had the high satisfaction of afterwards finding that I had thus anticipated the intentions of his majesty; your despatches (which I received by the messenger, Sylvester, on the 23rd) directing me to authorise that measure, in case the Portuguese government should pass the bounds which his majesty had thought fit to set to his forbearance, and attempt to take any farther step injurious to the honour or interests of Great Britain.

Those despatches were drawn up under the idea that I was still resident at Lisbon, and though I did not receive them until I had actually taken my departure from that court, still, upon a careful consideration of the tenor of your instructions, I thought that it would be right to act as if that case had not occurred. I resolved, therefore, to proceed forthwith to ascertain the effect produced by the blockade of Lisbon, and to propose to the Portuguese government, as the only condition upon which that blockade could cease, the alternative (stated by you) either of surrendering the fleet to his majesty, or of immediately employing it to remove the prince-regent and his family to the Brazils. I took upon myself this responsibility in renewing negotiations after my public functions had actually ceased, convinced that, although it was the fixed determination of his majesty not to suffer the fleet of Portugal to fall into the possession of his enemies, still his majesty's first object continued to be the application of the fleet to the original purpose, of saving the royal family of Braganza from the tyranny of France.

I accordingly requested an audience of the prince-regent, together with due assurances of protection and security; and upon receiving his royal highness's answer, I proceeded to Lisbon, on the 27th, in his majesty's ship *Confiance*, bearing a flag of truce. I had immediately most interesting communications with the court of Lisbon, the particulars of which shall be fully detailed in a future despatch. It suffices to mention in this place, that the prince-regent wisely directed all his apprehensions to a French army, and all his hopes to an English fleet; that he received the most explicit assurances from me that his majesty would generously overlook those acts of unwilling and momentary hostility, to which his royal highness's consent had been extorted; and that I promised to his royal highness, on the faith of my sovereign, that the British squadron before the Tagus should be employed to protect his retreat from Lisbon, and his voyage to the Brazils.

A decree was published yesterday, in which the prince-regent announced his intention of retiring to the city of Rio de Janeiro until the conclusion of a general peace, and of appointing a regency to transact the administration of government at Lisbon during his royal highness's absence from Europe.

This morning the Portuguese fleet left the Tagus. I had the honour to accompany the prince in his passage over the bar. The fleet consisted of eight sail of the line, four large frigates,

several armed brigs, sloops, and corvettes, and a number of
Brazil ships, amounting, I believe, to about thirty-six sail in
all. They passed through the British squadron, and his
majesty's ships fired a salute of twenty-one guns, which was
returned by an equal number. A more interesting spectacle
than that afforded by the junction of the two fleets has been
rarely beheld.

On quitting the prince-regent's ship, I repaired on board
the *Hibernia*, but returned immediately, accompanied by
Sir Sidney Smith, whom I presented to the prince, and who
was received by his royal highness with the most marked and
gracious condescension.

I have the honour to enclose lists of the ships of war which
were known to have left Lisbon this morning, and which were
in sight a few hours ago. There remain at Lisbon four ships
of the line, and the same number of frigates, but only one of
each sort is serviceable.

I have thought it expedient to lose no time in communicating to his majesty's government the important intelligence
contained in this despatch; I have therefore to apologise for
the hasty and imperfect manner in which it is written.

I have the honour to be, etc.

Strangford

Two days later, after the convoy had set sail and was about
sixty miles west of the Tagus, Sir Sidney sent a long report to the
Admiralty setting out, in greater detail, the events of the past
hectic few days. In it he referred to a previous letter, dispatched
a week earlier, in which he informed the Lords Commissioners
of the Admiralty the "misplaced terror of French arms" which
had influenced the Portuguese government to such an extent
that it had acquiesced to certain demands by the French that
certain action should be taken against the British. This, of
course, was a reference to the Prince-Regent's proclamation
mentioned above.

This action, Sir Sidney stated, made it necessary to inform
the Portuguese government that the Tagus should be declared
to be in a state of blockade. With the consent of Lord Strangford
this was done. Nevertheless, bearing in mind the first wise
intention of His Majesty's government which was to open a door
of refuge for the head of the Portuguese government, and considering the necessity of preventing the Tagus from becoming a

French naval base where the "wreck and remnant" of the French and Spanish navies could be reformed, Sir Sidney had thought it his duty to do all he could to endeavour to induce the Prince-Regent of Portugal to reconsider his decision to "unite himself with the continent of Europe" and to remind him that he had possessions on the continent of America, which would off-set any sacrifice he might be called upon to make at home.

Sir Sidney had, therefore, written to the Portuguese Minister of Foreign Affairs and War to this effect and had received the following reply.

Monsieur,

J'ai eu l'honneur de recevoir la depêche de votre excellence, et le prince-regent, maître, m'ordonne de vous déclarer qu'il vient de prendre la résolution de partir dans son escadre, avec toute la famille royale. Aujourd'hui toutes les dispositions pour cet effet seront hâtées, et elle sera prête à sortir après demain. Il souhaite que, pour la fréquence des communications, vous soyez à vue, ou à la baie de Cascaes, autant que les vents le permettront.

J'ai l'honneur d'être, etc.

D'Aranjo

Sir Sidney told the Admiralty that it was with great satisfaction that he was now able to announce that all his hopes and expectations had been realised and that during the night of November 28th the Portuguese fleet sailed down the Tagus and out to sea "with his royal highness the Prince of Brazil and the whole of the royal family of Braganza on board together with many of his faithful councillors and adherents, as well as other persons attached to his poorer fortunes . . . the scene impressed every beholder, except the French army on the hills, with the most lively emotions of gratitude to Providence that there yet existed a power in the world able, as well as willing, to protect the oppressed, inclined to pardon the misguided, and capable, by its fostering care, to found new empires and alliances from the wreck of the old ones, destroyed by the ephemeral power of the day, on the lasting basis of mutual interest."

Lord St Vincent, who could not stand Sir Sidney at any price, had ceased to be First Lord of the Admiralty in 1804 and did not, therefore, see this letter. It is not difficult to imagine what he would have said, had he read the flowery peroration with which it ended: "our Knight of the Sword is at it again!"

But the royal party only just got away in time and the convoy was still within sight of land when General Junot marched into Lisbon at the head of his bedraggled, half-starved troops. It was lucky that Lord Strangford had only allowed the Prince-Regent five hours in which to embark. Had he extended it by only a few hours the ships would not have been able to put out to sea, for the wind was getting up and by next morning a raging gale was blowing.

Had Junot arrived in time to oppose the flight of the royal family there might have been a very different story to tell, for something else had gone wrong. Sir John Moore had received orders from the War Office early in October to leave Messina at once, with his eight thousand troops, and proceed to Gibraltar where he was to leave two battalions, to reinforce the garrison, and return with the remainder of his force to England.

Owing to a certain amount of muddle and a little bad luck, including contrary winds, after a late start, he only arrived at Gibraltar on 1st December by which time, of course, the Royal family were already embarked and on their way to Brazil.

On arrival at Gibraltar, however, Sir John found fresh orders waiting for him. These instructed him to get in touch with Lord Strangford immediately in case the help of British troops was needed to cover the embarkation. If and when the royal family embarked, Sir John was to accompany them as far as Madeira and take possession of the island. Should the Prince-Regent decide not to go to Brazil, but to enter into a convention with France to close all her ports to British ships, then Sir John was to send a force to take possession of the island whose Governor already had orders to surrender if summoned to do so. Finally, should Lord Strangford be obliged to quit Lisbon, in consequence of the measures Portugal might take, Sir John was to proceed to the mouth of the Tagus and act in concert with Sir Sidney Smith's wishes. Sir Sidney, however, was to get in touch with Moore.

When Sir John arrived in Gibraltar, however, no word had come from either Sir Sidney or Lord Strangford. Neither of them had bothered to send any message or information to Sir John, to Admiral Purvis, who was carrying out a blockade of Cadiz, or even to Sir Hew Dalrymple, the Governor of Gibraltar. This omission was quite inexcusable, for the success or failure of the royal departure from Lisbon might well have turned upon the arrival of Moore and his troops. Sir John Fortescue, in his *History of the British Army*, calls Smith's conduct almost criminal but "knowing the man as we do," he wrote, "we shall probably not be wrong in ascribing his conduct to his incorrigible jealousy and selfishness."

Whatever may have been the motive for this failure, if, indeed, there was one, the complete silence from Lisbon did not help Moore, particularly as Dalrymple's information was that the general attitude of Portugal to England was decidedly hostile and that troops had been withdrawn from the frontier and concentrated in the forts at Lisbon to resist any attack.

Sir John wrote in his diary that as it would take at least eight days to get his troopships revictualled and supplied with water he decided to go at once by sea to Lisbon to get in touch with Sir Sidney and find out what the situation was. A strong wind had been blowing from the south-west and it was not until the afternoon of 4th December that Sir John was able to set sail. Twenty-four hours later they sighted some ships from Admiral Purvis's squadron, which was blockading Cadiz, and Sir John had an opportunity of talking to the Captain of the *Bulwark* who told him that as far as he knew Sir Sidney was still off the mouth of the Tagus, that Lord Strangford had sailed for England and that the Portuguese Prince-Regent had decided not to go to Brazil and had closed the port of Lisbon to all British ships. This was, of course, quite untrue; and it was not until two days later, 8th December, that Sir John learnt that the royal family were well on their way to Brazil and that his own brother, Captain Moore, was in command of the ships protecting the convoy. Sir John, therefore, decided to return to Gibraltar, but he never heard from Smith or Strangford. "This is most unaccountable conduct on their part," he wrote in his diary on 13th December. "I can only conclude that some other arrangement has been made which makes my aid in taking possession of Madeira unnecessary. I have, therefore, determined to return to England."*

Although Sir Sidney had not bothered to let Moore know what had happened he found time to write to the Secretary of the Admiralty from his flagship on 6th December.

* The expedition to Madeira had, in fact, been entrusted to General Beresford. He arrived off the island with 3,600 men on 24th December and received its surrender after guaranteeing that it would be returned to Portugal after the war. Two battalions were left there as a garrison.

Sir Sidney Smith to the Secretary of the Admiralty
                    Hibernia, at sea, lat. 37° 47¹ long. 14° 17¹,
                                        December 6, 1807.

Sir,

I have the satisfaction to acquaint you, for the information of my lords commissioners of the admiralty, that I succeeded in collecting the whole of the Portuguese fleet except a brig, after the gale, and that the weather was such as to allow the necessary repairs, and such distribution of supernumeraries and resources to be made, as to enable Vice-Admiral Don Manuel da Cunha, Sottomayor, to report to me yesterday all the ships capable of performing the voyage to Rio Janeiro, except one line-of-battle ship, which he requested might be conducted to an English port; I meant to escort her part of the way, but she did not quit the fleet with me last night as settled. I hope, however, she may arrive safe, as she is not in a bad state, being substituted for the *Martino de Freitas*, which was at first destined to go to England, in consequence of a fresh arrangement made yesterday, on the latter being found in the best state for the voyage of the two. I have detached Captain Moore in the *Marlborough*, with the *London*, *Monarch*, and *Bedford*, to attend the Portuguese fleet to the Brazils.

I have thought it my duty, in addition to the usual order, to direct him to take the above ships under his orders, and also to give him, Captain Moore, an additional one, to hoist a broad pennant after passing Madeira; in order to give him greater weight and consequence in the performance of the important and unusually delicate duties I have confided to him. I feel the most perfect reliance in that officer's judgment, ability, and zeal.

The Portuguese ships did not, after this repartition, want more provisions or slops from us than the list enclosed, which I supplied from this ship and the *Conqueror*.

This dispatch will be delivered by Captain Yeo, of his majesty's sloop *Confiance*, who has shewn great address and zeal in opening the communications by flag of truce, which it was the interest of those in power, who were against the measure of emigration, to obstruct. Lord Strangford speaks of his conduct in terms of warm approbation: on this ground I beg leave to recommend him to their lordships, to whom his general merits as an officer are already well known. Having been in Lisbon without restraint, during the intercourse, he is qualified to answer any questions their lordships may wish to put to him.

I have the honour to be, etc.

W. Sidney Smith

In reply he received unstinted praise from the Lords Commissioners which might have been less enthusiastic had the letter, written on their behalf by the Hon. W. W. Pole, not been despatched before Moore had returned to England to report to the War Office his scurvy treatment by Sir Sidney.

The Hon. W. W. Pole to Captain Sir Sidney Smith

Admiralty Office, December 28, 1807.

Sir,

I lost no time in laying your despatches, brought by Captain Yeo of his majesty's ship *Confiance*, and by the Trafalgar letter of marque, before my lords commissioners of the admiralty; and I am commanded by their lordships to express their high approbation of your judicious and able conduct, in the management of the service entrusted to your charge, and in the execution of the various orders you have received from time to time.

Their lordships are strongly impressed with the propriety of the whole of your conduct towards the royal family of Portugal: the respectful attention which you appear to have shewn to the illustrious house of Braganza, has been in strict conformity to their lordships' wishes, and they have directed me to express their complete satisfaction at the manner in which you have in this, as well as in every other respect, obeyed their instructions.

My lords are pleased to approve of your having supplied the necessary succours to the Portuguese fleet from his majesty's ships; and I am commanded to acquaint you, that, under the peculiar circumstances of the case, their lordships are satisfied of the necessity of your resuming in person the strict blockade of the Tagus, and they approve of your having detached from your squadron four sail of the line, under the command of Captain Moore, to escort the royal family of Portugal to Rio de Janeiro.

My lords concur in the propriety of your directing the officer in command of the squadron, destined for this important service, to hoist a broad pennant after he had passed

Madeira, and they approve of the instructions to Captain Moore, and of the selection you have made of that distinguished and judicious officer.

I have the honour to be, etc.

W. W. Pole

Towards the end of December Admiral Sir Charles Cotton was sent to relieve Sir Sidney of his command of the squadron off the Tagus, but it was not until 29th February 1808 that he handed over having, meanwhile, received orders from the Admiralty to proceed to South America and resume command of the squadron which had taken the Prince-Regent of Portugal to Brazil.

And so another of Sir Sidney's special missions was ended. His conduct while stationed off the Tagus came in for a great deal of criticism from many quarters and it cannot be denied that much of this was deserved. Sir Sidney's confidence in himself was overweening and there was nothing he liked more than to be number one. There is little, if any, doubt that his failure to keep Moore informed of the events then taking place in Lisbon was deliberate and that he hoped, in this way, to win all the credit for himself.

Nevertheless, he was never lacking in big ideas, nor was he diffident in conveying them to those in authority, and it is not surprising to learn that, within a few days of arriving off the coast of Portugal, he sent the following memorandum to his old chief Admiral Lord Keith, who was then at the Admiralty:

Sir Sidney Smith to Lord Keith:
On the Transfer of the Portuguese Government to the Brazils

If the Portuguese Government could be made sensible of the degradation, and probably the destruction which awaits them, or, if a sufficient degree of energy could be roused among them, there would still be time enough to snatch them from the destiny that is hanging over them, and lay the foundation of a mighty and magnificent empire, which would speedily compensate the loss of Portugal, and preserve (if it be considered worth preserving) the Portuguese name.

This might be effected by transporting the Court, and all its effects (as was once intended to be done) and a selection of the best troops, with all their ships of war to the Brazils. With the assistance of Great Britain, every preparation for such a step could be completed in a few days : their ships are in a sufficient state of forwardness to carry off whatever was intended to be removed to the island of Madeira, which is but three days sail from Lisbon, where, with two or three sail of British line-of-battle ships to protect them, they might remain as securely as in a British port from any attack of the enemy, until fully equipped for their ulterior destination. The Portuguese being firmly attached to their name, and to the family on the throne, there is little doubt that numbers would be disposed to take advantage of leaving the country for another, where nothing is wanting but an adequate population, to supply every kind of produce for commerce and consumption.

Although the Spaniards of Europe affect to despise the Portuguese, it is not improbable that the heterogeneous classes of which the population of South America is composed might gradually be brought under one government, and the more readily, as there is some similarity in their language and their religion is the same. The demand of this great empire for the manufacturers of Europe, and the valuable produce it would have to offer in return, especially of naval stores, is a consideration of no small moment to Great Britain.

13

THE BRAZILS

THERE was still much to be done, however, before Sir Sidney was ready to sail across the Atlantic, and it was not until 17th May that he sailed into the harbour of Rio de Janeiro in H.M.S. *London*. There he received a great welcome from the Prince-Regent, the Princess of Brazil and all the comrades-at-arms who had served under him off the Tagus.

His first report from Brazil was sent to the Admiralty on 20th June:

Sir Sidney Smith to the Honourable W. W. Pole

His Majesty's ship *London*, Rio de Janeiro,
June 20 1808.

Sir,

Commodore Moore will have so fully stated all the circumstances of the voyage and arrival of the combined squadron, and the establishment of the government of Portugal in this colony, that it is only necessary for me to state the events subsequent to my arrival on the 17th of May. The first public act, concerning the combined squadrons, was the appointment of his royal highness the Infant of Spain, Don Pedro Carlos, nephew to the prince-regent, as high-admiral of Portugal, by which appointment, I learn from the Viscount d'Anadia, minister of marine, that his functions as to all internal regulations of the navy had ceased; and they seem now to be confined to the ultra-marine governments, viz. the Islands, Africa, and Goa. This continental colony, that was in that department being now of course in that of the minister of the interior. His royal highness's flag is not flying, nor was it hoisted on board any ship the day the prince-regent did me the honour to dine on board the ship bearing my flag, on the 4th of June; when the king's birth-day was celebrated in due form; the whole royal family (except the Queen and Princess-dowager of Brazils), the ministers, and the whole court being present on board. On that occasion, his royal highness wore the standard of Portugal in his barge;

it was hoisted at the fore, while his majesty's royal standard was, as usual on his birth-day, at the main, where it remained till after his majesty's health, his own, and other appropriate healths were drunk, when his royal highness ordered his to be hauled down and presented to me, by the senior commodore of his royal navy present, desiring me 'to wear the arms of Portugal as thereon emblazoned, with those of my family and my descendants for ever, in memory of the 29th of November, 1807, and of that auspicious day when he was engaged in celebrating the birth-day of his august ally, on board one of the ships of his royal navy'.

His royal highness was pleased to express himself as highly gratified on this occasion, both by himself and his minister; and I, of course, cultivate the most perfect good understanding with every individual member of this government, from the highest to the lowest, for the advancement of the alliance and the good of his majesty's service. The injunction given by their lordships, in their letter, as to avoiding giving offence to the inhabitants of these countries, has been duly circulated by me; and I am happy to be able to say there has been no complaint of aggressions on our part, nor has the government been deficient in endeavouring to trace the authors of disturbance, when individuals of this nation have been in some few instances guilty thereof. The discipline preserved by Commodore Moore and the captains of the squadron I detached under his command, and the hospitality shewn by them was such as to lay the basis of the harmony which so happily exists; and his royal highness has been pleased to decorate them with medals, and to revive the Order of the Sword established by Alphonso V., commemorative of the great event of the translation of an European government to this side of the Atlantic and to this hemisphere. His royal highness the prince-regent and his ministers look with anxiety to the prevention of the arrival of any French force in the River Plate, or of arms being landed on the south shore. I accordingly mean to keep the squadron cruising in succession, which will preserve them in health and in a proper state as to efficiency.

I have the honour to be, etc.

W. Sidney Smith

For a short time Sir Sidney was in his element and was

treated like a little tin god. The Portuguese royal family and the aristocracy lionised him and he was given permission to quarter the royal arms of Braganza with his own, and the British government were congratulating themselves on having the right man in the right place. It was not long, however, before he found himself, once again, in serious trouble. Brazil was the only large Portuguese colony and the possibility of a French landing in the River Plate was an ever present danger to its safety. The Prince-Regent and the Minister for War and Foreign Affairs, therefore, approached Sir Sidney for naval assistance to patrol the coast and ward off any attempted French landing and at the same time informed him that he had sent a senior army officer, Marshal Curado, to Buenos Aires to negotiate for the return of St Sacramento, on the River Plate, which had formerly been Portuguese territory, in exchange for a commercial treaty.

If these negotiations were to fail, however, it would be necessary for Portuguese troops to occupy the north bank of the river as the only means of preventing the French from doing it. In that event the Prince-Regent would expect Sir Sidney to cover the operation from the sea with the naval force under his command, and hoped that the Admiral would take command of the whole expedition.

Smith reported all this to the Admiralty, for he doubtless recognised its gravity. His Royal Highness, he wrote, had urged this upon him with much persuasion and enthusiasm and seemed surprised when Sir Sidney did not appear to share it. Nevertheless there was no suggestion in the report that he had definitely refused to play any part in the affair and he specifically stated that he did not refuse the request that he should command the Portuguese element of the force as there was no British army officer there competent to do so.

It was not long before he went a step further and began talking of "reducing the refractory people in Buenos Aires in the provinces of La Plata by the force of our combined army (in which combination I should hope to include the Spanish royal forces) by sending Portuguese men-of-war round Cape Horn to those coasts under the command of the Spanish prince Don Carlos, nephew of King Charles IV and, therefore, a cousin of the Prince-Regent's wife who was the King's daughter."

Sir Sidney ended his letter by saying that he trusted that it would be considered by H.M. Government that he was, so far, acting within his sphere but he also, rather unwisely, concluded his letter with a threat. "If the general confidence I enjoy here is withheld from me I may be allowed respectfully to withdraw from so weighty, responsible and ruinous a situation as the chief commandant afloat here, and take another line of service, till the country's interests may no longer be in danger, when I can conscientiously retire altogether."

Very soon after sending this letter home Sir Sidney received information that another flag officer, Rear Admiral de Courcy, was coming out to join him. There was, however, no suggestion that de Courcy had been sent to supersede him. Meanwhile Strangford, who had been re-appointed British Ambassador to the Portuguese Court at Rio de Janeiro, and resented Sir Sidney's great influence at the Court, had been frantically pulling strings to get him recalled, so far without any success. There had always been great rivalry between them, Strangford was young and ambitious and Smith's intransigeance had become a household word. Both of them had tried to obtain the sole credit for persuading the Prince-Regent to leave his invaded country, whereas all the documentary evidence shows that it was due to neither of them and that the suggestion had been conveyed through Strangford personally from George Canning long before Sir Sidney ever reached the Tagus.

H.M.S. *Diana*, however, with Rear Admiral de Courcy on board, arrived at Rio early in May 1809, and had hardly dropped anchor before de Courcy received the following letter from the British Ambassador:

Lord Strangford to the Honourable M. de Courcy
Rio de Janeiro, May 12, 1809.

Sir,

I have been officially called upon to procure the execution of the arrangement which I announced to this court several days ago, as well in his majesty's name, as by his majesty's command.

It is earnestly desired by this court that you should assume the command of his majesty's squadron upon this station. It was supposed (in consequence of the assurances which I was authorised to give to that effect) that on your arrival at Rio de Janeiro, the command of the squadron would immediately have devolved upon you; and that an application of this nature would have been altogether unnecessary.

It is not my design to interfere in any manner with the rules of his majesty's naval service. But it is absolutely my duty to state to you the just expectations which have been formed by the Portuguese government, and thus to secure the attainments of the objects which his majesty had most undoubtedly in view, when you were commanded to proceed to this station.

I have the honour to be, etc.

Strangford

De Courcy was extremely embarrassed when he was invited next day to be present at a review of the Portuguese troops and, at the same time, to be officially received at Court. Very properly, he replied saying that he thanked His Royal Highness for the invitation but that as the objects mentioned in the Ambassador's letter could only be brought into effect with the concurrence of Sir Sidney, who was his senior as a rear-admiral, he had taken the opportunity of showing Sir Sidney the Ambassador's letter and he now had the honour to enclose a copy of the reply which he had received.

Sir Sidney Smith to the Hon. M. de Courcy

H.M.S. *Foudroyant*, Rio de Janeiro, May 13 1809.

Sir,

In answer to your letter of yesterday's date, enclosing one and a note from his majesty's envoy of the same date, which you have very properly laid before me, with your request that I will instruct you how you shall act upon, and reply to, them; and these letters containing requisitions to you, that I do not think it proper that you should comply with, in the exact manner therein pointed out, as being contrary to the rules of his majesty's naval service; and as his majesty's envoy expresses himself as not having the design to interfere in any manner therewith, it will, I hope, be sufficient for you to explain to him, that the commission you bear from the Lords Commissioners of the Admiralty directs you to obey all orders that you may receive from a superior officer; that I am such superior, that I have given orders by signal, which I hereby repeat, for all persons belonging to the fleet to repair on board their respective ships immediately, and that no boats are to be sent on shore after this signal has been made, without leave from the admiral, which you cannot disobey; consequently that you cannot meet him at the appointed time and place without my leave which you have not obtained.

I have the honour to be, etc.

W. Sidney Smith

De Courcy carried out the Admiral's instructions and the fat was now really in the fire. Two days later Lord Strangford sent a long despatch to Canning about the whole incident and Sir Sidney's days in Rio were numbered.

"Sir Sidney," Lord Strangford wrote, "still avails himself of his professional seniority to retain chief command of his majesty's naval forces upon this station and he has not hitherto manifested any inclination to relinquish that authority.

"On the 12th inst. (the day preceding the anniversary of the prince-regent's birth-day) I received from Condé de Linhares a note, of which a copy is enclosed herewith, together with an intimation from the prince-regent, conveyed to me by General Montaury, the commander-in-chief of the Portuguese forces in this district, that, on the following morning a review of several regiments would take place, and that it was his royal highness's wish that I should invite Admiral de Courcy and his officers to come on shore to view it from the windows of the palace. His royal highness did me the honour personally to make similar communications to me in the course of that day; and accordingly, I wrote to Admiral de Courcy a letter and note, of which copies are enclosed.

"On the following day the prince-regent was grieved and mortified to find that Admiral de Courcy did not appear at the palace at the appointed time. But the astonishment of his royal highness exceeded all bounds when he was informed, in the very words of Sir Sidney Smith, that he (Sir Sidney Smith) 'had not judged proper to give permission to Admiral de Courcy to leave his ship.'

"It is true that Admiral de Courcy did afterwards attend at the palace to pay his respects to his royal highness the prince-regent, but not until the end of the spectacle to which his royal highness had invited him, but which he was prevented from witnessing by this exercise of Sir Sidney Smith's authority as a senior officer.

"I have the honour to enclose herewith a copy of the letter which I received from Admiral de Courcy, explaining to me the cause of his apparent inattention to the commands of the prince-regent, and transmitting to me the letter addressed to him by Sir Sidney Smith, (of which a copy is also enclosed,) which had deterred him from accepting his royal highness's invitation.

"I have likewise the honour to annex a copy of a letter which I have written to Admiral de Courcy, by desire of the prince-regent, expressive of the feelings with which his royal highness the prince-regent has regarded the conduct of Sir Sidney Smith in this very singular affair."

After that events moved quickly, and on instructions received from the Admiralty Sir Sidney handed over his command to de Courcy only eight days later. When he did so, which was on 24th May, he drew up very lengthy written instructions for the new admiral in which he gave him a full picture of the strategic position of Brazil and then went on to tell de Courcy that it was more than likely that he would experience similar trouble.

"Having now communicated everything which occurs to me as useful for your guidance," he wrote, "it remains for me only to express my readiness to give you any explanation you may require, on any point where I may not have been sufficiently explicit, my sole and earnest wish being, that success may crown your endeavours for the public service, in which I trust and hope you will have less trouble than I have had.

"In making over a copy of instructions, under which you are to act, containing an injunction grounded on the admitted necessity, that the person accredited by his majesty to the prince-regent should obtain the undivided confidence of that sovereign, I cannot refrain from remarking to you, the impossibility of that ever taking effect. Where that confidence has been impaired by the mistatements of the individual so accredited confidence cannot be commanded, and it cannot be in the power of the British admiral to aid him, in obtaining what has been sacrificed to the objects of impairing the degree of confidence, which his royal highness has been pleased to place in an officer of that rank, at whose discretion, as to destination, he placed his person, royal family, fleet, and treasure, without waiting for any other guarantee than the honour of the individual, and towards whom his royal highness has often expressed gratitude for the mode in which that discretion was exercised, manifesting his entire confidence on various occasions since, and which he has expressed himself to be sensible has never been abused.

"It would be necessary, for the attainment of the above desideratum, that his royal highness should be able to obliterate from his memory the real motives and facts, relative to and connected with his emigration from Lisbon, and then to admit the truth of the record, as it appeared in the 'Gazette' of December, 1807, which his royal highness has denied in conversation with me, and many other respectable persons. If intercourse with all such persons, who might be able to undeceive him, and enlighten a mind thirsting after knowledge and truth, opportunities for attaining which were denied in early life, would have been precluded, as was and is attempted, this accredited person might have obtained an exclusive influence, such as he is endeavouring in vain to exercise on less general principles; but as long as his royal highness shall prefer frankness, candour, and benevolence, as he does, to the opposite qualities in mankind, he will seek general intercourse, in the hope of finding them; and on this ground it is that I earnestly solicit you, sire, *not to allow yourself to be excluded, or allow those officers to be so, of sufficient rank to be admitted to the confidential intercourse.* His royal highness has repeatedly told me he wishes to cultivate the British navy and to be excluded from such intercourse with the person exercising the sovereign authority here who is deserving of every respectful attention from us collectively and individually and by these means his royal highness will preserve and cultivate the predilection for the British character, which he professes and evidently feels.

"Before concluding I feel it incumbent upon me, in my public duty, to warn you officially and distinctly, that I have not found his majesty's minister plenipotentiary to act frankly and cordially with me, as the admiral on this station, and that my experience does not warrant my giving you any ground for expectation, that he will do so with you, or for placing any confidence in the uniformity of any system on which he may be apparently acting with you, in his occasional vague and rare communications with a British admiral, whom he arrogantly manifests himself to consider, as a subordinate officer under his command, even in a sphere beyond the limits of his accreditation, not admitting, that where responsibility is placed a power of acting according to instructions must necessarily reside in the same person."

This was strong stuff but there was probably a good deal of

truth in it. As things turned out Sir Sidney's warning was unnecessary for Strangford himself was recalled a few weeks later.

At the time he handed over command to de Courcy the two
admirals changed ships and on the 9th August Smith arrived at
Spithead in H.M.S. *Diana*. He lost no time in going to see the
Foreign Secretary to discuss Strangford's letter and give
Canning his own version of the incident. Of what happened at
that interview there is no record, but the Foreign Secretary
must have had some reservations about the degree of blame
which really rested on Smith's shoulders as the ensuing correspondence, written more than ten months later, clearly shows.

In the first of these letters, which was written by Canning to
Smith on 21st July 1810, the former Foreign Secretary, who was
no longer a member of the Cabinet, stated that he had discussed the whole matter with Lord Wellesley since the interview
on the subject of Smith's conduct in Brazil, and had told him
that the main reason for recalling Smith was because at that
time Canning was under the impression, obviously given to him
by Strangford, that Smith had "arrogated to himself in his
transactions respecting Spanish America an authority not
derived from any instructions given him by H.M. Government". This impression Canning wrote, "was completely
removed by the secret despatch addressed to you from the war
department on 5th August 1808 which you communicated to
me in our first interview, and of which I had previously no
knowledge whatever." There still remained, however, one other
aspect of the matter which, in Canning's opinion, was the most
"extraordinary and reprehensible part" of Smith's conduct,
namely, his witholding the information from Lord Strangford.
On this he had not been misinformed; he had not been
informed at all. It was only at the first interview with Sir Sidney
that the Foreign Secretary learnt, for the first time, that the
'Mr B' who had delivered the secret despatch was authorised,
or professed to be authorised, to caution Sir Sidney not to
communicate the contents of the despatch nor any of the
circumstances connected with his mission to Lord Strangford.
The real reason for writing this letter, after such a long interval
of time, was that Canning wanted to make sure that in his
desire to do justice to Sir Sidney he had not been "led beyond
the exact truth", and he asked the Admiral to confirm that this
was so.

Sir Sidney was delighted to receive such a letter and hastened to confirm in writing what he had said at the interview, namely, that 'Mr B' made a special point about not communicating the information to Strangford and in such definite terms as to leave Sir Sidney absolutely no discretion whatever in the matter.

"I might confine my answer to this simple fact, in exculpation of myself after your distinct and frank admission of it on this ground, if I thought myself alone," he wrote, "and I might leave my case to your candour and liberality, my confidence in which, under the conviction of my correctness, has induced me to wait thus patiently for justice at your hands as a voluntary act, when the whole truth should be known to you, rather than press you on the subject, or appeal formally otherwise than to yourself, from the decision you made against me on the *ex-parte* statement of Lord Strangford, and the prince-regent's premature expressions of momentary disapprobation, not being aware of their real character and motives; but, a regard for truth and the good of the king's service, render me apprehensive lest an error should subsist in your mind as to the origin of this caution, on a supposition that it had reference to the *official situation* of Lord Strangford; whereas the person communicating it to me expressly stated, that it originated with himself, as the condition *sine qua non* of his undertaking such a delicate commission, and regarded Lord Strangford personally; his own experience of his lordship's conduct towards himself in Portugal rendering any connexion with him in such affairs repugnant to his feelings, and occasioning an apprehension for his safety, which made him anxious not to expose himself to such risks again. A sentiment which has been painfully awakened in me, and which I have found to be general among all who have had occasion to transact business of a delicate nature with Lord Strangford; at all events, the caution was imperative on me, as the despatch referred me distinctly to the discretion of the bearer."

Canning's reply put an end to the matter once and for all. He began by saying that the existence of the secret despatch made it quite clear that there was no justification for the specific charge of Sir Sidney "having arrogated to himself an authority not derived from any instructions". He did not want it to be thought, however, that he necessarily agreed with the manner in which the 'discretion' had been exercised. What he still thought about that was now no longer relevant nor, in his

opinion, were the *motives* which were the reason for the pro-
hibition to communicate with Lord Strangford, at all material
to the case, as far as Sir Sidney was concerned. "The charge
against you," Canning wrote, "was that you had withholden
from the knowledge of the king's minister at Rio de Janeiro the
instructions under which you acted and your answer to that
charge is that you were positively directed to do so. This defence
is perfect and satisfactory. For the propriety of the restriction
you are not responsible."

Sir Sidney must, indeed, have been glad to put that incident
behind him but there was still one more vexation with which he
had to deal, for Lord Strangford, just before he was recalled
from his appointment in Rio, had tried to give him one last
stab in the back.

In October 1809 Sir Sidney had sent Captain Sir James Yeo,
in command of two cruisers in his squadron one of which, the
Confiance, was commanded by Yeo himself, down the coast as
far as the Rio de la Plata to find out whether the French were
active in that vicinity either on sea or on land. If he sighted any
French ships or troops he was to take such action as he thought
warrantable in the circumstances. Putting in at Para he conferred with the Portuguese Governor there and they decided
to mount a joint expedition on the nearby island of Cayenne,
which belonged to France and it was captured without much
difficulty. Cayenne was not of any particular strategic importance but the value of the stores captured there, cloves,
nutmegs and pepper, was considerable in the region of a
hundred and eighty-five thousand pounds.

It is true that the credit for this operation was Yeo's alone but
there was no reason to suppose that Smith would do anything to
take it from him. Whatever his faults all his despatches to the
Admiralty in the past had proved beyond any doubt that the
Admiral was the first to praise and give credit to his sub-
ordinates when they had earned it. In any event the *Confiance*
only returned to Rio with news of the surrender of Cayenne
to the forces under Yeo's command three days after Smith had
handed over his command and it would have been de Courcy's
duty to report the result of the action to the Admiralty.

There was, therefore, no justification for the letter which
Strangford wrote to Canning on 7th June 1809 and it can only
have been written for reasons of personal spite.

Lord Strangford to Mr Canning

Rio de Janeiro, June 7, 1809.

Sir,

On the 27th ult. his majesty's ship the *Confiance* arrived here with intelligence of the surrender of Cayenne to the combined British and combined forces.

It is certain that the success of this achievement has been principally owing to the valour and conduct of Captain Yeo, and of the British officers and seamen under his command. And it is but justice to Captain Yeo to mention another circumstance, which will very probably be *suppressed* in any details of the affair which that officer may transmit to his majesty's government. It is not only the actual success of the enterprise against Cayenne which is due to Captain Yeo: the original plan of the expedition was solely conceived by himself and even the Portuguese governor of Para does not hesitate to declare frankly that the entire merit of the design is to be attributed to Captain Yeo.

I have the honour to be, etc.

Strangford

14

MEDITERRANEAN AGAIN

WHEN Sir Sidney struck his flag on returning home on 9th August 1809 there was no immediate prospect of further employment and he was to enjoy almost three years leave on half-pay. This, according to John Barrow,* he appears to have done, as he "entered into society and enjoyed all its gaieties and amusements to which he had for some time been a stranger". He also took to himself a wife, the widow of Sir George Rumbold who had, at one time, been the British consul in Hamburg.

On 12th July 1812, however, at Portsmouth he hoisted his flag once more, this time in the *Tremendous* and was appointed second in command of a fleet which was about to join Sir Edward Pellew, the new commander in the Mediterranean theatre of war. *En route* to join Pellew he put in at Carthagena where he helped General Ross strengthen its defence. A report of his activities was sent by him to the Horse Guards, instead of to the Admiralty, which would have been the correct procedure, with the request that it should be communicated to Lord Wellington. This got him into more hot water and he was reprimanded, not for the first time, for not sending it through the proper channels.

Throughout his service life Sir Sidney had always believed in going straight to the fountain head whenever possible, and as the recommendations made in his letter concerned His Majesty's land forces he decided that Wellington was the right man to see them. It is often the best way to get something done, but it does not endear one to those who take umbrage at having been short circuited. His letter is set out below.

Sir Sidney Smith to The Horse Guards
> *Tremendous*, in Escombrera Bay, Carthagena,
> Sept. 21, 1812.

Sir,

As Vice-Admiral Sir Richard Keats, whom I have relieved

---

* The author of *The Life and Correspondence of Admiral Sir Sidney Smith* (1848).

on the Mediterranean station, will probably not have intercourse with Cadiz, I think it right to communicate to you the
information I have received from the eastward by him, who
called off this port yesterday. I therefore send for your
perusal the enclosed documents, the contents of which you
may perhaps think proper to communicate to Lord Wellington, together with my earnest recommendation to his lordship
that this important and only port by which the navy can
effectually supply the army in the south of the peninsula, be
defended by a competent body of troops. Those at Alicante
may be, and I believe are, very well posted for their own
safety, but they there defend a comparatively unimportant
part of the coast, whereas here they not only defend *themselves*
while inferior to the armies concentrating here against them,
but a *naval station*, the only one on the coast, and of more use
than Cadiz, in our operations in the heart of the Peninsula.
I have not withheld this opinion from Admiral Hallowell,
who may communicate it to General Maitland if it is
required.

   I have thought it my duty while Soult was pointing this
way by the Lorca road, to devote every hour of the time a
Levant wind gives me, by retarding my progress eastward
towards the fleet off Toulon where the presence of the
second in command thereof is requisite, to co-operating with
General Ross in making every arrangement for the defence
of this place against a *coup de main*, to which it was absolutely
exposed before the wall on the eastern height of St Sult was
built as high as it is now by twelve feet, and before the
approaches to it were flanked by a fire from a battery commanding those forces of the (illegible)* which it could not
itself see or flank. An order from the Spanish government
seems requisite, as also the means such as *pitch*, of which there
is none, and wages for a few shipwrights, to put the remaining
Spanish gun-boats here in a state for action. We have but
three of the whole number, brought out in an active state.
The order for the frigate *Solidad* to go round to Cadiz
fortunately cannot be executed for want of sailors to navigate
her; she is more useful where she is at present, as a rendezvous
and shelter for the men employed in the gun-boat service in
winter, and I hope she may be allowed to remain, and
Captain Carrol, whose division I have ordered may be

* Some words in this letter are illegible.

authorised to make use of her for that purpose till an English frigate under his command may be so appropriated. I name him as being most competent, most richly deserving post rank, and most anxious to continue to serve. The garrison of Ceuta is useless where it is and starving. Here it would earn and might receive its bread.

I have the honour to be, sir,

Your most obedient humble servant,

W. Sidney Smith

Ten days later, however, on 30th September, when off Toulon, he did write to the Admiralty announcing that he had joined up with Sir Edward, and he enclosed copies of correspondence relating to the vulnerability of Carthagena which was almost surrounded by a large French army.

"I trust I have left it out of immediate danger of a *coup de main*," he wrote, "whatever may be the enemy's intention, and I have no reason to think he will afford himself time to make a regular siege of the place; however, he might desire to possess himself of the valuable park of artillery there, containing a supply of all the western army under Marshal Soult, which has been observed to be left behind. Joseph Buonaparte, it is understood, is withdrawn with the force he brought with him from Madrid, towards the Ebro, where it is expected Marshal Soult will take a position, as he has sent his heavy ordnance to Tortosa and in that direction."

On this occasion, also, Sir Sidney was told by the Secretary of the Admiralty, through Sir Edward Pellew, "that their lordships are greatly surprised at receiving these communications direct from him, which, if necessary to be communicated at all, should have been transmitted to his commander-in-chief whom their lordships cannot permit to be set aside and passed over by a flag-officer serving under his command."

Most of what proved to be the last two years of Sir Sidney's service life did not provide the excitement without which he found life extremely tedious, and except for one assignment of the kind he most enjoyed, when he was sent by Sir Edward to Cagliari in Sardinia, he had plenty of time on his hands. He set up a printing press in the *Hibernia*, started a library, and organised an amateur dramatic society to amuse the ship's company and pass the time.

As there appeared to be little likelihood of the French fleet coming out to do battle, the Commander-in-Chief sent several of his ships to show the flag in some of the countries bordering on the Mediterranean with which England was not at war and Sir Sidney, in his flagship, was ordered to proceed to Cagliari where one of His Majesty's ships had been fired on while she was trying to examine a French ship.

As usual, he by-passed all the local officials and went straight to the King, Victor Emmanuel, and his principal Minister, Chevalier Rossi. After a number of private audiences with the King Sir Sidney wrote to Sir Edward:

I have obtained the most distinct assurances of a ready co-operation against the common enemy . . . The King of Sardinia was graciously pleased to mark, in the eyes of his subjects, the mutual confidence existing between the two nations, by selecting the fourth of June, being the birth-day of his Majesty, George III, to pay me (as his Sardinian Majesty was pleased to say) a personal visit on board the *Hibernia* on that day, with his queen, royal family, and court. I, of course, received them with the honours due to crowned heads, and royal persons connected with the imperial family of Austria, by a double marriage; the Archduke Francis and his Archduchess, the King of Sardinia's eldest daughter, being with their majesties, although they had before visited the ship.

Previously to the repast, customary on such anniversaries and on such occasions, their majesties and the royal family visited every deck of the ship, and their admiration and satisfaction were manifested, in the most condescending and obliging manner. On this occasion I should be wanting in justice to the captain and first lieutenant and other officers of the *Hibernia*, if I did not record my own satisfaction at the good order and cleanliness, in every respect constantly maintained on board her, and the consequent fitness to bear the very minute inspection which hath been bestowed upon her by his Sardinian majesty, and many thousands of his subjects, who thronged daily to see her, as an object of stupendous and awful novelty to them.

The queen was graciously pleased to send, as a present to the ship's company, a handsome proportion of refreshments, consisting of five bullocks and three pipes of wine, which it was thought respectful gratefully to accept.

My mission ended by closing the official correspondence in the way you will observe, by the enclosures, in perfect harmony and good understanding, and I am now on my way to join your flag on your rendezvous.

The Commander-in-chief, however, does not appear to have been very impressed; he dismissed the whole affair as just another of Smith's junketings. He also wrote to the Admiralty and suggested that as the British Chargé d'Affaires in Sardinia happened, at that moment, to be in London it gave His Majesty's ministers an opportunity of preventing any recurrence of cause for complaint in the future "as it did not appear that any security had been obtained from the result of Sir Sidney's mission. No formal treaty or agreement had been executed and only royal assurances had been obtained."

This was very uncharitable of Sir Edward as Smith's visit to Sardinia had, in fact, been another diplomatic triumph which was probably why his commander-in-chief did not want to give his second in command any credit for it. Nevertheless, when in the following spring Sir Sidney asked permission to return to England for reasons of health Sir Edward made amends, and expressed "his grateful sense of the cordiality with which he had duly and uniformly acted with him during the period of his service on the station".

Sir Sidney had thoroughly enjoyed his trip to Sardinia but he had entertained so lavishly on board the *Hibernia* that he was considerably out of pocket, and, shortly after his return to Plymouth in July 1814, he wrote to one of the under-secretaries of State, Mr Hamilton, at the Foreign Office, giving a long and graphic description of the hospitality which he had felt bound to provide and asking that he be reimbursed. As the mission was a diplomatic one he felt that it was not the responsibility of the Admiralty to do this but that of the Foreign office. His claim was granted and an entertainment grant was paid to him, though the amount is not known.

"You are already, I believe, apprized," he wrote to Mr Hamilton, "that I was sent to Cagliari on a peaceable mission, although in a first-rate man-of-war, to heal a breach occasioned by an actual act of hostility against one of our cruisers, committed by one of the forts on the north-west end of Sardinia, and at the same time to demonstrate that we could not require of subordinate officers, in *the execution of their duty*, such a degree

of forbearance as to bear being fired at with *grape-shot*, by a
soi-disant friend protecting a common enemy, without firing
again, in which case, had it come to that, such was the tenacity
of the king to support his 'territorial rights', such the formal
mechanical mode of reasoning always exhibited by the first
minister according to his Ratisbon education; and such the
absolute barbarism of the savage inhabitants of Sardinia, that
if matters had not been settled, *à l'aimable*, we should have been
in a most uncomfortable state of hostility, affecting our trade by
so much that the island would have been a harbour for French
privateers in the track to Malta and the Levant, and we should
in the fleet have been deprived of our only resource for beef
and vegetables in case, as we apprehended, that of Africa should
fail us, from the monopolizing rapacity of the local governors,
and the absolute resistance of the natives against the exactions
by which we were supplied—'*On n'attrappe pas les mouches avec
du vinaigre*', in any country; it became necessary, therefore, to
bait with sweets, but these cost money; and where ten thousand
individuals at least choose to profit by the welcome given them,
that they may come and handle the rod that is to chastise them
if they should provoke it; where a crowned head, with his royal
family, and his son-in-law a member of an imperial family,
coming round into our scale, condescend to visit a public officer
in his place, whose appointments and allowances are not
calculated to meet such a contingency, it would require the
power of working a miracle, like that of the loaves and fishes,
to meet it without expense, for, on such an occasion, a man of
my rank in the world, independent of the flag, could not set a
leg of mutton and turnips before such guests. I did as became
me and the country; I completely succeeded not only in re-
establishing harmony, but inspiring a degree of confidence,
giving us ascendancy in the direction of the combination then
going on for the recovery of Modena, the archduke Francis
d'Este's maternal inheritance, and the king of Sardinia's
continental dominions, combining also the attack on Genoa,
against which it would have been impolitic to allow Austria or
Murat to operate alone.

"I succeeded in the object of my mission and more. Mr Hill
as you know, was absent, and the consul (a Sardinian subject)
could not act as I could and did; *by all* as his representative,
Mr Smith, not being there, I did not flinch from the duty, but,
as this cost me *more than my income*, I am reduced to claim re-

imbursement from the department, which can take cognizance of, and duly appreciate, such sort of disbursement, incident to extra duty, not in the least naval. I was situated much in the same way as to the obligation of expense incident to numerous royal and illustrious volunteer guests, as I was at Rio de Janeiro. I earnestly beg the favour of you to examine and liberally consider the items of the enclosed account of the expenditure having been unavoidable, considering the honour and advantage of the country; and economical, inasmuch as peace and friendship is cheaper than hostility or mistrustful observation of our neighbours and doubtful allies. You may not be aware that at Valencia (in sight of which the last three-coloured flag was flying on the impregnable fortress of Murviedro, under orders from Suchet, to hold that link of communication with his dukedom of Albufera to the last) *one half* of the Spanish army considered the peace of Valençay, signed by the Duke of St Carlos, as valid and binding on them, and that the news of the events of Paris, in April, which I brought, so far from creating the exultation that might have been expected, was received *most coldly*; under these circumstances, it was as well that my old Monte Video correspondent and *friend*, the hot-headed Elio, the Empecinado, the Duke of St Carlos, Palafox, Seyas, etc. etc. on one hand, and Luyando on the other, should have a hunger and thirst for my moderate corrected ideas, and come on board to me to seek them,— could I let such personages go on shore hungry in any way, after a four-mile row in a boat? Could I do otherwise than make due preparations, when I am officially told that my old Madrid acquaintance, the Infant Don Antonio, *just nominated Lord High Admiral*, intended to honour my ship with a visit, and my table with their presence, together with his nephew the king's brother, Don Carlos, and that the king himself would come also if his gout would let him? Ought *I* to pay for such an entertainment, or my family-table to be curtailed for a year afterwards, to square such an expenditure in my agent's books? I put it to the candour of such liberal men as Lord Castlereagh and his colleagues; and particularly with confidence through such a liberal and experienced man in such matters as yourself, whether as the *state gains* by such arrangements I shall be *taxed my whole income*, and even to the *being in debt*, to realise these peaceable objects. If Sir Henry Wellesley had heard Capons the constitutionalist commander of the first army, '*primero exercito,*' and Elio, the *anti-* constitutionalist, commanding the second, express their sentiments, as they did confidentially to me, in direct opposition to each other, he would have seen how near he was to a scene of confusion, beyond his control or the control of anything but a superior military arbitration. I was as economical as possible, which you will see by the account herewith. . . . While writing I receive your discouraging letter of yesterday : where I have right and reason on my side, and have to do with right and reasonable men, I am never discouraged, and will make my application in any and every quarter and form till I obtain what I consider to be as justly my due, as in any of the many similar cases where the chief secretary of the Foreign Department has had occasion to reimburse a public servant his expenses for conciliatory or etiquette purposes in foreign courts. The *Admiralty* may not choose to make a precedent of allowing table-money to a flag-officer, *second* in command, I therefore look to the Foreign Office, which may exercise a discretionary power in my *peculiar* case, under *peculiar* circumstances."

Before twelve months had passed Napoleon had been defeated at Waterloo and Sir Sidney's career in the navy had come to its end.

15

EARLY RETIREMENT

DURING his years of service in the Levant, and along the coasts of Tunis, Algiers, Tripoli and Morocco, Sir Sidney had witnessed the atrocities carried on by the Barbary pirates in connection with the white slave trade and he had, for some time, been considering the formation of an international Christian Society to bring about the liberation of these slaves. That this desire was soon to become a reality was no mere coincidence, for the abolition of Negro slavery had recently become a political issue of some importance in England. Owing to the efforts of William Wilberforce, public opinion was beginning to be roused, and an address had been moved and carried in the House of Lords on the subject of the abolition of the African slave trade on 5th May 1814.

Address Voted on the 5th of May, 1814, by the House of Lords to His Royal Highness the Prince-Regent, for the Abolition of the African Slave Trade.

We humbly represent to your royal highness, that we have seen with unspeakable satisfaction the beneficial and happy consequences of the law by which the African slave trade has been, throughout all his majesty's dominions, prohibited and abolished; and that we rely with the fullest confidence on the gracious assurances, which both his majesty and your royal highness have condescended to give to us, of your endeavours to obtain from other powers that co-operation which is still necessary for the completion of this great work. It well became Great Britain, having partaken so largely in the guilt of the inhuman and unchristian traffic, to stand forward among the nations of Europe and openly to proclaim the renunciation. This duty we have discharged; but our obligations do not cease here. The crimes countenanced by our example, and the calamities created or extended by our misconduct, continue to afflict an unoffending people. Other European nations stilll carry on this commerce, if commerce it can be called, in the lives and liberties of our fellow-creatures. By their intervention its clandestine continuance is encouraged and facilitated in our dependencies. By the same cause the desolation and barbarism of a whole continent are prolonged; and unless some timely prevention be applied, the returning tranquility of Europe, the source of joy and exultation to ourselves, will be the era only of renewed and aggravated miseries to the wretched victims of an un-principled and relentless avarice. With all humility, therefore, but with the utmost earnestness, we supplicate your royal highness that the whole weight and influence of the British crown may be exerted, in the approaching negotiations, to avert this dreadful evil. In the name of our country, and on the behalf of the interests of humanity, we entreat that the immediate and total abolition of the slave trade may be solicited from all the sovereigns of Europe. No moment we think was ever yet so favourable for stipulating a joint and irrevocable renunciation of those barbarous practices, and for promulgating, by the assembled authority of the whole civilised world, a solemn declaration, that to carry away into slavery the inhabitants of unoffending countries, is to violate the universal law of nations, founded, as it must ever be, on the immutable principles of justice and religion. It is on those sacred principles, the safe-guards of all lawful governments, the bulwark of all national independence, that we wish our proposal to be rested; on them we rely for its success: recommended as it will be, not by the exhortations only, but by the example of Great Britain, and addressed to the rulers of those states, which have themselves so signally been rescued by providence from danger and destruction, from eternal desolation, and from subjection to a foreign yoke. On all it must, we think, impress itself with equal force; for whether they be ranked among the deliverers or the delivered, among those whom a merciless oppression has already overwhelmed, or among those whose moderation and justice in success have added lustre even to the firmness of their resistance and to the glory of their victories, no worthier thanks, we confidently believe, can be offered to providence for past protection; on no better grounds can future blessings be solicited, than by the recognition and discharge of the great duties which we all owe to the rights, the liberty, and the happiness of our fellow-creatures.

Having conceived the idea and being determined to bring it

to fruition Sir Sidney was not content with half measures. The Congress of Vienna was to open in September and he managed to arrange for a meeting of his new organisation to take place there while the Congress was still in session. He first wrote to the Knights of several orders then in existence and got them to join the society which he called The Knights Liberators of the Slaves in Africa and then became its president. He also wrote to kings, statesmen, admirals and generals and obtained widespread support for the movement.

His efforts to get his old friend William Wilberforce interested in the Knights Liberators failed miserably. Before Sir Sidney left London for Vienna he had written a long letter to Wilberforce asking for his support because of his interest in the abolition of the Negro slave trade. A few weeks later he received a reply which was not only unhelpful but, in parts, scarcely coherent. He does not appear to have heard from Wilberforce again for several years and when at last he did receive a letter it did not contain a single word about the object so dear to Sir Sidney's heart.

Lord Exmouth, however, became very interested in the Knights Liberators and he and Sir Sidney corresponded frequently on the subject. Before he was given a peerage Lord Exmouth had been Sir Edward Pellew, Smith's Commander-in-Chief during his last spell of service in the Mediterranean. Then they had not been on the best of terms and this change of heart was much appreciated by Sir Sidney.

"It is a pride and pleasure to me to recollect," wrote Lord Exmouth, "the many proofs I have experienced of your regard and support. . . . I had read with much interest your address to the sovereigns of Europe, and I believe the feeling of interest it has created is general. . . . I had hoped the Congress of Vienna would either have made an appeal to arms or have dictated a code of maritime law for them* by which, in future, they should regulate themselves, and I think if a qualified person like yourself, acquainted with their manners, temper etc. could have been sent over to them, all such arrangements might chance to be made as would have ended depredation and Christian slavery. I am greatly obliged to you, my dear Sir Sidney, for thinking of me among your knights, and your good intentions towards me. . . . I shall give it all the support I can."

Encouraged by Lord Exmouth's support, and more still by

*The Barbary pirates.

the thousands of letters and offers of help which he received from almost every country in Europe, Sir Sidney spent all his time, most of his energy and much of his money, of which he had very little, sending appeals to all the sovereigns of Europe and potentates of Africa. He wrote to them all himself and varied his style to suit the recipient. The following is a typical example, written to a Turkish Bey.

Vice-Admiral Sir W. Sidney Smith, Knight Grand Cross of the Tower and Sword, Knight Commander of the Bath, Companion of the Imperial Ottoman Order of the Crescent, President of the Knights Liberators of the Slaves in Africa, to His Highness the High and Puissant Prince Bey.

Salut! Salut! Salut!

High and Mighty Sir,

The fame of your exalted virtues has reached us. The many instances of your justice, benevolence, and hospitality are known to us. We therefore address you in confidence, and offer you the opportunity of becoming a member of our illustrious society of knights liberators of slaves in Africa. This illustrious and highly noble association being composed of the persons of the most exalted rank and highest endowments in the world at large, you will no doubt be as desirous to enrol yourself a member thereof, as the members are to see you belonging to their body. What certain detached members of our community have done in South Africa, at Algiers, in Tripoli and in Egypt, towards the abolition of slavery among men, is well-known to you; what remains to be done is daily before your eyes; and we call upon you, as a good Mussulman whom we respect, and as the descendant of the illustrious and high-minded (name purposely obliterated), our respected and lamented friend, whose virtues and power you inherit, to aid us in this great work. You have been graciously pleased to liberate the white slaves, and we doubt not you will discourage the practice of buying and selling black men, in deference to the precepts of the Koran, and remembering the saying of Sidna Mohammed.

In giving liberty to slaves you will follow his sublime example when he, at an advanced age, liberated as many as he was years old, hoping thereby to do a thing pleasing to God. In giving us the satisfaction of knowing that you do so, by a friendly letter, you will extend to us the supreme pleasure you will yourself feel, and merit the title we wish to extend to you, of a knight liberator. This letter having no other object, we wait your friendly answer, and the expression of your wish, that we should do something agreeable to you; which we are ready and willing to do at all times; and we pray God to exalt you in dignity, and to have you in his holy and especial keeping.

Your true friend,
W. Sidney Smith

Sir Sidney's career as a sailor had ended when he struck his flag after giving up his appointment as second in command of the British fleet in the Mediterranean under Sir Edward Pellew. The defeat of Napoleon at Waterloo, however, in 1815 gave him his last opportunity of seeing war again, not from the quarter-deck of his flag ship, but as a spectator in the front row of the stalls.

It must have intrigued him to see his old antagonist at what was to be his last performance. Napoleon's active military career had begun at Toulon where he had been a helpless witness of the destruction of a large part of the French fleet and naval arsenal by Sir Sidney, who at the siege of Acre had the satisfaction of making Napoleon 'miss his destiny'.

On the eve of Waterloo Sir Sidney happened to be in Brussels with his wife, but when he realised that the great decisive battle of the Napoleonic war was about to take place he quickly made his way to Waterloo. In the battle, of course, he could take no part but the following letter was later discovered among Sir Sidney's papers. Captain Arabin, his son-in-law, later confirmed that it was Sir Sidney who procured the waggons to carry off the wounded to the hospitals from the battlefield as described in the letter. It was signed 'C.G.C. Kierulff' but the address is missing.

Brussels, June 28th 1815.

Sir,

I have the honour to inform you that, agreeable to your orders, I took your waggon with four horses to the place where the battle was fought. I arrived there at half-past four o'clock, p.m. The first six wounded as I found were Dutch-men, whom I sent to a village to be dressed, as some of our surgeons were there; on the return of the waggon I sent five more, two Dutch, two Belgic, and one Frenchman to the

Jesuit hospital at Bruxelles, as it was too late for them to be dressed in the village; and before I left the field, through the assistance of the Boors (to whom I promised two francs for each wounded man they would bring me), I had collected eighteen Frenchmen, whom I placed under straw, it being impracticable to get them into any house so late at night; and I am happy to state to you that on the morning of the 21st, when I arrived on the ground, I was informed that sixty-seven wounded were brought to different villages, where I went and found that the Boors had kindly fulfilled my wishes, by washing their wounds and dressing them as well as they could with the shirts which I had stript from the dead men for that purpose. I was also informed that a farmer had brought to the Jesuit hospital (in two waggons) sixteen men. About one o'clock on the 22nd, I found in two small huts four British soldiers of the Guards, one of the 30th, and six Hanoverians who had not been dressed since they were wounded; I sent immediately two surgeons of the Guards to dress them. I met these surgeons afterwards, who informed me that these men had been dressed and sent to Bruxelles.

I reported to the inspector of hospitals, the names of the villages where those wounded men are, as well as to different surgeons I met; before I left town I called at the Jesuits' hospital, where I had sent the five wounded men on the 20th, and I informed the inspector of the very great want of conveyance for transporting the wounded to Bruxelles, and I am happy to add that through this means he has sent fifty waggons and carts.

I also went to the place where the Prussians had the first engagement, and with the aid of Boors and some Prussian soldiers, I had the wounded (about thirty) conveyed to a village about a league and a half from the main road; these wounded had a surgeon to attend them.

It is impossible for me to convey to you the gratitude of the soldiers for your humanity, their blessings for you and your family came from their grateful hearts. I had also the heartfelt pleasure to partake of their blessings, for my endeavours to fulfil that duty you had commanded me for.

I have the honour to be, Sir,
C. G. C. Kierulff

P.S. Immediately after the wounded were found, they had

some bread and water, which I bought of the Boors and the wounded that could not be accommodated in the houses the first night, I had well covered with straw. I had also the Boors to bury the dead men and horses; on the 22nd, with permission of Lady Smith,* I called on the minister of state, Baron Capellan, to inform him that, on the field of battle and in the road, lay more than three thousand dead men and horses; on the 23rd, I also called on this good and noble man, to inform him that the inspector of hospitals told me, that he was in want of two hundred and eighty waggons, besides what the British government could send, to convey the wounded to Bruxelles, which the minister promised to send.

It is to your humanity the following were saved:—
June 20th—Dutch 8; Belgians 2; French 1.
June 21st—British 4; Hanoverians 6; of the 30th 1; French 67; Prussians 30.
June 22nd—Hanoverians 3; Prussians 12.—Total 134.

This incident confirms the following assessment of his character by a friend whose name is not known: "That deep-seated vice, which with equal power freezes the miser's heart and inflames the ruffian's passions, was to Sir Sidney a total stranger; he was always rich and always poor; frugality fled before the carelessness of his mind, and left him too frequently the victim of his liberality; and of course, in many instances, a monument of ingratitude. His character was entirely transparent; it had no opaque qualities, his were open, his prepossessions palpable, his failings obvious. He was a friend, ardent but indiscriminate, even to blindness. He lost his dignity by the injudiciousness of his selections; and sunk his consequence in the pliability of his nature. To the first he was a dupe, to the latter an instrument."

It was, again, typical of Sir Sidney that he should be somewhere near the battlefield, accompanied apparently by his wife, and this last humane act towards his old enemies was done at considerable expense to himself. The financial straits in which he found himself at that time are described in a fragment of a letter, the rest of which was burnt, found amongst his papers after his death.

. . . expenses, after twelve years, having neither time nor

* Sir Sidney Smith's wife.

paper to keep accounts, with the enemy's red feathers never out of my eyesight, and generally within shot; they acknowledge that historical fact hour by hour, however it may be out of mind elsewhere. It is my duty now to take care of my sword, with the inscription on it which you well know, and which is, under all circumstances, so invaluable to me, it not melted down for its nominal value, and yet that must be its fate, if it is in my possession when I am asked upon honour to surrender all my property to pay my debts, *as I shall be*; therefore, rather than part with it to profane hands I place it in deposit in yours, begging the city of London to save my credit so far, by sending the nominal, or at least, the intrinsic value to Messrs Coutts, to my credit account, that I may not be accused of cheating my creditors in Brussels of it, they having lent me the means of moving onwards to the enemy, when they were within a few miles of the gates, and of sending my family into the rear, if my inspection of the state of things, beyond the Forest of Soigny should decide me to indicate that direction to them.

In another fragment Sir Sidney described his meeting with Wellington on the field of battle after Napoleon's defeat:

Meeting Sir G. Berkeley returning from the field wounded, and thinking his sword a better one to meet my old antagonist on horseback I borrowed it. Things went ill and looked worse at that time in the afternoon of the 18th June. I stemmed the torrent of the disabled and the *givers-in* as I best could; was now and then jammed among broken waggons by a drove of disarmed Napoleonist janissaries, and finally reached the Duke of Wellington's person and rode in with him from St Jean to Waterloo. Thus, though I was not allowed to have any of the fun, not to be one too many, like a fifth wheel on a coach, I had the heartfelt gratification of being the first Englishman, that was not in the battle, who shook hands with him before he got off his horse, and of drinking his health at his table; a supper I shall no more forget than I can the dinner at Neuilly when Fouché came out to arrange the quiet entry into Paris without more bloodshed.

His money troubles, however, and the shabbiness with which, in his opinion, he had been treated by the authorities were still uppermost in his mind when he was writing this letter, for he

7*

ended it with these words: "I cannot help feeling that if I am not to be rewarded as others, and as I have been taught to expect, it would be fair *to place me as I should be if I never had been, or done anything in, the service.* Had I chosen to sit down early in life, with a life annuity of my present nominal income, I am told (but I don't understand these things) that by selling my estate before it was involved I might have purchased that income by merely walking into an insurance office, without going to the east or the west, through storms and showers of hail, lead or iron; you gentlemen of the city know best how that is. All I know is that I have to sit down at the end of this long contest without a home in my own country, or the means of living out of it. I have got to Paris, the object of my thoughts and hopes, *and in the way I wished,* with a victorious army, but I don't see how I am to get out of it creditably, without the aid of my fellow-citizens of London, by a LOAN, if my country grants me that."

Although it was some time before Sir Sidney received any financial compensation for the various expenses to which he had been put in the service of his country, he did receive some recognition before the year was out. On 29th December, at the Elysée Palace in Paris he was invested by the Duke of Wellington with the insignia of Knight Commander of the Most Honourable Order of the Bath.

16

FINANCIAL EMBARRASSMENT

FROM 1815 onwards Sir Sidney took up residence in Paris where he was very happy, for he loved France and liked the French against whom he had been fighting off and on for nearly a quarter of a century. He spent most of his time carrying on an unending correspondence with his Knights Liberators and, later, became Regent of the Order of Knights Templars, into which Society he had first been introduced when he visited Cyprus after the siege of Acre was raised in 1799.

While in Cyprus he had put down an insurrection, and in recognition of this the Archbishop of the island awarded him the Cross of St John of Jerusalem, which had been worn by Richard Coeur de Lion during the crusades.

Sir Sidney has described the incident in a document found in his papers, addressed to no one, but believed to have been written for Dr Luscomb, the Anglican bishop in Paris:

"In the exercise of my duty," wrote Sir Sidney, "representing the King in his dignity, as his minister plenipotentiary at the Ottoman Porte, and being decorated by Sultan Selim with his imperial aigrette, and with a commission to command his forces by *sea and land*, on the coast of Syria and Egypt, consequently representing that sovereign in his authority, in the absence of the grand vizier (his highness being the one to exert it when present,) and as the Capitan Pasha was expressly put personally under my orders, I thought it my duty to land at Cyprus, for the purpose of restoring subordination, and the hierarchy of authority, on a sudden emergency, which arose from the bursting out of an insurrection of janissaries, Arnauts and Albanians, in the year 1799, after the raising of the siege of Acre. The insurgents having murdered their local immediate chief in the island, the Greek population was at their mercy, and under dismay and terror. I landed on the instant, and exercising the delegated authority of Sultan Selim, as if he had been there in person, and wearing his imperial aigrette, or plume of triumph, I restored order by re-establishing the hierarchy of authority and causing the disbanded troops to go down to the beach, like sly slinking wolves, foiled in their blood-thirsty career, and there to embark, leaving the island, tranquil and free from the previous apprehension of plunder and massacre.

"On visiting the venerable Greek archbishop afterwards, at the capital (Nicosia), to prevent him from disgracing himself by a visit to me, which I understood was his intention, his grace met me outside the city gates. I of course dismounted to receive his welcome and animated harangue, at the termination of which he embraced me paternally, and, at the same moment, adroitly threw the Templar's Cross, which he wore as an episcopal decoration on his breast, around the neck of his English guest, saying, 'This belonged to an Englishman formerly, and I now restore it. It belonged to Saint Richard, "*Agio Ricardo*", surnamed "*Coeur de Lion*", who left it in this church at his departure, and it has been preserved in our treasury ever since; eighteen archbishops, my predecessors, have signed to the receipt thereof, in succession. I now make it over to you, in token of our gratitude for saving all our lives— the archbishops, ecclesiastics, laymen, citizens, and peasantry.' With other complimentary expressions, I found myself thus, in the consideration of the Greek population, invested with ecclesiastical authority, which also the Turkish authorities, and comparatively minor Mahomedan population, respected as such; and I was thus enabled to quell a Greek insurrection by my good offices between the conflicting parties, disarming the Greek insurgents, and sending them home with their grievances redressed.

"You are aware that the Grand Master of the Knights Templars was at Cyprus when he received the mandate of the king of France, Philip the Fair, and the contemporary pope to go to Paris, and justify himself and the order against the foul charges of two apostate knights, suborned by those who speculated on their spoils from confiscation. The grand master never returned, but was burnt near the *Pont Neuf*, with other knights, then falsely accused and unjustly dealt by. You may not be aware that the surviving knights, justly despising the impotent bull that pretended to abolish an order, not created by, and totally independent of, the papal authority, the forced terms of which bull '*suspendo in perpetuo*', admitted the impossibility of abolition and extinction, and forthwith, that a new grand master was elected in secret, and has continued to maintain the order in due form and consistence ever since.

"Thus it has not ceased to exist; and the Grand Master and his council recognising me as a new Knight Templar elect, duly received me, and voting me to be qualified by the above antecedents, recorded me as Grand Prior of England, an authority which Richard I exercised after he had become the purchaser of the land of the order in Cyprus.

"I have ceded this dignity to a most illustrious and a more worthy personage, (nevertheless I do not thereby cease to belong to the order, having received a higher dignity therein), —and it is unquestionably a holy order, considering its origin and attributes among the primitive Christians; and considering that I did not understand the whole of the Greek archbishop's speech, at the moment of the investiture, I may have been ordained without being quite aware of it; and if so, or under the doubt in my mind, which suddenly arises by learning that the Grand Prior of Portugal is a candidate for church preferment, which proves him to be an ecclesiastic; *I hesitate to take the oath as tendered to me (to enable me to receive my half-pay) in its precise form, requiring me to assert that I am not in holy orders;* my appeal to your Lordship is to have my mind satisfied on the historically recorded quality of the Knights Templars in England, previous (probably) to my taking the said required oath."

But he was still very short of money and in considerable debt, and the first two years after he settled down in Paris were occupied with the submission and re-submission of claims for compensation and an additional pension. A schedule of his active service between 1792 and 1814, which he submitted direct to his Royal Highness the Prince-Regent makes impressive reading.

When the American war began he was serving under Lord Howe and, shortly afterwards, at the commencement of the French and Spanish wars he was under Sir George Rodney who promoted him at such an early age to the rank of Captain.

Then came Toulon where, after volunteering for the task, he was put in command of the operation which resulted in a large part of the French fleet being destroyed, together with the naval arsenal. On that occasion, because he was, at the time, on half-pay he did not qualify for a share of the gratuity awarded.

For the next two years, 1794–5, he commanded a squadron of frigates cruising up and down the English Channel to give warning of any attempted landing on the English coast and break up any concentration of French ships assembled for that purpose. This led to his capture and confinement in the Abbaye and Temple prisons, and the planning and carrying out of his escape involved him in considerable expense. As he reminded the Prince-Regent he never received any compensation for this although the Treasury agreed that his claim for it was "a sacred national obligation".

1798 saw the first of his joint diplomatic and military assignments when he was sent, as Captain of the *Tigre*, to Constantinople to explore the possibility of an alliance between the British and the Turks. He then defended St Jean d'Acre against Napoleon's army in Egypt and finally succeeded in getting H.M. Government, who, first of all were opposed to it, to carry out the terms of the Convention of El Arish which led to the evacuation of Egypt and the Levant from the enemy's forces. For this he did, in fact, receive the thanks of Parliament and a pension of a thousand pounds per annum but he got no compensation for the heavy expenses incurred.

Sir Sidney then reminded His Royal Highness of the invaluable service which he had given, after being recommended for it by Lord Nelson just before he was mortally wounded at Trafalgar, along the coasts of southern Italy and Sicily from 1805–7. During this time he captured Capri, helped in the defence of Gaeta, assisted Sir John Stuart at the Battle of Maida, and made several raids on the coast of Calabria which resulted in his incurring extra expenses of more than four thousand pounds in respect of which he never received even one halfpenny.

In addition to all this there were the Dardanelles, Portugal and Rio de Janeiro and, lastly, two final years in the Mediterranean as Second in Command to Sir Edward Pellew. No mention was, of course, made of his period of mercenary service with the Swedish navy. He concluded this memorial to the Prince-Regent with these words:

"Your memorialist humbly submits that after a life spent in the public service of his country, seizing every opportunity of active employment and declining none; and having on some occasions been so fortunate as to render to the great cause in which Europe has now fought for twenty years, he finds himself materially and seriously injured in his private fortune, and with no accession to it whatever from public sources; that he has served in many situations of great and unavoidable expense and sacrifice; and he humbly hopes his distressing case, with a large family to support, may be taken into your royal highness's serious consideration. And that your royal highness will shew your memorialist such favour, and grant him such relief as to your royal highness's wisdom, justice, and humanity may seem meet."

He had previously submitted another protest in which he complained that others who had never held such important posts as he had, and had never been entrusted with such responsible assignments, had been better rewarded. It is not known to whom this appeal was made but it was probably to Lord Melville who was First Lord of the Admiralty when Sir Sidney struck his flag for the last time in 1814.

"Identified as I always have been with my work," he wrote, "and pursuing only the interests of my country, I could not pursue my own; for in fact I had none, even in contemplation, that could be considered separate from those of my country. I had no right to expect, or even the wish, to survive its wreck, supposing we had not succeeded in the glorious struggle for our independence and pre-eminence. But I have lived through it, to my astonishment, and lived to see the day when, on winding up the long account current, I find myself the victim of my zeal and disinterestedness, without the means of existence in my own country, which I have served with loss of fortune and of health.

"Rigidly just, as I have ever been and am towards others, and disinterested as I have ever been in the pursuit of *advantage for the state*, while I never gave my own interests a single thought, and not having been enabled, by any of those contingent and collateral chances of prize-money, etc., which have been put in the way of other officers, to meet my engagements; but, on the contrary, having been selected by the confidence of successive governments to be employed on services of greater importance to the state, of more personal risk and of no pecuniary advantage whatever, I may now, nay I must, in justice to myself and others, *earnestly* urge my claims to any of the professional appointments or advantages that may be at the disposal of Lord Melville; not doubting but that his lordship or any other impartial statesman, looking back to the history of the long and arduous struggle in which we have been engaged, the services rendered by me at different times in responsible situations, and the manner in which those services were spoken of and complimented *from the throne*, and by the leading politicians of the day, must admit that some *substantial* reward is due to a successful and indefatigable labourer in the service of the state, considering that *others, who have not* filled the situations I have of minister plenipotentiary and of *commander-in-chief*, have been rewarded, not only with greater pecuniary advantages, but with rank and honorary distinction beyond the second class of the Order of the Bath, which I have had in common with lieutenant-colonels of the army, who were subalterns at the time that the thanks of Parliament were conveyed to me, in such flattering terms, for a service of great *national* importance."

In March 1817, Sir Sidney's long held opinion that it paid to go to the fountain head was justified, and as a result of his memorial to the Prince-Regent, he received a letter from Captain Arabin who was employed at the Foreign Office.

Captain Arabin to Sir Sidney Smith
                                        Foreign Office, March 21 1817.
My Dear Sir Sidney,
    My joy is indeed excessive in having to announce to you the favourable result of my exertions. Mr Vansittart has just informed me that the government have agreed to reimburse you the 4,500 £ for the Sicily claim. The official communication will shortly be made;* in the meantime Sir Charles Stuart will be written to, to give you immediate credit for 2,000 £, on account to afford present relief. . . .
                                        And believe me, etc.
                                        Septimus Arabin

This good news clearly confirmed Sir Sidney's conviction that persistence in time of peace brought the same success as continuous offensive action on the battlefield, but he was still not wholly satisfied. On the same day as Captain Arabin had written, he wrote the following letter to the Lords of the Treasury.

* In fact, the news of the Government's decision had been conveyed to Sir Sidney three days earlier by William Hamilton to whom he had written after completing his mission to Cagliari about the expenses necessarily incurred in Sardinia.

Sir Sidney Smith to the Lords of the Treasury

Paris, March 26 1817.

My Lords,

Mr Wm. Hamilton, under secretary of state in the foreign department, having informed me by his letter of March 18th, that he had Mr Vansittart's authority to authorise me to draw for 2,000 £. immediately; and Captain Arabin, by his letter of the 21st, having informed me that Mr Vansittart has informed him that government have agreed to reimburse me the 4,500 £. claimed by me for carrying the service committed to my guidance and direction on the Sicilian station, and that Sir Charles Stuart would give me immediate credit for 2,000 £., I beg leave to inform your lordships that I have this day drawn on you for 1,000 £. in favour of Messrs Baquenault & Co., under the authorization of Sir Charles Stuart, to them addressed, to pay my bills on the Treasury, to the extent of 2,000 £.; no banker here choosing to advance money on a private agent without a previous letter of credit from London; and you will please to hold the other 1,000 £. at my disposal in like manner. The remaining 2,500 £., I beg may be paid to my agents, Messrs Toulman and Copland, of Surrey-street, Strand, on their exhibiting my general power of attorney, of which they are in possession. I have now to call your lordships' attention to a point of great importance to my interests, and, I will venture to say, to the honour of the country. The sum advanced by me to carry on the operations by which Sicily was saved in 1807; in fact, 4,700 £. (although not having access to my agent's books, I estimated and stated it from memory at 4,500 £., in order to be conscientiously within the mark,) was the sum in fact advanced *to* me, *and I have been paying interest for it ever since* now a diminution of my pension of 900 £. per annum net, granted for a former service of 230 £. interest annually, has been a heavy charge, occasioning me to contract other debts for subsistence, and it must be admitted, that I ought not to be out of pocket in the performance of a service commanded and indicated by Mr Pitt and Lord Nelson. I therefore presume respectfully to claim its reimbursement.

Your Lordships', etc.

W. Sidney Smith

It was almost twelve months to the day before Sir Sidney

received any reply to this letter but when it came it contained the welcome news that he had been granted an additional pension of one thousand pounds, ante-dated to 1814.

Sir Sidney appears at last to have decided to 'call it a day' and he wrote to the Prime Minister from Paris on June 12 to tell him so:

Sir Sidney Smith to the Right Hon. the Earl of Liverpool
Paris June 12 1818.

My Lord,

I learn with much satisfaction that the prince-regent's government has been pleased to grant me an additional pension of 1,000 £. per annum, from the close of the war in 1814 and I beg leave through him and to your lordship, to make my humble acknowledgements for the same. I learn that I am required to consider and acknowledge this additional pension to be in full compensation of all pecuniary claim on the government, which I hereby do accordingly.

I beg to be considered as ready and willing, under all circumstances, to serve my country to the utmost of my power and ability, when called upon, and to subscribe myself with respect and regard,
Your Lordship's, etc.
W. Sidney Smith

On reflection Sir Sidney appears to have thought that the persistent claims which he had made during the past few years might one day be criticised, for he took steps to safeguard his reputation in the future by setting out the full circumstances in a memorandum which was found filed with his other papers after his death. If the facts in this document be true, and there is no reason to suppose that they are not, it is evident that it was not without considerable reluctance that the pension was granted.

Memorandum of the circumstances under which the Pension of 1,000 £. per annum was granted to Sir Sidney Smith, about the year 1817 or 1818.

During the services of Sir Sidney Smith in the Levant, in the years 1799, 1800, 1801, and subsequently on the coasts of Italy, in 1806, 1807, he was exposed to considerable expense for the public service beyond what his pay and allowances could cover. These services were officially recognised and publicly acknowledged; but the monies, which he had

actually expended from his private resources in the execution
of those services, had not been reimbursed to him, and in
fact remained in dispute during successive administrations,
until about 1816, his agent becoming a public defaulter,
called upon the government to impound Sir Sidney Smith's
income, to discharge the balance which had accumulated in
his books, and which would thus by so far diminish the
agent's debt to the Crown.

This compelled Sir Sidney Smith to prove that those sums
had been actually expended by him in the public service, and
he did establish satisfactorily that a sum of between eight
and nine thousand pounds was fairly due to him by the
government.

Lord Liverpool resisted the claims, upon which Sir Sidney
Smith was about to present a petition to the House of
Commons, which petition was actually prepared, and taken
to Lord Liverpool by Mr Wilberforce, who had undertaken
to present it; Sir James Mackintosh to second it; Mr Lamb
(Lord Melbourne) to support it; and Mr Nicholson Calvert,
also to support it.

Lord Liverpool finding the petition so powerfully supported, yielded the point; and in lieu of the money acknowledged to have been fairly expended in the public service,
being close upon 9,000 £., proposed a pension of 1,000 £.
per annum, upon the 4½ per cent. West India fund. This
proposal was accepted, and by Sir Sidney Smith very
reluctantly, from its giving him the odium or appearance
with the public of having that additional pension, whereas
the real fact of the case is, that it was a bad and inadequate
reimbursement to him of monies acknowledged to have been
expended upon important public services.

These circumstances are well known to Lord Melbourne,
who kindly and duly appreciated them at the time, and to
Lord Bexley, who was Chancellor of the Exchequer.

Sir Sidney's financial difficulties were now over but, although
he still enjoyed life in Paris, time must have begun to weigh
heavily on his hands because he asked Captain Arabin to apply
to Lord Melville, on his behalf, for some employment in the
public service, preferably in the Royal Navy.

Arabin did his best, as the letter written to Sir Sidney on
18th May 1820 clearly shows:

London, 18th May 1820.

My Dear Sir Sidney,

I should have written to you before the result of my communication with Lord Melville on the subject of your succeeding to some of the commands shortly about to become vacant, but that I thought it better to let you know at the same time what Lord Grenville might say on the subject. To secure Lord M's not refusing to see me, I waited first upon Mr Hay, to tell him that I had a communication of a private nature from you to Lord M., and that I would wait upon him on his next levee day for the purpose. This I accordingly did, and found him very courteous and willing to hear anything I might have to say. I told him that you thought it of importance he should understand that the pension recently granted to you was not as a reward for services, but as compensation that you were compelled to accept in satisfaction and in lieu of a principal sum of greater value. All this he appeared to perfectly comprehend. My next point with him was to say, that your private affairs were now in such a state as to admit of your accepting any beneficial appointment that he might have it in his power to give. He looked at the list, and said that he did not see what could be given to an officer of your standing except Portsmouth or Plymouth. I told him you had named those commands, but that Jamaica was the most advantageous in a pecuniary point of view, and that vice-admirals were frequently appointed to rear-admiral's commands. To this he gave no answer, but said your claims were very strong. Upon the whole, as far as one can judge of a cool, cautious Scotchman, I left him as I thought favourably disposed. I gave him an extract, which I send you a copy of, being *passages* that I selected from some of your former letters to me and others, as expressive of your feelings, the latter part altered and some additions to make it applicable to the present case. I have seen Lord Grenville on this same subject and shewed him the same extract, and told him that you had desired me to do so, in case it should come in his way to forward your wishes. He said he would be glad to do so if he had opportunity.

Nothing came of this application and Sir Sidney evidently realised that it would be useless pursuing it further during the lifetime of the Liverpool Government, but when the Duke of Wellington became Prime Minister in 1828, after breaking with the Canningites, he renewed his application. Wellington's short ministry was a great failure and he never felt that he was on safe ground. This was probably why his reply to Sir Sidney was a definite, though courteous, 'No'.

From the Duke of Wellington to Sir Sidney Smith
Cheltenham, August 29th 1818.

Dear Sir,

I have had the honour of receiving your letter of the 28th instant and I assure you that nothing could give me greater satisfaction than to have it in my power to forward your views, or to improve your situation in life.

I am convinced you will see that it is difficult, if not impossible, for me, entering into office in January, 1825 (my predecessors, under whose directions your services and others, such as yours, were performed, being either dead or disabled from conveying their sentiments upon those services) to find means for his majesty to reward them all, as I am willing to admit they deserve to be rewarded. The question which naturally occurs is, why did not Mr Pitt, Lord Melville, Mr Percival, Lord Liverpool, or Mr Canning, under whom these services were performed, and who had a knowledge of all the circumstances of the cases, respectively reward these services?

The answer is, they have rewarded them, but inadequately, and thus the question occurs again,—why did not they provide adequately for that for which it was their duty to provide, if the claim really existed, as it appears it did? These are not questions sought for in order to defeat a claim, they naturally occur, and if I did not consider them, they must be brought to my recollection by those who must be consulted and must decide upon these subjects.

Under these circumstances, and as I really have no means at my disposition of rewarding such services, I feel great objections to recur back to transactions, however honourable and meritorious, which occurred many years ago, and which ought, and indeed must have been considered by my predecessors in office.

In respect to the employment of you in your profession, in the manner pointed out in your letter, it is a subject with

which I have no more to do than I have with the employment of an officer in the navy of the king of France.

I don't think either, that considering the nature and state
of the diplomatic service in this country, I ought to do otherwise than decline to recommend to Lord Aberdeen that you
should be employed in that branch of the service.

I really feel most sensibly for your situation, and most
particularly because I have no means of relieving you.

I have the honour to be, etc.
Wellington

Even after this rebuff Sir Sidney never gave up trying to get
back into Government service, but he met with no success.
However he did become a full admiral, though he still remained
in retirement, and in July 1838 he received a letter from Lord
Minto, which must have pleased him greatly for it contained
the announcement of his promotion in the Order of the Bath.
It had long been his moan that although he had held the
appointments of minister plenipotentiary and commander-in-
chief he only shared the second class Order of the Bath with
lieutenant-colonels of the Army who were subalterns at the time
when the thanks of Parliament were conveyed to him "in such
flattering terms for a service of great national importance".

"I feel great pleasure," Lord Minto wrote, "in announcing
her majesty's gracious intention of conferring upon you the
grand cross of the Order of the Bath. The navy generally will,
I am sure, rejoice to see one of its most illustrious chiefs thus
invested with the highest honours of professional distinction."

Sir Sidney did, indeed, receive many congratulations from
within and without the services on this belated honour, but
none can have pleased him more than the letter he received
from General C. J. Doyle who had written to him so kindly and
so forcefully on the occasion of the Admiral's recall from Egypt.

"My dear old friend," he wrote, "accept my warmest congratulations at the fact that TARDY *justice has at length overtaken
thee!* The gazette announces your being made a grand cross of
the Order of the Bath, that *ought* to have been the case *many
many years ago.* However, better late than never. In my heart do I
rejoice, and so will all those who saw, as I did, how you worked
to merit that, and every other distinction your country could
confer upon you. Long may you live to enjoy your new honour
is the sincere wish of your old ally and friend, Charles Doyle."

17

THE LAST TWO YEARS

GENERAL DOYLE's hope that his "dear old friend" would live long to enjoy this new honour was not realised. Sir Sidney's beloved wife had died in 1826 and he had never been the same man since. The Order of Knights Templars and his own Knights Liberators kept him more or less occupied, for he wrote incessantly about them and received letters from all over the world, all of which he answered.

But his health was failing and his thinking muddled. Only two months before he died he wrote to his friend Bishop Luscomb after he had decided to accept the honorary appointment of Regent of the Templars. The letter is no longer in existence but a draft of it was with his other papers. It was very nearly illegible and ended in the middle of a sentence. Perhaps the letter was never sent to the Bishop, but the draft shows to what extent Sir Sidney was living in a world of dreams. He imagined that by accepting the title of Regent he had exposed himself "to the effect of the most malignant calumnies, such as formerly brought discredit on members of the order, and, finally, brought the grand master and other worthy members to the stake to be burnt to death." He also seems to have thought that his becoming Regent might be thought to impair his allegiance to "our gracious queen", and he wanted it to be clearly understood that it was exactly the opposite, it meant that he gave "additional support to her, and to all other Protestant thrones." He thought of little except the Star of Jerusalem and Coeur de Lion.

On 9th May, according to an entry in Captain Arabin's diary, "the bishop came to me to announce that Sir Sidney had been taken seriously ill. We went together to see him and, finding him in a state not to be left with strangers, I caused him to be removed to my house. In fact he had received a stroke of apoplexy, which was followed by paralysis; and the second or third day after he had been with us, he became totally paralysed, and on the 26th May he departed this life, in the seventy-sixth year of his age."

This was, indeed, the crowning mercy, for a paralysed Sir Sidney is beyond imagination.

During the twenty-four years he had been living in Paris he had become quite a respected figure and had made many friends. When his wife had died he had buried her in the cemetery of Père Lachaise and gave direction that, at his death, he should be buried by her side. And so he was. The funeral service was held at the Anglican Church in Paris and in the procession which walked there on foot from Captain Arabin's house the pall-bearers were, most appropriately, a British and a French admiral and a British and a French general. More than fifty private carriages followed the coffin to the cemetery and, it was said, more than a hundred ordinary people from the quarter in which he lived followed it on foot.

On the Sunday after the funeral Sir Sidney was the subject of Bishop Luscombe's sermon.

"The loss which we and the country have just sustained," he said, "in the person of one of our bravest of her heroes, naturally raises in our bosoms serious regret and many a solemn reflection. . . . You will not expect, however, unguarded flattery or unmeasured censure. You all know the high character which our deceased countryman bore during a long life of glorious and hardy enterprise, through every scene of which he was distinguished not more by deeds of heroism, than by mercy and forbearance to the vanquished—generous in victory, and intrepid until he obtained it. This point of his character is, however, better suited to the pen of the historian than to the mouth of the Christian preacher. The corrupt nature of man leads to strife and war and to every consequent misery; and whilst this nature shall remain unsubdued by the mild influence of the Gospel, there will exist, it is to be feared, a tendency to war and desolation—to a sad waste of human life, causing heartbreaking privations, to which individuals and families are exposed, during the continuance of its destructive consequences.

"The Christian, in calm consideration of events, turns with pain and horror from the scene; but he cannot refrain from admiring a faithful discharge of duty, even in harrowing deeds, to which a deep and honest sense of it leads a brave servant of his country.

"In this light you, my Christian friends, have regarded him whose loss you now deplore; but you have regarded him, not only as the brave and intrepid hero, who shone so conspicuous

among our naval heroes (all brave and intrepid in their turn)
but you reflect upon his numerous and amiable qualities, which
in private life, endeared him to us all.

"Yes—you have hearts which have felt, and generosity which
acknowledges the warmth and sincerity of his friendship, and his
utter freedom from cold and selfish feeling; his even lavish
bounty to all who solicited, and who, he believed, deserved
support and assistance; his ardent zeal in promoting every
humane and charitable institution, and his honest enthusiasm
in every undertaking which he thought likely to promote the
welfare of mankind. All this, you will say, is characteristic of
the profession of which he was so great an ornament—and you
say well: it is our country's pride to see so many of her sons
distinguished in the annals of history by all these generous
sentiments; but there is not one of them who will refuse to the
character of our deceased friend, a pre-eminence in all that is
lofty, and great, and generous in thought and in action. They,
who shared his confidence, can bear witness to the singleness of
his heart, for which they respected and loved him; they watched
the inspirations of his genius and talents; they listened to his
instructive and scientific conversation; and they saw them all
directed to benefit his country, and to ameliorate the condition
of all mankind."

"Sir Sidney," as Brian Tunstall has pointed out,* "never
had the good fortune to command a fleet in set battle but
defeated Bonaparte with a handful of seamen and marines.
Many of his contemporaries received peerages and baronetcies
for a single day's action; Graves and Bridport were made peers
and Pasley and Bowyer baronets solely for their conduct on the
First of June;† Jervis became an earl as a result of the battle of
St Vincent; Captain Berry was knighted for bringing home
Nelson's despatches after the battle of the Nile; and Duncan
was made a baron for defeating an inferior Dutch fleet off
Camperdown. Pensions flowed in abundance. This does not
mean that such honours were undeserved or that their recipients
had not thoroughly earned them by previous service, but it is
remarkable that until 1815, Smith was only 'Sir Sidney' by
courtesy of the King of Sweden."

But was it really so remarkable? Sir Sidney did not have a
very high opinion of politicians or of diplomats. He hated red

* In his book, *Flights of Naval Genius*.
† Generally known as 'The glorious First of June'.

tape and did not suffer fools gladly. As he was frequently brought into contact with all four it is not surprising that there were differences, to put it mildly. He also believed, as has been mentioned before, that if one wanted something done, and done quickly, it was better to by-pass the 'usual channels', and go straight to the top. Very often it works but it does not increase one's popularity.

The diplomats did not like him, for he frequently trespassed on their preserves, sometimes with authority but frequently without. The government officials, who were then the equivalent of the civil service of today, also disliked him for obvious reasons. Nor was this all. He was not very popular with the Admiralty or the War Office. He was often right but sometimes wrong, but when he had definite views about anything he was determined that they should be considered. The trouble was that some of his views on warfare were almost a hundred years before his time. Had he been born a hundred and thirty years later he would have been either the Chief-of-Staff of the Commandos, or head of S.O.E., dropping agents in France to help the Maquis.

It is not surprising, therefore, that he was not popular with his superiors although many of them secretly admired him. He was theatrical, garrulous, self-opinionated, and an exhibitionist. Most of the commanders under whom he served, whether in the navy or the army, had little time for him. Lord St Vincent, Nelson who subsequently changed his opinion, Collingwood, Abercrombie, Stuart and, last but not least, Sir John Moore could not stomach him. Colonel Bunbury, Chief-of-Staff to Sir John evidently shared his General's opinion of Smith.

"He was an enthusiast," Bunbury wrote, "always panting for distinction, restlessly active, but desultory in his views, extravagantly vain, daring, quick sighted, and fertile in those resources which befit a partisan leader; but he possessed no great depth of judgment, nor any fixity of purpose save of persuading mankind, as he was fully persuaded himself, that Sidney Smith was the most brilliant of chevaliers. He was kind tempered, generous, and as agreeable as a man can be supposed to be who is always talking of himself."

Whatever else may be said of Sidney Smith, Our Knight of the Sword as he was disparagingly known, it cannot be denied that although he was prone to talking hot air to an immoderate degree, he also had fire in his belly.

SHORT BIBLIOGRAPHY

Public Record Office
Adm 1/411–17 (Admirals' Despatches, Mediterranean).
Adm 2/150–7 (Orders and Instructions).
Adm 2/1365–70 (Secret Orders and Letters).
Adm 50/41, 45, 46, 49, 53, 74 (Admirals' Journals, Collingwood and Duckworth).
Adm 51/1642 (Captain's Log of *Royal George*).
Adm 52/3730 (Master's Log of *Alceste*).
W.O. 1/280–1, 304–9, 348 (Despatches from Mediterranean).
W.O. 6/56–7, 149–50, 164, 185 (Secretary of States out-letters).
F.O. 65/54–7, 63, 65, 67–9 (Russia).
F.O. 70/21–7, 29, 30, 32, 33, 36, 39 (Sicily and Naples).
F.O. 78/51, 52, 55, 60, 62–5 (Turkey).
F.O. 352/60 (Stratford Canning Papers).

British Museum
Add MSS 14273–80 (Collingwood's letter-books and journal).
Add MSS 34932 (Nelson Papers).
Add MSS 37050, 37053 (Bunbury Papers).

Windsor Castle
Letters of General Sir John Stuart and Sir Sidney Smith.

Books, pamphlets and articles
Adolphus, I. H. *The Royal Exile, or, Memoirs of the Private Life of Queen Caroline.*
Anderson, R. C. *Naval Wars in the Levant.*
Annual Register, The.
Barrow, J. *Life and Correspondence of Admiral Sir Sidney Smith*, vols. I and II (1848).
Boothby, C. E. *Under England's Flag.*
Browning, Oscar. *England and Napoleon in 1803.*
Browning, Oscar. *Hugh Elliott at Naples* (English Historical Review 1889).
Brownrigg, Beatrice. *The Life and Letters of Sir John Moore* (1923).
Bunbury, Lt. Gen, Sir Henry. *Narratives of some Passages in the Great War with France* (1854).
Castlereagh. *The Correspondence, Despatches and other papers of Viscount Castlereagh*, vols. V–VIII.
Charnock's *Naval Biography.*
Colletta, Pietro. *History of the Kingdom of Naples* (1858).
Cooper, G. E. *Methods of Blockade and Observation employed during the Napoleonic Wars* (Journal of the R.U.S.I. 1916).

Denton, Sydney. *Admiral the Lord Collingwood* (U.S. Magazine 1905).

Dictionary of National Biography.

Driault, J. E. *Napoléon en Italie, 1800–12* (1906).

English Historical Documents, vols. X and XI.

Fortescue, Sir John. *History of the British Army,* vols. IV, V, and VI.

Fugier, A. *Napoléon et l'Italie* (1947).

Hargreaves, R. *The enemy at the gate.*

Historical Manuscripts Commission. *Manuscripts of the 7th Earl of Bathhurst* (1923).

Historical Manuscripts Commission. *Dropmore Papers.*

Hoste, Sir William. *Memoirs and Letters* (1833).

Hoste, Sir William. *Service Afloat* (1887).

Howard, Hon. E. G. G. *Memoirs of Sir Sidney Smith,* vols. I and II (1839).

James, William. *Naval History of Great Britain 1793–1820.*

Johnston, R. M. *The Napoleonic Empire in Southern Italy.*

Laughton, J. K. *Letters and Papers of Charles, Lord Barham.*

Lewis, M. A. *The Navy of Britain* (1948).

Lord, W. F. *England and France in the Mediterranean.*

Mackesy, Piers. *The War in the Mediterranean 1803–10* (1957).

Mahan, A. T. *The Influence of Sea Power upon the French Revolution and Empire* (2 vols. 1892).

Mahan, A. T. *Sea Power in its relation to the War of 1812* (2 vols. 1905).

Maurice, Sir Frederick. *Diary of Sir John Moore,* vol. II.

Morier, J. P. *Memoir of a Campaign with the Ottoman Army in Egypt* (1801).

Naval Chronicle, The. Volumes XV–XX.

Navy Records Society. Volumes XXVIII, XXXIX.

Navy Records Society. *The Keith Papers.*

Nicholas, Sir N. H. *The Despatches and Letters of Vice-Admiral Lord Nelson,* vols. III, IV.

Oman, Sir Charles. *Studies in the Napoleonic Wars.*

Oman, Carola. *Nelson.*

Parkinson, C. N. *War in the Eastern Seas 1793–1815* (1954).

Rose, J. H. *Napoleonic Studies.*

Rose, J. H. *Lord Hood and the Defence of Toulon.*

Rose, J. H. *Napoleon and Sea Power* (Cambridge Historical Journal, vol. I).

Russell, W. C. *Collingwood.*

Tunstall, Brian. *Flights of Naval Genius.*

Ward, A. W. and Gooch, G. P. *The Cambridge History of British Foreign Policy,* vol. I (1922).

Wellesley Papers, The (ed. L. S. Benjamin) (1914).

Windham Papers, The (ed. L. S. Benjamin) (1913).

INDEX